Hamlyn's FAMILY COOKBOOK
by Marguerite Patten

HAMLYN
London · New York · Sydney · Toronto

Contents

Published by
THE HAMLYN PUBLISHING GROUP LIMITED
London · New York · Sydney · Toronto
© Copyright The Hamlyn Publishing Group Limited 1975

ISBN 0 600 33555 0

Printed in England by Tinlings (1973) Limited, Prescot,
Lancashire
Line drawings by Jackie Grippaudo

Introduction

I have tried to make this a true Family Cookbook and to cover the kind of situations I and many of my friends and acquaintances experience during our everyday lives. If you consider an average year in a home there are many different things that happen to an 'average' family. For example, there are the occasions, all too frequent for most of us, when the housekeeping budget is very low and one must adjust the cooking accordingly. This is a challenging situation and one I have dealt with at some length in the chapter starting on page 5.

Even though your family is usually very fit, you may suffer a 'flu epidemic or other illness which means lighter meals for the invalids. I have provided some appetising, but quickly prepared, invalid dishes on pages 124 to 133, and suggested ways of adapting these meals for the fit members of the family. Since it could well be that it is the lady of the house who is the invalid, there are chapters especially for the menfolk and for the children, so they can 'take over' the cooking with success and enjoyment too.

However well organised you may be there are occasions when you are particularly short of time, so the chapter starting on page 160 covers dishes that can be prepared and cooked within less than 30 minutes.

In most households there will be times when we want to celebrate; it may be a birthday, special anniversary, or the visit of relations and friends. In the entertaining section there are menus for such occasions. In each case there are hints on pre-preparation of the dishes and suggestions on how to keep the food hot, or prevent it from drying, before the meal is served.

I have a very large post-bag during an average year. I welcome this, for it has given me a splendid opportunity to appreciate the problems of running an average home today. I hope this book will give you pleasure and help to solve some of the difficulties of cooking and catering for the family.

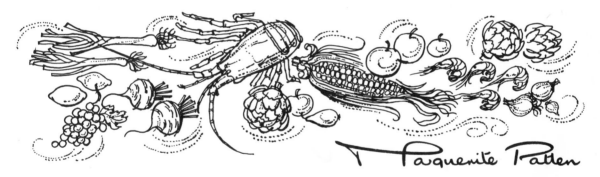

Marguerite Patten

Acknowledgements
The author and publishers thank the following for their co-operation in supplying photographs for the book:

American Rice: pages 15, 23, 34, 55, 59, 135, 143
Apple and Pear Development Council: pages 35, 63, 150, 163, 195
Atora Beef Suet: page 46
Australian Recipe Service: page 199
British Sausage Bureau: page 211
Cadbury Typhoo Food Advisory Service: pages 67, 158, 183
Cape Fruit: page 122
Charbonnier Wines Counsel Limited: page 139
Cheese Information Bureau: page 155
Cherry Valley Farms: page 179

Colman's Mustards: page 118
Danish Centre: page 99
Dutch Dairy Bureau: pages 111, 191, 207
Flour Advisory Bureau: page 94
Fruit Producers' Council: page 79
Hassy Perfection Celery: pages 14, 119, 171
Lea and Perrins Worcestershire Sauce: page 127
George Newnes Limited: page 82
New Zealand Lamb Information Bureau: pages 127, 142
Olives from Spain: page 151
Pasta Information Centre: page 175
White Fish Kitchen: page 7

Useful Facts and Figures

Oven Temperatures

The following chart gives the conversions from degrees Fahrenheit to degrees Celsius (formerly known as Centigrade) recommended by the manufacturers of electric cookers.

Description	Electric Setting	Gas Mark
very cool	225°F.–110°C.	0–$\frac{1}{4}$
	250°F.–130°C.	$\frac{1}{2}$
cool	275°F.–140°C.	1
	300°F.–150°C.	2
very moderate	325°F.–170°C.	3
moderate	350°F.–180°C.	4
moderate *to*	375°F.–190°C.	5
moderately hot	400°F.–200°C.	6
hot	425°F.–220°C.	7
	450°F.–230°C.	8
very hot	475°F.–240°C.	9

Note This table is an approximate guide only. Different makes of cooker vary and if you are in any doubt about the setting, it is as well to refer to the manufacturer's temperature chart. Some gas cookers have a mark labelled low or even 0 which is lower than $\frac{1}{4}$. This is best for meringues.

Comparison of Weights and Measures

Imperial and Metric weights and measures have been used throughout this book. In addition, it is useful to note that 3 teaspoons equal 1 tablespoon; the average English teacup is $\frac{1}{4}$ pint; the average English breakfast cup is $\frac{1}{2}$ pint; and when cups are mentioned in recipes they refer to a B.S.I. measuring cup of $\frac{1}{2}$ pint or 10 fluid ounces.

American equivalents are given throughout the recipes. It should be noted that an American tablespoon is smaller than the British Imperial tablespoon so I have increased the number of spoons used under the American measures, *except for 1 tablespoon*. American readers should therefore fill the 1 tablespoon a little more generously to compensate for its smaller size. The American pint is 16 fluid ounces as compared to the British Imperial and Canadian pints, which are 20 fluid ounces. The American $\frac{1}{2}$-pint measuring cup is 8 fluid ounces and is therefore equivalent to $\frac{2}{5}$ British pint. In Australia, the new metric cup of 250-millilitre capacity is now the standard measuring cup, replacing the 8-fluid ounce cup formerly used. The Australian standard spoon is 20 millilitres, larger than the British one, so use scant measures.

Metrication

For quick and easy reference when buying food it should be remembered that 1 kilogramme (1000 grammes) equals 2·2 pounds (35$\frac{3}{4}$ ounces) – i.e. as a rough guide, $\frac{1}{2}$ kilogramme (500 grammes) is about 1 pound. In liquid measurements 1 litre (10 decilitres or 1000 millilitres) equals almost exactly 1$\frac{3}{4}$ pints (1·76), so $\frac{1}{2}$ litre is $\frac{7}{8}$ pint. As a rough guide, therefore, one can assume that the equivalent of 1 pint is a generous $\frac{1}{2}$ litre.

A simple method of converting recipe quantities is to use round figures instead of an exact conversion, and in this book a basic equivalent of 25 grammes to 1 ounce, and a generous $\frac{1}{2}$ litre to 1 pint has been used. Since 1 ounce is exactly 28·35 grammes and 1 pint is 568 millilitres it can be seen that these equivalents will give a slightly smaller finished dish, but the proportion of liquids to solids will remain the same and a satisfactory result will be produced. The following tables show exact conversions to the nearest whole number and alongside the recommended amount.

Liquids/Fluids

Imperial	Exact conversion to nearest whole number (dl. = decilitre)	Recommended equivalent used only in some recipes
Pints	**Millilitres**	**Litres**
1 pint (20 fl. oz.)	568 (or 6 dl.)	$\frac{1}{2}$ litre – generous
$\frac{3}{4}$ pint	426 (or 4$\frac{1}{2}$ dl.)	$\frac{3}{8}$ litre – generous
$\frac{1}{2}$ pint	284 (or 3 dl.)	$\frac{1}{4}$ litre – generous
$\frac{1}{4}$ pint	142 (or 1$\frac{1}{2}$ dl.)	$\frac{1}{8}$ litre – generous
1 fl. oz.	28	25 ml.

Note The B.S.I. tablespoon holds 18 ml., the B.S.I. teaspoon 5 ml.

Solid and Dry Ingredients

Imperial	Exact conversion to nearest whole number	Recommended equivalent
Ounces	**Grammes**	**Grammes**
1	28	25
2	57	50
3	85	75
4	113	100
5	142	125
6	170	150
7	198	175
8	226	200

(herrings and kippers are excellent for a change). Blend about 8 oz. (200 g.) flaked fish and the same amount of mashed potato together. Bind with an egg or a little white sauce. Form into flat cakes, coat in seasoned flour then beaten egg and crumbs and fry until crisp and golden brown. Drain on absorbent paper and serve with lemon and parsley.
If you form the mixture into finger shapes instead of cakes they are known as fish croquettes.
The fish mixture may be flavoured with chopped parsley, grated lemon rind and juice, or anchovy essence (extract).

Fish Meunière Season, then fry small ribbons or fillets or even whole small fish in butter until tender. Lift the fish out of the pan. Add a little extra butter to the pan and cook until this turns a dark golden colour. Add a squeeze of lemon juice or a few drops of vinegar to the butter together with chopped parsley and/or capers. Pour over the fish and serve. The most suitable fish are cod and plaice, or whole trout, but sole or turbot or large prawns (scampi) can be served this way for special occasions.
If the butter is allowed to turn dark brown the dish is then *au beurre noir* and it has a very delicious flavour. Take care the butter does not burn.

Fish Risotto Chop 1 onion and 2 oz. (50 g. — $\frac{1}{2}$ cup) mushrooms, toss in 2 oz. (50 g. — $\frac{1}{4}$ cup) butter or margarine or in 2 tablespoons (3 tablespoons) oil. Add 4–6 oz. (100–150 g. — $\frac{1}{2}$–$\frac{3}{4}$ cup) long grain rice; mix with the vegetables. Pour in a generous $\frac{1}{2}$ pint (3 dl. — $1\frac{1}{4}$ cups) water or fish stock (made by simmering fish skin and bones). Cook for 10 minutes then add 8–10 oz. (200–250 g.) finely diced white (lean) fish. Season well and cook for another 10 minutes. Spoon on to a hot dish, then top with grated cheese and chopped parsley.
This recipe can be varied in many ways, e.g. you can fry sliced tomatoes with the onion and mushrooms. Cook the rice until nearly tender, then add flaked cooked or canned fish (salmon or tuna is excellent), or chopped shell fish. Heat for a few minutes only and serve.
Cooked peas, diced cooked carrots may also be put into the mixture.

Potted Fish This is very like a fish pâté, see page 169, but quicker to make. Cream 2 oz. (50 g. — $\frac{1}{4}$ cup) margarine or butter with a squeeze lemon juice, seasoning and a few drops anchovy essence (extract)

then blend in about 8 oz. (200 g.) flaked cooked or canned fish (most white (lean) or shell fish can be used, so can canned salmon or tuna). Put into small dishes, top with a little melted margarine or butter and grated nutmeg. Chill, then serve with hot toast.

Spanish Fish Salad Blend 6–8 oz. (150–200 g. — 1–1$\frac{1}{3}$ cups) warm cooked rice with a little mayonnaise and a small quantity of French dressing (see recipes page 65). Cool. Add 1–2 grated raw carrots, a few cooked peas, diced red and/or green pepper (discard core and seeds) and 8–10 oz. (200–250 g.) cooked or canned flaked fish. Mix well and serve on bed of salad.
To vary this salad use a mixture of shell and white (lean) fish; add more cooked vegetables.

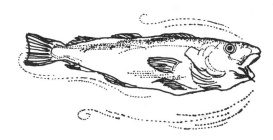

Spaghetti Marinara For this very adaptable dish you mix cooked spaghetti with some kind of sea-food. Fry sliced onions and/or tomatoes and/or mushrooms in margarine or oil. Blend with anchovy fillets and/or flaked cooked or canned fish and/or shell fish. Blend with the well drained spaghetti, pile on to hot plates and serve with bowls of grated Parmesan cheese.

Stuffed Mushrooms Remove stalks from 12 large mushrooms. Fry mushroom heads in hot margarine or butter. Put on to rounds of fried or toasted bread, keep hot. Fry chopped stalks, 1 chopped onion, 1 clove garlic in more margarine or butter, add 3 eggs, seasoning and 6 oz. (150 g.) flaked cooked or canned fish or chopped shell fish. Cook until eggs are set. Spoon on to mushrooms.

More Meal Starters
You will find suggestions for fruit and vegetable starters on pages 125 and 168.
Pâtés and other hors d'oeuvre are given on pages 169 and 170.

Making Soups

Soups can be so varied that they never should be monotonous. One of the most adaptable recipes is the creamed vegetable soup, below. This can be the basis for most vegetable soups.

Cream of Celery and Carrot Soup

Imperial/Metric	American
1 large head celery	1 large bunch celery
3–4 large carrots	3–4 large carrots
1 large onion	1 large onion
about 1 pint (6 dl.) chicken stock or water and 1 chicken stock cube	about $2\frac{1}{2}$ cups chicken stock or water and 1 chicken bouillon cube
seasoning	seasoning
1 oz. (25 g.) butter or margarine	2 tablespoons butter or margarine
1 oz. (25 g.) flour	$\frac{1}{4}$ cup flour
$\frac{1}{2}$ pint (3 dl.) milk	$1\frac{1}{4}$ cups milk
little thick or thin cream	little whipping or coffee cream
1 tablespoon tomato purée	1 tablespoon tomato paste
to garnish	**to garnish**
little red and green pepper	little red and green sweet pepper

Cooking time 30 minutes
Serves 4–6
Advance Preparations Make soup without cream; reheat gently, adding cream.

Wash celery, peel carrots and onion. Cut 1 carrot into matchstick strips. Cook in a little well seasoned water until tender. Save for garnish. Chop celery, rest of carrots, onion. Simmer in the stock, or water and stock cube, until tender, season. Sieve or emulsify in a warmed liquidiser (blender) and just sieve any 'stringy' pieces of celery. Make a white sauce with the butter or margarine, flour and milk, add vegetable purée, heat gently. If the mixture is too thick add a little more liquid. Stir in the cream and tomato purée; spoon into soup cups, top with carrot and sliced pepper.

Rice and beef chowder (see page 16)

Vegetable Cream Soups

The recipe on page 14 gives a good idea of the basic way to make a creamed vegetable soup. Choose vegetables in season that are economical. Remember some vegetables, such as Jerusalem artichokes, potatoes and other root vegetables, produce a much thicker mixture than leafy-type vegetables (i.e. cauliflower, etc.). A too-thick soup is very unappetising, that is why I suggest in the recipe on page 14 that you may need to dilute the soup with a little more liquid (this can be stock or water or milk).

It is more difficult to make a too-thin soup thicker, so when using leaf vegetables I would reduce the amount of stock or water slightly and make rather more white sauce of a slightly thicker consistency, i.e. use 2 oz. 50 g. – $\frac{1}{4}$ cup) butter or margarine with 2 oz. (50 g. – $\frac{1}{2}$ cup) flour and $\frac{3}{4}$ pint (4$\frac{1}{2}$ dl. – just under 2 cups) milk. This gives a soup with more body, which can always be diluted with more stock, etc., if necessary.

Vegetable Purée Soups

These are made by cooking the prepared vegetables in stock or water and stock (bouillon) cubes or just water. Sieve or emulsify the vegetables and reheat. If the mixture is a little thin it can be thickened by using a small quantity of flour, cornflour (cornstarch) or potato flour, or instant (dehydrated) potato.

Remember a bunch of herbs (*bouquet garni*), tied with cotton, or good pinch of dried herbs, gives any vegetable soup more flavour, so do garlic cloves or garlic salt.

Rice and Beef Chowder

Imperial/Metric	American
1 lb. ($\frac{1}{2}$ kilo) shin of beef	1 lb. foreshank of beef
2 pints (1$\frac{1}{4}$ litres) water	5 cups water
seasoning	seasoning
bouquet garni *or good pinch mixed dried herbs*	bouquet garni *or good pinch mixed dried herbs*
3–4 medium carrots	3–4 medium carrots
2–3 medium onions	2–3 medium onions
1 clove garlic (optional)	1 clove garlic (optional)
2 medium leeks	2 medium leeks
few sticks celery	few stalks celery
approximately 4 oz. (100 g.) runner or green beans	approximately $\frac{1}{4}$ lb. string, wax or green beans
8–12 oz. (200–300 g.) tomatoes	$\frac{1}{2}$–$\frac{3}{4}$ lb. tomatoes
approximately 4 oz. (100 g.) peas (shelled or frozen)	$\frac{3}{4}$ cup peas (shelled or frozen)
4 oz. (100 g.) long grain rice	just over $\frac{1}{2}$ cup long grain rice

Cooking time 2$\frac{1}{2}$ hours
Serves 4–6
Advance Preparations This soup may be cooked and reheated, in which case do not over-cook when rice is added, as reheating could make this too soft.

Dice the meat fairly finely, put into the saucepan with the cold water. Bring the liquid to boiling point, skim if necessary, add seasoning and the bunch of fresh herbs (tied with cotton or in a muslin bag) or the dried herbs. Lower the heat, cover pan tightly and simmer for 1$\frac{1}{2}$ hours. Peel and dice the carrots and onions; crush the garlic; clean and chop the leeks and celery; prepare and slice the beans; skin the tomatoes, quarter these if fairly large. Add all the

vegetables, except the tomatoes, to the meat, simmer for $\frac{1}{2}$ hour then add the tomatoes, rice and any extra seasoning required. Continue simmering for another 30 minutes. Remove *bouquet garni* and serve. *Illustrated on page 15.*

For Economy Use rather less meat and more vegetables.

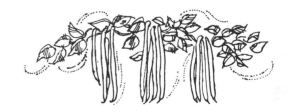

Soups Make a Meal

Some soups are so satisfying that they can form the basis for a complete meal. A good example is the chowder on page 16 and the two soups on this page.

If you want to turn a vegetable soup into a complete meal all you need to do is either top it with a good layer of cheese, or serve cheese and fruit after the soup.

Dutch Cheese Soup

Imperial/Metric	American
1—2 medium onions	*1—2 medium onions*
2 medium carrots	*2 medium carrots*
2 medium potatoes	*2 medium potatoes*
2—3 sticks celery	*2—3 stalks celery*
2 oz. (50 g.) butter	*$\frac{1}{4}$ cup butter*
1$\frac{1}{2}$ pints (9 dl.) chicken stock or water and 1—2 chicken stock cubes	*4 cups chicken stock or water and 1—2 chicken bouillon cubes*
small piece cauliflower	*small piece cauliflower*
seasoning	*seasoning*
4—6 slices bread	*4—6 slices bread*
4—6 oz. (100—150 g.) Dutch Gouda or Edam cheese (in one piece)	*$\frac{1}{4}$—$\frac{3}{8}$ lb. Dutch Gouda or Edam cheese (in one piece)*

Cooking time 30 minutes
Serves 4—6
Advance Preparations Prepare basic soup, reheat, add bread and cheese topping just before serving.

Peel and dice the onions, carrots and potatoes. Chop the celery into small pieces. Toss these vegetables in the hot butter for several minutes then add the stock or water and stock cubes. Bring to the boil, cover the pan, lower heat and simmer for 10 minutes. Meanwhile, divide the cauliflower into very tiny sprigs (flowerets). Add to the soup together with seasoning. Simmer for another 7—10 minutes. Spoon into a flameproof casserole or individual dishes. Remove crusts from the bread, slice the cheese and place on the bread. Arrange on the soup and heat for a few minutes under the grill (broiler), or in the oven, until the cheese melts.

Mulligatawny Soup This soup may be made in advance and reheated when required. Peel and chop 2 large onions, 1—2 large carrots and 1 dessert apple. Toss in 2 oz. (50 g. — $\frac{1}{4}$ cup) hot dripping, work in 1—2 tablespoons curry powder and 1 oz. (25 g. — $\frac{1}{4}$ cup) flour. Stir for a few minutes. Blend in 2 pints (1$\frac{1}{4}$ litres — 5 cups) water, bring to the boil, stir until thickened slightly. Add a few pieces of uncooked neck of mutton or lamb, 2 tablespoons (3 tablespoons) sultanas (seedless white raisins), few drops vinegar, good pinch sugar and 1 tablespoon chutney; cover the pan and simmer for 1$\frac{1}{4}$ hours. Remove meat from soup, sieve or emulsify, season well and return to pan. Take all meat from bones, add to soup and heat. *Serves 6.*
For Economy Use just bones of mutton, omit meat.
Freezing This soup freezes well; use within 4 months.

Variations

Cook 2 tablespoons (3 tablespoons) rice in hot soup after sieving or emulsifying.
Cook rather more meat in the soup, lift this out and serve as main course with caper sauce, page 44, sieve or emulsify liquid as soup.

Cold Soups

There are many occasions when a cold soup will be very popular. Obviously in summer time this is an ideal choice, but even in winter you will find a refreshing soup is very popular. The curried vegetable soup below, plus variations, is a good basic recipe that you can serve hot or cold according to the weather or your menu. Some other suggestions for easy and economical cold soups are also given on the next pages. If preferred, serve the soups hot, but if there is cream, soured cream or yoghourt in the recipe either heat the soup very gently or add these ingredients *after* heating the soup. Where quantities are given the soup serves 4–6.

Curried Vegetable Soup

Imperial/Metric	American
lamb or mutton bones and 2 pints (1¼ litres) water or lamb stock	lamb or mutton bones and 5 cups water or lamb stock
2 carrots	2 carrots
2 onions	2 onions
1 turnip	1 turnip
1 parsnip	1 parsnip
1 tablespoon curry powder	1 tablespoon curry powder
seasoning	seasoning
1–2 oz. (25–50 g.) raisins	¼–⅓ cup raisins
to garnish	**to garnish**
chopped parsley	chopped parsley

Cooking time 1 hour
Serves 4–6
Advance Preparations Make soup and reheat if required hot, or allow to cool.

Put all ingredients into pan, cover and simmer for 1 hour. Remove any scraps of meat from bones. Rub all ingredients through a sieve or emulsify in liquidiser (blender). Reheat, top with parsley, or allow to cool then top with parsley.

For Economy Use vegetables only with water; omit bones and meat pieces. See also variation under navarin of lamb, page 44.
Freezing This freezes excellently, can be stored for 4 months, but if you use the vegetables only and omit the meat bones, etc., it will keep up to 1 year.

Variations

Frosted Curry Soup Frost soup lightly in the freezing compartment of a refrigerator or freezer. Spoon into cold soup cups, top with chopped cucumber and natural yoghourt.
Jellied Vegetable Soup Turn the soup into a light jelly consistency. Sieve or emulsify soup. Soften ½ tablespoon gelatine (gelatin) in 2 tablespoons (3 tablespoons) water or lemon juice or tomato juice.

Add to the hot soup, stir until dissolved. Cool the soup then pour into cold soup cups, top with soured cream and chopped parsley.
Creamed Potato Soup (Illustrated) Follow basic recipe, but use all potatoes plus 1 onion instead of mixed vegetables. Use just white stock or lamb stock, and omit meat so you have a creamy colour. Sieve or emulsify the soup, add a little cream and serve hot or cold topped with cayenne pepper and chopped watercress. The curry powder can be omitted.

Frosted Tomato Soup Cook 2 chopped onions, 2 crushed gloves garlic and 1½ lb. (¾ kilo) tomatoes in 1½ pints (9 dl. – 3¾ cups) water. Season well. Sieve or emulsify and frost lightly. Serve topped with yoghourt and chopped mint.

Speedy Gazpacho Add garlic salt, a little lemon juice and olive oil to tomato juice. Serve with diced cucumber, diced onions, diced green pepper.

Cucumber Cream Soup Peel and chop a whole cucumber and 2 onions. Cook in 1½ pints (9 dl. – 3¾ cups) chicken stock or water with 2 chicken stock (bouillon) cubes for 15–20 minutes. Sieve or emulsify, then cool and blend with ¼ pint (1½ dl. – ⅔ cup) soured cream or thick (whipping) cream and 1 tablespoon lemon juice. Season well. There are many interesting ways in which this soup may be altered in flavour, e.g., add 2–3 chopped cloves garlic; add little curry powder; cook a few apricots with the cucumber, omit the onions; cook a few tomatoes

with the cucumber and onions. Top with parsley, cucumber, see picture.

Vichyssoise Verte

Imperial/Metric	American
8 oz. (200 g.) potatoes	½ lb. potatoes
8–10 oz. (200–250 g.) shelled or frozen peas	1½–1¾ cups shelled or frozen peas
sprig of mint	sprig of mint
6–8 spring onions	6–8 scallions
1½ pints (9 dl.) chicken stock or water and 2 chicken stock cubes	3¾ cups chicken stock or water and 2 chicken bouillon cubes
½ oz. (15 g.) butter	1 tablespoon butter
½ oz. (15 g.) cornflour	2 tablespoons cornstarch
½ pint (3 dl.) milk	1¼ cups milk
¼ pint (1½ dl.) thin cream	⅔ cup coffee cream
seasoning	seasoning
to garnish	**to garnish**
chopped chives	chopped chives

Cooking time 25–30 minutes
Serves 4
Advance Preparations Make in advance.

Peel and chop potatoes, defrost peas. Heat potatoes, peas, mint, chopped onions, stock or water and stock cubes. Simmer for 20 minutes. Remove the mint and sieve the soup or emulsify in the liquidiser (blender). Melt the butter, add cornflour, cook over a low heat for 1 minute. Stir in the milk, bring to the boil and stir until thickened. Blend in the vegetable purée, cool, then add the cream. Season to taste. Chill thoroughly. Serve cold, garnished with chives.

Variations
This could be served hot if desired, in which case use a little less stock.
Use half white wine and half stock.
Vichyssoise Use leeks instead of peas.
Creamed Pea Soup Use the recipe above, but omit potatoes and use 1¼–1½ lb. (⅝–¾ kilo) shelled peas or equivalent in frozen peas. Cook as above.

Fruit Soups

Many countries make a speciality of fruit soups and they are most delicious. Basically they are prepared rather like a thin fruit purée but there are certain things to remember:

The soup is generally served cold, but you can have it hot if preferred.

Never make the mixture too sweet – the soup must be refreshing.

While you can use water as the liquid, try using cider or a mixture of water and cheap wine, or to give a piquant 'savoury' flavour use chicken stock or water plus a limited quantity of chicken stock (bouillon) cubes. Cooking time and quantities as rhubarb soup, this page.

If you are sieving the fruit there is no need to peel or stone it, but if you are putting the mixture into a liquidiser (blender) then you must remove most skins and all stones.

Here are some quick ideas for economical fruit soups:

Apple Soup Use the type of dessert apple that has a good 'bite' or a cooking (baking) apple, or crab apples. Prepare the fruit, simmer in water, cider, wine and water or stock. Sweeten lightly. Sieve or emulsify.

Try flavouring apples with a little ginger or cinnamon or lemon juice, or use half water and half ginger ale.

Apricot Soup Cook fresh apricots as apples, and flavour with a little lemon juice or with curry powder.

Cherry Soup Use fairly sharp (tart) cherries or the small cherry plums, and cook as apples.

This soup is delicious if flavoured with a little orange juice.

Cranberry Soup Cook 1–2 small chopped onions and about 12 oz. (300 g.) cranberries in about 1½ pints (9 dl. – 3¾ cups) liquid (see under apple soup). Sweeten to taste and flavour with a little port or red wine. This can be served without sieving or emulsifying.

To thicken fruit soups you can use a little cornflour (cornstarch) or you can cook 1–2 tablespoons rolled oats in the fruit mixture, then sieve the mixture.

Rhubarb Soup

Imperial/Metric	American
1½ lb. (¾ kilo) rhubarb	1½ lb. rhubarb
1 pint (6 dl.) water or use half water and half white wine	2½ cups water or use half water and half white wine
1 lemon	1 lemon
sugar	sugar
ground cinnamon	ground cinnamon
to garnish	**to garnish**
soured cream or yoghourt	sour cream or yogurt

Cooking time 15–20 minutes
Serves 4–6

Wipe rhubarb, dice, then simmer with the water or water and wine, sliced lemon and enough sugar to give a fairly sharp flavour. Remove the lemon slices when the rhubarb is tender, and sieve or emulsify the mixture in a liquidiser (blender). Taste and stir in a little cinnamon, as liked. Serve hot or cold topped with soured cream or yoghourt.

Freezing This freezes excellently; can be stored for up to a year.

Variation

Use cider or ginger ale instead of water.

Tomato and Orange Soup

Imperial/Metric	American
2 lb. (1 kilo) ripe tomatoes	2 lb. ripe tomatoes
2 oranges	2 oranges
¼ pint (1½ dl.) white wine	⅔ cup white wine
½ pint (3 dl.) water	1¼ cups water
1 oz. (25 g.) cornflour	¼ cup cornstarch
seasoning	seasoning
pinch sugar	pinch sugar
to garnish	**to garnish**
1 tablespoon chopped chives	1 tablespoon chopped chives
1–2 oranges	1–2 oranges

Cooking time 25 minutes
Serves 4–6
Advance Preparations Make soup, reheat to serve.

Chop the tomatoes, grate the rind from the oranges. Use the top 'zest' only and none of the bitter pith. Simmer the tomatoes and rind with the wine and water for 15 minutes. Sieve or emulsify in a liquidiser (blender), then tip back into the saucepan. Mix the cornflour and orange juice, stir into the tomato mixture and continue stirring over a low heat until thickened. Season well, add the sugar. Serve hot garnished with chives and small pieces of orange.

Freezing Freeze tomato pulp plus orange juice *before* thickening. Use within 1 year. Heat gently until defrosted, then blend cornflour (cornstarch) with the wine and water and thicken.

If you freeze the completed soup you may find it becomes rather thin when defrosted (in which case add a little more thickening). Also the wine loses some of its potency.

Variation
For a more savoury soup add a chopped onion to the tomatoes.

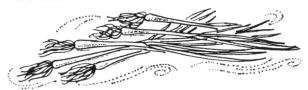

Accompaniments for Soup
Top soups with fried croûtons of bread, chopped nuts, parsley, etc., or the dumplings, below.

Potato Dumplings

Imperial/Metric	American
1 lb. (½ kilo) potatoes	1 lb. potatoes
seasoning	seasoning
1 oz. (25 g.) margarine	2 tablespoons margarine
2 oz. (50 g.) self-raising flour*	½ cup self-raising flour*
1 egg	1 egg
to cook	**to cook**
boiling salted water or stock	boiling salted water or stock

* or use plain (all-purpose) flour and ½ teaspoon baking powder (double-acting).

Cooking time 40 minutes
Serves 4–8 depending on the dish
Advance Preparations Prepare dumplings but do not cook before required.

Scrub potatoes and boil in their skins. When tender, skin and mash. Season well and add the rest of the ingredients. Form into small balls and poach in boiling salted water or stock for 15 minutes, or cook in the soup as in the stew recipe on page 43.

Economical Fish Dishes

It is very important to choose fish carefully, for if the food is not really fresh it can be both harmful as well as unpleasant.

It is difficult to be too dogmatic about what fish is the most economical, for this is a seasonal food and often weather conditions dictate the cost. When you go shopping for fish, therefore, inspect it critically to see it is fresh, i.e. that there is no unpleasant smell of ammonia, the flesh looks firm and, in the case of whole fish, the eyes are bright and clear. A good fishmonger will often advise you as to the best 'buy'. There may have been a glut of cod, in which case this will be relatively inexpensive.

Often the commercially frozen fish are a wise purchase as the price of these remains constant.

Never over-cook fish – if you do it loses both texture and flavour. The cooking times given in the recipes are the average ones, you can always test if the fish is cooked by feeling it with the tip of a knife; when the flesh comes away from the bones or skin the fish is done.

Basic methods of preparing and cooking fish are to be found below and on pages 24 to 30.

White Fish (Lean Fish) This term is used to cover such fish as cod, fresh haddock, plaice, sole, etc. White fish is suitable for practically every method of cooking. The picture on this page shows an interesting way of serving grilled (broiled) cod. The recipe for cutlets espagnole is on page 25. The picture opposite shows another white (lean) fish, i.e. skate (ray), and the recipe for skate with curried rice is on page 24.

Oily Fish Covers herrings (these fish can be cooked in most ways) and mackerel, and the more luxurious salmon and trout.

Shell Fish Includes clams, crab, lobster, oysters, prawns, etc. Most shell fish is fairly high in price so you will find recipes using these fish on pages 160 and 198, for they are delicious for party occasions. Shell fish is boiled to cook it, but can be served in many different ways.

Smoked Fish Varies from smoked haddock and cod to the luxurious smoked salmon, eel, trout and the smoked forms of herrings, i.e. bloaters, kippers, buckling. Smoked haddock and cod is usually poached; smoked salmon, eel, etc., served without cooking, and bloaters, etc., grilled (broiled) or fried. When buying fish allow approximately 5–6 oz. (125–150 g.) fish per person. Naturally, if the fish is on the bone you must be rather more generous.

Canned Fish There are many interesting varieties of canned fish:
Salmon or Tuna Flake and use cold in salads or sandwich fillings; add to other ingredients, e.g., in fish cakes, see page 12.
Fish Pie Make a white sauce as page 61, add flaked salmon or tuna, put into an ovenproof dish, top with creamed potato and heat in the oven or under the grill (broiler).
Sardines Serve as part of a mixed hors d'oeuvre; on hot toast; or mash and use as a sandwich filling. Remember canned fish is highly perishable when once the can is opened.

Frozen Fish Most frozen fish can be cooked from the frozen state; substitute frozen white (lean) fish for any fresh fish in the recipes that follow.

Cutlets espagnole (see page 25)

Skate with curried rice (see page 24)

Boiling Fish

This is really an incorrect term to use, for if fish is boiled rapidly the outside breaks before the inside is cooked. The correct term to use is poaching, see page 27, and recipe below. Raw shell fish is boiled to cook ready for use. Prawns (scampi), lobster, etc. can either be put in cold water and the water brought gradually to boiling point, or plunged straight into boiling water. There are differences of opinion as to which is the most humane, personally I prefer the former method. Small prawns will take just 2–3 minutes boiling, where a lobster will take approximately 7 minutes per lb. ($\frac{1}{2}$ kilo). The fish is cooked when the shells turn bright red.

Skate with Curried Rice

Imperial/Metric	American
wing skate – $2\frac{1}{2}$–3 lb. ($1\frac{1}{4}$–$1\frac{1}{2}$ kilos) in weight	*wing skate (ray) – $2\frac{1}{2}$–3 lb. in weight*
juice $\frac{1}{2}$ lemon	*juice $\frac{1}{2}$ lemon*
seasoning	*seasoning*
1 bay leaf	*1 bay leaf*
sprig lemon thyme or pinch dried herbs	*sprig lemon thyme or pinch dried herbs*
8 oz. (200 g.) long grain rice	*just over 1 cup long grain rice*
1 pint (6 dl.) water	*$2\frac{1}{2}$ cups water*
1 tablespoon curry powder	*1 tablespoon curry powder*
few black olives	*few ripe olives*
for the sauce	**for the sauce**
$1\frac{1}{2}$ oz. (40 g.) butter	*3 tablespoons butter*
1 oz. (25 g.) flour	*$\frac{1}{4}$ cup flour*
$\frac{1}{2}$ pint (3 dl.) fish stock (see method)	*$1\frac{1}{4}$ cups fish stock (see method)*
1 tablespoon tomato purée	*1 tablespoon tomato paste*
2 egg yolks	*2 egg yolks*
$\frac{1}{4}$ pint ($1\frac{1}{2}$ dl.) thin or thick cream	*$\frac{2}{3}$ cup coffee or whipping cream*
1–2 tablespoons capers	*1–2 tablespoons capers*
to garnish	**to garnish**
1 lemon	*1 lemon*
chopped parsley	*chopped parsley*

Cooking time 35 minutes
Serves 4–6
Advance Preparations Prepare all ingredients but this dish is better freshly cooked.

Put the skate (ray) into a large pan with enough water to cover, add lemon juice, seasoning and herbs. Simmer for 15–20 minutes or until fish is nearly tender, *do not over-cook.* Strain off $\frac{1}{2}$ pint (3 dl. – $1\frac{1}{4}$ cups) fish liquid for the sauce, leave the fish in the pan, cover tightly and put into a warm place. Meanwhile, put the rice with the water, curry powder and seasoning into a large pan. Bring to the boil, stir briskly, cover pan and simmer steadily for 15 minutes, then add the olives. Heat the butter in another pan, stir in the flour then the fish stock and tomato purée. Bring to the boil, stir over a low heat until thickened. Blend the egg yolks and cream, stir into the sauce, add the capers and any extra seasoning required. *Do not boil* but allow to simmer very gently; too quick cooking would cause the sauce to curdle. Spoon the curried rice on to a dish, top with the well drained fish, coat with some of the sauce, serve the remainder of the sauce separately. Garnish with the lemon and parsley. *Illustrated on page 23.*

For Economy Use cheaper cod, hake or huss instead of skate.

Variation
If you do not have a pan big enough to take the large fish, cut into 4–6 portions and simmer for 8–10 minutes only.

Grilling Fish

This method of cooking is suitable for most fish, especially white (lean) and oily kinds.

Pre-heat the grill (broiler), make sure the fish is well moistened with melted butter or margarine before and during cooking, season lightly and add a little lemon juice if wished.

Cooking times to follow:

Thin fillets of fish – 3–4 minutes on either side or cook without turning.

Thicker fish – cook quickly for 2–3 minutes on either side, then reduce the heat and cook for a further 3–4 minutes. Whole fish may need a little longer with the heat turned low.

Barbecuing Fish

Fish may also be cooked over a barbecue fire. This is one form of grilling (broiling) that is becoming increasingly popular. The recipe for herb stuffed herrings, page 26, gives one way of barbecuing fish, but most fish can be cooked in this way. Either brush the fish with melted butter or margarine or with oil, or use the mixture under the herring recipe, or the barbecue sauce on page 207.

Cutlets Espagnole

Imperial/Metric	American
4 large cod cutlets	4 large cod steaks
juice 1 lemon	juice 1 lemon
seasoning	seasoning
1 oz. (25 g.) melted butter	2 tablespoons melted butter
1 small onion	1 small onion
6 oz. (150 g.) grated cheese	1½ cups grated cheese
1 tablespoon mixed herbs	1 tablespoon mixed herbs
1 oz. (25 g.) butter	2 tablespoons butter
1 lemon, sliced	1 lemon, sliced
1 large tomato, sliced	1 large tomato, sliced
to garnish	**to garnish**
parsley	parsley

Cooking time 10 minutes
Serves 4
Advance Preparations Prepare cheese topping.

Wash the cutlets and dry thoroughly. Squeeze some of the lemon juice on each cutlet, season well and brush with the melted butter. Grill (broil) on one side only for 3–5 minutes. Chop the onion finely and mix with the grated cheese and herbs, add a little more lemon juice. Divide the mixture into 4 portions and form each portion into a firm ball. Place a portion of cheese mixture on each of the cutlets, top with knobs of butter (from half the remaining butter). Place under the hot grill, cook for 4–5 minutes, or until the cutlets are tender. Add the lemon and tomato slices, topped with the rest of the butter, towards the end of the cooking time. Dish up immediately as the cheese mixture may toughen with standing. Garnish with parsley. *Illustrated on page 22.*

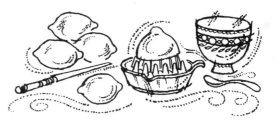

Note The cheese must be formed into a ball otherwise it will have melted long before the fish is cooked.

Freezing Fish cutlets may be cooked from the frozen state.

Variations

Use cutlets (steaks) of haddock, turbot or other white fish instead of cod.

This cheese mixture may also be used as a stuffing for whole fish, and baked in the oven.

Herb Stuffed Herrings

Imperial/Metric	American
8 herrings	8 herring
8 large tomatoes	8 large tomatoes
for the stuffing	for the stuffing
3 oz. (75 g.) butter or margarine	generous ⅓ cup butter or margarine
2 oz. (50 g.) soft breadcrumbs	1 cup soft bread crumbs
2 tablespoons chopped parsley	3 tablespoons chopped parsley
2 tablespoons chopped chives or spring onions	3 tablespoons chopped chives or scallions
1 tablespoon capers	1 tablespoon capers
1 teaspoon made mustard	1 teaspoon made mustard
1–2 cloves garlic	1–2 cloves garlic
seasoning	seasoning
for the basting sauce	for the basting sauce
1 lemon	1 lemon
3 oz. (75 g.) butter or margarine	generous ⅓ cup butter or margarine
1 tablespoon tomato ketchup	1 tablespoon tomato catsup
1 teaspoon Worcestershire sauce	1 teaspoon Worcestershire sauce
to serve	to serve
wholemeal bread	wholewheat bread
watercress	watercress

Cooking time   12–14 minutes
Serves 4–8
Advance Preparations Stuff fish ready for cooking.

Cut the heads from the herrings, split the fish along the stomach, remove the backbones. Chop any roes and mix with the stuffing. To make the stuffing, cream the butter or margarine, add the crumbs, parsley, chives or spring onions, capers, mustard and crushed garlic. Season, put the stuffing inside the fish. Grate the lemon rind and squeeze out the juice. Put this into a pan with the butter or margarine, the ketchup and sauce. Season well and warm. Put foil or a flat baking tray over the grid of the barbecue fire and lay the fish on this. Spoon the sauce over the fish and cook for 10 minutes or until tender, turn once or twice. Add the tomatoes towards the end of the cooking time. Serve with wholemeal bread and watercress.

Variations
Use other fish instead of herrings – the most suitable would be mackerel, trout, whiting or small cod or haddock.
Use other stuffings, e.g. page 56.
Prepare the fish as above, cook under the grill (broiler).

Poaching Fish

This method of cooking is used for white (lean) fish, as in the recipe below, for some oily fish such as salmon or salmon trout, and for smoked fish like haddock, see page 29. Poaching means *simmering* the fish steadily in a limited amount of liquid. You can either put the fish into cold liquid, water, water and wine or fish stock (made by simmering fish bones and skin), or put the fish into liquid that has just come to boiling point. Allow approximately 5–6 minutes gentle simmering for medium thick fillets of fish, if put into very hot liquid, or less if the fish is put into cold liquid.

Macaroni Fish Pie

Imperial/Metric	American
3 oz. (75 g.) macaroni	3 oz. (just under 1 cup) macaroni
water	water
salt	salt
1 lb. (½ kilo) white fish	1 lb. lean fish
for the cheese sauce	**for the cheese sauce**
1 oz. (25 g.) butter or margarine	2 tablespoons butter or margarine
1 oz. (25 g.) flour	¼ cup flour
½ pint (3 dl.) milk	1¼ cups milk
seasoning	seasoning
pinch dry mustard	pinch dry mustard
3 oz. (75 g.) grated Cheddar cheese	¾ cup grated Cheddar cheese

Cooking time 15–25 minutes
Serves 4
Advance Preparations Prepare beforehand and heat in the oven. As the macaroni absorbs liquid when standing use rather more milk in the sauce.

If using long macaroni break into pieces, cook in nearly 2 pints (1¼ litres – 5 cups) boiling salted water until tender. If using elbow-length macaroni, cook as directed on the packet. Meanwhile, simmer fish in a little salted water until tender but not too soft. Lift fish out, break into fairly big flakes. Heat butter or margarine in pan, stir in flour, cook 'roux' for 2–3 minutes over low heat. Remove from heat, add the milk and seasonings. Bring to the boil, cook until thickened, add cheese, do not boil after this. Put drained macaroni and fish into a hot dish, top with cheese sauce. Put for 2–3 minutes under a hot grill (broiler) until the top is bubbly. Serve with green vegetables – broccoli or green salad. Potatoes are not necessary.

Variation

Au Gratin Top with breadcrumbs and grated cheese before browning.

Baking Fish

This is suitable for most fish, see recipe below, and it means cooking the fish in the oven.
The fish can be cooked in a buttered dish or it can be cooked with milk or other liquid, etc.
Baking time varies, of course, appreciably, but fillets of fish, without liquid, etc., would take approximately 15 minutes in a moderate to moderately hot oven, where whole fish would take over 30 minutes at a slightly lower heat. This makes certain the fish is cooked through to the centre.
The recipes below and right for plaice and soused fish illustrate two methods of baking.

Frying Fish

This method of cooking is suitable for most fish. There are three basic methods of frying fish:

1 **Frying fish without coating** This is the method sometimes used for white (lean) fish, generally used for smoked fish such as bloaters, kippers, and for small fish such as trout. The fish is washed, dried and seasoned, then fried in hot butter or fat (shortening) until tender. The cooking times will be similar to shallow frying. Fish meunière, page 13, illustrates this method of cooking.

2 **Shallow frying with a coating** This method is used for white (lean) fish and for large shelled prawns (shrimp or scampi) and can be used for fish such as herrings. Wash and dry the fish, coat with seasoned flour then beaten egg and crisp breadcrumbs (raspings); herrings can be coated in seasoned oatmeal.
Fry quickly in hot fat (shortening) or oil until the fish is brown on either side, then reduce the heat and cook until tender. Drain on absorbent paper. Cooking times:
Thin fillets of fish – allow approximately 3 minutes on either side.
Thicker fish – fry quickly on either side until brown, lower heat and cook for 3–4 minutes or a little longer for thick whole fish.

3 **Deep frying** The fish can be coated as for shallow frying, or coated in seasoned flour and then dipped in a fritter batter as page 68. A pan half full of oil or fat (shortening) is heated until a cube of bread turns golden within less than a minute. Lower the frying basket into the oil or fat (shortening), this makes certain the fish will not stick to the basket. Lift the coated fish out of the batter, allow any surplus batter to drop back into the basin. Fry the fish quickly for 1–2 minutes until the coating is really set and golden, lower the heat and continue frying for a few minutes until tender. Drain on absorbent paper. Total cooking times are slightly shorter than for shallow frying above.

Plaice au Gratin

Imperial/Metric	American
8 medium fillets plaice	8 medium fillets flounder
seasoning	seasoning
1¼ oz./40 g. butter	3 tablespoons butter
2–3 tablespoons milk or thin cream	3–4 tablespoons milk or coffee cream
1 oz./25 g. soft breadcrumbs	¼ cup soft bread crumbs
1 oz./25 g. grated cheese	¼ cup grated cheese
parsley and lemon	parsley and lemon

Cooking time 25–30 minutes
Serves 4
Advance Preparations Prepare dish for cooking.

Season the fish and put into a well buttered ovenproof dish. Pour over the milk or cream then top with the breadcrumbs and grated cheese. Spoon over the remaining butter, melted. Bake for 25–30 minutes, uncovered, in the centre of a moderate oven, 350°F. (180°C.), Gas Mark 4. Garnish with parsley and lemon.

For Economy Use other fish in season.
Freezing Fish does not need defrosting before use.

Variations

Plaice Niçoise Use sliced, well seasoned chopped fresh or canned tomatoes instead of cream.

Poached Smoked Haddock

Imperial/Metric	American
1 smoked whole haddock or haddock fillet	1 smoked whole haddock (finnan haddie) or haddock fillet
water	water
butter	butter

Cooking time see method
Serves 4
Advance Preparations Cook as required.

Cut the haddock (finnan haddie) into neat portions,
discard fins and tail from whole fish.
Either put into enough cold water to cover and bring
steadily to the boil, then allow 3—4 minutes
simmering, or put into boiling water and allow 6—8
minutes simmering. Serve topped with butter.

For Economy Cook a little extra haddock and use in
risotto, page 153, or kedgeree, see variations.
Use smoked cod if cheaper than haddock.
Freezing If using frozen haddock cook from frozen
state; a very sharp knife (designed for frozen foods)
will cut it into portions.

Variations

Add pepper to the liquid to season — but *not* salt;
use half milk and half water. For a more substantial
dish top with poached egg.
Kedgeree Heat a good knob of butter or margarine
in a large pan together with 2—3 tablespoons (3—4
tablespoons) milk or cream. Add equal amounts of

cooked flaked smoked haddock (finnan haddie) and
cooked rice, heat gently.
This dish may be varied by adding chopped
hard-boiled eggs and/or fried onions or snippets of
fried bacon or grated cheese to the mixture.

Steaming Fish

This is a method of cooking fish that is often advocated for children and invalids. It is particularly suitable
for fillets of white (lean) fish. The easiest method of steaming is to put the fish on a buttered ovenproof plate
or dish and balance this over a pan of boiling water, cover the plate with another plate or foil and steam
gently. Fairly thin fillets of fish generally take about 10 minutes.

Soused Fish This dish can be cooked and reheated
or served cold; the vinegar acts as a preservative so
it keeps for some days in the refrigerator. Herrings or
mackerel are the most usual fish for this dish, but
portions of white (lean) fish are equally good.
Bone herrings or mackerel, see instructions on page
30 for boning, etc. Fillet if wished. Roll fish neatly
towards the tail. Pieces of white (lean) fish can be
skinned. Put the fish into a dish with enough
vinegar (or use half vinegar and half water) to cover.

Add 1—2 thinly sliced onions, sliced apple (optional),
seasoning, 1—2 teaspoons mixed pickling spices; you
can also add a little grated nutmeg or ground
cinnamon. Cover the dish and cook for about 1 hour
in a slow to very moderate oven, 300—325°F.
(150—170°C.), Gas Mark 2—3. Serve hot or allow to
cool in the liquid. The liquid can be strained and
used in a dressing with salad.
This dish also makes an excellent hors d'oeuvre.

Filleting Fish, etc.

Most fishmongers will fillet fish for you, but you may find you need to do this yourself.

To Fillet Flat Fish, such as Plaice (Flounder) or Sole

Make a slit down the centre of the fish (over the backbone). Cut round the edge of the fish. Make a slit just above the tail of the fish. Dip the blade of a sharp flexible knife into salt and insert this under the flesh at the tail end. Gently ease the flesh away from the bones.

To Fillet Whole Fish, such as Herrings, Mackerel, Codling, etc.

First remove the bone. To do this split the fish along the underside of the belly. Then cut into the flesh until you feel the knife touching the backbone. Either ease this out with the knife or put the fish, cut side downwards, on to a chopping board. Press along the backbone with your fingers (this loosens the bone), turn the fish over again and pull away the bone. You can then divide the fish into two fillets and remove the fish from the skin as below.

To Skin Fish

Make a small cut at the tail end of each fillet of fish, dip your knife in salt as suggested under filleting. Now gently ease the fish away from the skin — you will find this is quite easy to do if you keep the knife between the flesh and the skin and make small gentle cutting actions. The salt on the edge of the knife helps in cutting; if you feel you have used rather a lot of salt, rinse the fish in plenty of cold water.

Stuffed Fillets of Plaice

Imperial/Metric	American
2 medium sized plaice	2 medium sized flounder
seasoning	seasoning
lemon juice	lemon juice
stuffing — see recipe	stuffing — see recipe

Cooking time   20 minutes
Serves 4
Advance Preparations Stuff the fish and put into the dish ready for cooking.

Fillet the plaice (flounder) as directions above, then remove the skins. Season the fillets and sprinkle with lemon juice. Spread each fillet with the chosen filling and roll. The filling can be a suitable stuffing from pages 56–60 or a very thick cheese sauce or potted fish. The stuffing shown in the picture is made by mixing 4 oz. (100 g.) diced peeled cucumber, 2 oz. (50 g.) diced gherkins, 2 oz. (50 g.) chopped capers, 1 tablespoon vinegar, a little lemon juice and seasoning. Put the rolled fillets into a greased dish, cover with a lid or foil and bake in the centre of a moderate oven, 350°F. (180°C.), Gas Mark 4, for approximately 20 minutes. Serve hot or cold with white sauce, see page 61, and garnish with prawns (shrimp).

Seafood Timbale

Imperial/Metric	American
1–1½ lb. (½–¾ kilo) potatoes	1–1½ lb. potatoes
seasoning	seasoning
1 oz. (25 g.) butter or margarine	2 tablespoons butter or margarine
little milk	little milk
1 lb. (½ kilo) whiting	1 lb. whiting
¼ pint (1½ dl.) milk	⅔ cup milk
mixed herbs	mixed herbs
¼ pint (1½ dl.) water	⅔ cup water
1 oz. (25 g.) flour	¼ cup flour
1 oz. (25 g.) butter	2 tablespoons butter
2 oz. (50 g.) cooked lean ham	2 oz. cooked lean ham
chopped parsley	chopped parsley
1 hard-boiled egg	1 hard-cooked egg

Cooking time   25–30 minutes
Serves 4
Advance Preparations Prepare potatoes, fish and egg.

Boil the potatoes in salted water. Mash, add seasoning, butter or margarine and little milk. Meanwhile, poach the fish in the ¼ pint (1½ dl. – ⅔ cup) milk with salt, pepper and mixed herbs. Remove and flake the fish. Strain the milk, add the ¼ pint (1½ dl. – ⅔ cup) water. Make into a thick white sauce with the flour and butter. Add the chopped ham, parsley, sliced egg and flaked fish. Spread a layer of mashed potato into a shallow buttered pie dish and press well up the sides or pipe into rosette shapes. Pour in the fish cream and brown under the grill (broiler) for 2–3 minutes. Serve immediately after cooking with vegetables, including grilled (broiled) tomatoes.

Variations

Use shell fish and white (lean) fish.
Prepare whole dish ahead and heat for 20 minutes in moderate oven.
Seafood Flan Omit potato mixture in the recipe above. Make and bake a 7–8-inch (18–20-cm.) flan case (using short crust pastry made with 6 oz. (150 g. – 1½ cups) flour, etc., see page 72). Prepare the filling – do not be too generous with the water as the filling needs to be a little stiffer for a pastry case. Spoon the hot filling into the hot pastry and serve at once.
Seafood Scallops Use the recipe for seafood timbale, above. Pipe the mashed potato round the edge of 6 scallop shells. Spoon the fish mixture into the centre of the shells. Top with soft breadcrumbs, a little grated cheese and small pieces of butter or

margarine. Brown under a hot grill (broiler), or in the oven, and serve at once. This makes a good meal starter or supper dish.

Economical Meat Cookery

There are many different ways of cooking meat, these are described on page 33, opposite. Often the method of cooking must be determined by the quality of the meat. *Never* try and cook the cheaper, and less tender, cuts of meat by any of the quicker methods, i.e. roasting, grilling (broiling) or frying. If you do, the result will be most unsatisfactory. Tougher meat needs the gentle, slow cooking of boiling, stewing, etc., to tenderise it, whereas the prime cuts are at their best when given the minimum cooking time. When buying meat off the bone allow about 6 oz. (150 g.) per person, or a little less for stewing if you are using a great variety of vegetables too. When buying a joint, where there is a high proportion of bone, allow a weight of 10–12 oz. (250–300 g.) per person. Below and right are the cuts to choose and suggested cooking methods.

Beef This should have bright red lean meat and firm creamy-white fat. A certain amount of fat on the joint is important, for it ensures good quality meat and prevents the cooked meat becoming dry.

Lamb and Mutton Remember that mutton will be less tender than lamb and will be better with longer, slower cooking. Lean should be firm and pink, the fat white and firm and slightly transparent looking in lamb.

Pork The pale pink lean and white fat should both be firm and never appear flabby.

Veal Make sure the meat is firm and not flabby looking; the lean should be very pale pink and any fat (there is little on veal) should be firm and white. * means prime cuts can also be used.

Gravy Good gravy 'sets the seal' on a roast joint and many people like gravy with fried or grilled food. One golden rule for a well flavoured gravy is to use some of the fat from the tin in which the meat was roasted and any residue of meat juices. To make a thin gravy, pour away all the fat in the tin except about 1 tablespoon. Stir in 1 tablespoon flour and any gravy browning you may wish to use, then blend with approximately $\frac{1}{2}$ pint (3 dl. – $1\frac{1}{4}$ cups) vegetable stock or meat stock. Stir until slightly thickened and strain. For a thicker gravy increase the amount of flour slightly. Either the gravy may be made in the roasting tin, or you can pour any fat, etc., from the tin into a saucepan and make it in this.

Beef

Imperial/Metric	American
for roasting	**for roasting**
aitchbone, fresh brisket, topside (all must be good quality), rib, sirloin, rump, fillet	standing and rolled rib, standing and rolled round, rump, sirloin tip roast, whole tenderloin
for frying and grilling	**for frying and broiling:**
fillet, rump, porterhouse, sirloin, chateaubriand, minute, entrecôte	round tip steak, short loin steaks – club, porterhouse, T-bone, tenderloin – rib steak, sirloin
for braising*, stewing, etc.	**for braising*, stewing, etc.**
aitchbone, brisket, topside, flank, chuck, silverside, shin (generally used for stock), skirt, bladebone	eye and heel of round, top round, sirloin tip, chuck, foreshank, brisket, short plate, flank steak, arm steak

Lamb and Mutton

Imperial/Metric	American
for roasting	**for roasting**
loin, leg, shoulder, best end of neck, saddle (double loin), crown roast, breast	leg, loin, saddle, crown roast, square or rolled shoulder, cushion shoulder, breast or rolled breast
for frying and grilling	**for frying and broiling**
chops or cutlets from loin or best end of neck, slices (fillets) from leg	leg steaks, rib or rack chops, English chops, loin chops, boneless shoulder chops, Saratoga chops
for braising*, stewing, etc.	**for braising*, stewing, etc.**
middle and scrag end of neck, breast, head (for brawn, etc.)	shoulder – arm/blade chops, neck slices, breast, foreshank, hindshank, head (for brawn, etc.)

Pork

Imperial/Metric	American
for roasting	**for roasting**
leg, knuckle, loin, spare ribs, tenderloin	loin, shoulder (butt, picnic shoulder, cushion), fresh ham, ham butt half or shank portion, spare ribs
for frying and grilling	**for frying and broiling**
slices (fillets) from leg, chops or cutlets from loin or spare ribs	ham or shoulder steaks, chops from loin or rib
for braising*, stewing, etc.	**for braising*, stewing, etc.**
belly, spare ribs, trotters, head (for brawn, etc.)	spare ribs, fresh shoulder hock, feet, head (for brawn, etc.)

Veal

Imperial/Metric	American
for roasting	**for roasting**
breast, loin, thick fillet (from leg), leg, best end of neck	center and rolled leg, loin, rump (round), blade, arm, rib, crown roast
for frying and grilling	**for frying and broiling**
slices (fillets) from leg, chops and loin or best end of neck	round steaks (sometimes called cutlets), chops from loin, rib chops
for braising*, stewing, etc.	**for braising*, stewing, etc.**
breast, feet, knuckle, middle or scrag end of neck, head (for brawn, etc.)	neck, arm steak, rolled shoulder, breast, foreshank, loin and kidney chops, heel of round, hindshank, head (for brawn, etc.)

Boiling This is suitable for most of the inexpensive cuts of meat. It is often used for salted meat, such as bacon and ham, see page 147; beef, see page 42, and ox (beef) tongue or other kinds of tongue, page 51. Soak as recipe. Always discard the water in which the meat has been soaked and use fresh cold water or other liquid.

The term 'boiling' is really incorrect, for the liquid should simmer gently and *never* boil rapidly. Times for boiling are given under the specific recipe.

Braising While this is a suitable method of cooking cheaper cuts of meat it is also used for prime cuts too, as well as for poultry and vegetables. The food is first browned, then cooked above a layer of savoury ingredients, known as a *mirepoix*, which is used as a rich thick sauce for the meat. The recipe for braised kidneys on page 49, with suggestions for braising meat, etc., gives a basic recipe to follow.

Casseroling This method is suitable for cheaper cuts of meat, see this chapter. If you adapt a stew recipe for casserole cooking use a little less liquid, since you do not have as much evaporation as you have in a saucepan.

Frying This is ideal for steaks, chops and small portions of tender meat. Always seal the outside of the meat quickly in a little hot fat, then cook more steadily until the meat is tender. For full details see pages 136–7.

Grilling (Broiling) This is ideal for really tender cuts of meat. It is described in detail on page 136. Remember to pre-heat the grill (broiler) when cooking all meats except bacon and ham.

Roasting Although slower roasting can tenderise medium tender cuts of meat, see tables, you cannot roast the kind of meat meant for stewing, etc. I have not included full details for roasting in this budget chapter, but you will find full details on page 141.

Pot Roasting This is a slow method of cooking in a pan; cheaper joints can be used as well as the better ones, see page 216.

Stewing This slow, gentle method of cooking in liquid produces a delicious dish from really cheap cuts, see this chapter.

Veal niçoise (see page 44)

Lamb and apple curry (see page 45)

Using Minced Meat

An excellent way to buy meat is in the minced (ground) form. The most usual minced meat is beef, but there is no reason why other meats cannot be used instead in some recipes. The following recipes show the versatility of minced meat. Make quite certain the meat is pleasantly moist when you buy it; if dry and hard it has been stored for too long a period. Use quickly after purchase, or freeze, see information below recipe.

Minced Beef Sauce

Sauces made with minced (ground) beef make an excellent accompaniment to pasta and rice. Where beef is not obtainable use mutton or veal, but pork is a little over-rich for this purpose.

Imperial/Metric	American
1 tablespoon olive oil	1 tablespoon olive oil
1 oz. (25 g.) butter	2 tablespoons butter
1 onion	1 onion
1 clove garlic	1 clove garlic
2 tomatoes	2 tomatoes
¾ pint (4¼ dl.) stock or water and 1 stock cube	just under 2 cups stock or water and 1 bouillon cube
12 oz. (300 g.) minced beef (or other meat, see above)	¾ lb. ground beef (or other meat, see above)
seasoning	seasoning
1 tablespoon chopped parsley	1 tablespoon chopped parsley
good pinch mixed herbs	good pinch mixed herbs
1 green pepper	1 green pepper

Cooking time just over 1 hour
Serves 4
Advance Preparations Make sauce, reheat as required – see comments about storing minced meat on page 38.

Heat the oil and butter, then fry the finely chopped onion and crushed garlic and skinned chopped tomatoes. Add the liquid and the stock cube (if using this), then stir in the minced meat. Allow this to simmer gently in the liquid for about 30 minutes. Add the seasoning, parsley, herbs and diced green pepper (discard core and seeds). Continue cooking for another 30 minutes until a fairly thick consistency. Do not thicken with flour or cornflour (cornstarch). Serve over cooked pasta or cooked rice, or over a bed of cooked creamed potatoes.

Freezing Cooked minced meat freezes excellently. Use within 3 months. Where rice or spaghetti or noodles are suggested as an accompaniment I prefer to cook these freshly when reheating the mince. If the rice, etc. is part of the recipe as in savoury risotto, page 40, I prefer *not* to freeze the dish as the rice loses its texture.

Recipes Based on Minced Beef Sauce

Shepherd's Pie Make the sauce as above, but omit the green pepper. When nearly cooked put into a pie dish, cover with mashed potato, plus a little margarine or butter. Heat in a moderately hot oven for approximately 25 minutes, until crisp and brown. If you prefer a firmer mixture use mince stew, page 38. Leftover cooked meat blended with fried onions, tomatoes and stock is often used instead of fresh meat.

Soufflé Topped Pie Make the meat sauce as the recipe above, put into a pie dish. Beat the yolks of 2 eggs with seasoning and 2 oz. (50 g. – ½ cup) finely grated cheese. Fold in the stiffly whisked egg whites and spoon very carefully over the meat sauce. *This must be very hot as the cooking time for the topping is very short.* Bake for 10–12 minutes in the centre of a moderately hot oven until well risen and golden coloured. Serve at once.

Spaghetti Bolognese This is probably the best known dish using the sauce. For 4 people, cook 8–12 oz. (200–300 g.) spaghetti in boiling salted water until tender. Strain, top with the sauce and serve with grated Parmesan cheese.

Aspic Flan Make the meat sauce as given on previous page, but use 1 pint (6 dl. – 2½ cups) water or water and 1 stock (bouillon) cube. Cook as the recipe. Meanwhile make a flan case with 6 oz. (150 g. – 1½ cups) flour, etc., see page 72, and bake 'blind' until crisp and golden brown. Strain the meat sauce and dissolve a packet of aspic jelly in the liquid. Allow to cool, then mix with the meat, etc. Put on one side until this begins to stiffen slightly, then spoon into the *cold* flan case. When quite cold garnish with rings of cucumber and raw tomato.

Savoury Pancakes Make about 8 pancakes (using 4 oz. (100 g. – 1 cup) flour, etc. for the batter), see page 66. Make the sauce mixture as the basic recipe on previous page. Put the sauce into the pancakes, roll and serve at once.

Pancake Gâteau Make about 8 pancakes, see page 66. Put the first one on to a hot dish, top with some of the meat sauce, given on previous page, then a layer of grated cheese. Continue like this, adding a pancake, then some of the sauce and cheese. When the last pancake is put on top, cover with a thick layer of grated cheese and heat for about 10 minutes in a moderately hot oven.

Cannelloni in Cheese Sauce Make about 8 pancakes, see page 66, and fill with the meat sauce, given on previous page; roll the filled pancakes and put into a shallow flameproof dish. Make a cheese sauce with 1 oz. (25 g. – 2 tablespoons) butter or margarine, 1 oz. (25 g. – ¼ cup) flour, ½ pint (3 dl. – 1¼ cups) milk, seasoning and 4 oz. (100 g. – 1 cup) grated cheese. Pour over the hot pancakes and brown under the grill (broiler) for a few minutes. If the pancakes and filling have become a little cool, then make the sauce a trifle thinner (add 2–3 extra tablespoons milk) and heat the dish in a moderately hot oven for 25 minutes.

To Serve au Gratin Top the cheese sauce with fine breadcrumbs and grated cheese before browning under the grill (broiler) or in the oven.

Durham Cutlets

Imperial/Metric	American
2 oz. (50 g.) fat	¼ cup shortening
1 onion	1 onion
1 oz. (25 g.) flour	¼ cup flour
¼ pint (1½ dl.) stock or milk	⅔ cup stock or milk
12 oz. (300 g.) minced raw meat	¾ lb. ground raw meat
2 oz. (50 g.) soft breadcrumbs	1 cup soft bread crumbs
seasoning	seasoning
to coat	**to coat**
1 egg	1 egg
crisp breadcrumbs (raspings)	crisp bread crumbs (raspings)
for frying	**for frying**
oil or fat	oil or shortening

Cooking time 20 minutes
Serves 4
Advance Preparations Make cutlets, coat and leave for several hours in refrigerator.

Heat the fat in a pan, stir in the finely chopped onion and cook for several minutes, then gradually blend in the flour. Cook for 2–3 minutes, then blend in the stock or milk. Bring to the boil and cook until thickened. Add the meat, breadcrumbs and seasoning. Let the mixture stand for a short time, then form into 4 large or 8 small cutlet shapes. Brush with beaten egg and roll in crisp breadcrumbs. Fry steadily in hot shallow oil or fat until crisp and brown on either side. Serve hot or cold.

Freezing Freezes excellently, whether fried or just coated. Reheat or fry from frozen state. Use within 2–3 months.

Basic Mince Stew

Imperial/Metric	American
1–2 oz. (25–50 g.) fat	2–4 tablespoons shortening
1 large onion	1 large onion
1 lb. (½ kilo) minced beef or other raw meat	1 lb. ground beef or other raw meat
1 oz. (25 g.) flour	¼ cup flour
¾ pint (4½ dl.) stock or water and 1–2 stock cubes	just under 2 cups stock or water and 1–2 bouillon cubes
seasoning	seasoning

Cooking time just over 1 hour
Serves 4–5
Advance Preparations Cook and reheat when required. Never store uncooked or cooked mince for too long, even in a refrigerator, as it deteriorates very rapidly.

Method 1 (This has the advantage that the pieces of meat keep separate with the minimum of stirring and also it gives the meat a richer flavour.)
Heat the fat in a pan, stir in the chopped onion and fry for several minutes, then add the meat and cook, stirring well, until golden brown. Blend in the flour, then the liquid. Bring the mixture to the boil, stir until thickened, add seasoning to taste. Cover the pan and simmer gently for about 1 hour until tender.
Method 2 (This has the advantage of giving a more moist texture and I prefer this way of cooking minced meat myself.)
Fry the onion in the fat as method 1, blend in the flour then the liquid. Bring to the boil, cook until thickened. Add the meat and seasoning and stir very well to break up the lumps of meat. Cook as method 1, stirring once or twice.
Serve the minced meat with cooked pasta, boiled or mashed potatoes, cooked rice or crisp toast.

For Economy Cook small dumplings, as page 43, or potato dumplings, as page 21, in the mince stew. Check you have sufficient liquid in the pan before putting these in.
Add canned haricot (navy) beans (a good source of protein) to the mince stew. Add just before serving; heat for a few minutes only.
Freezing Cooked minced meat freezes excellently. Use within 3 months. See comments page 36.

Variations
Add chopped herbs or a good pinch of dried herbs to to the basic recipe.
Add sliced carrots or other vegetables to the mince halfway through the cooking period so they retain their firm texture.
Use tomato juice instead of stock, or use canned tomato soup instead of stock in the basic recipe. If the soup is fairly thick you can omit the flour. Other soups can also be used.
Curried Mince Blend a little curry powder with the flour in the basic recipe, add 1–2 tablespoons chutney and a little dried fruit to the mixture; serve with the same accompaniments as curry, page 45.

Recipes Based on Basic Mince Stew
Either method of cooking the basic mince recipe above may be used, unless stated to the contrary, and choose any meat, unless the recipe states otherwise.

Economy Moussaka Prepare the basic recipe. Meanwhile, slice and fry 2 aubergines (eggplants) and several peeled and sliced potatoes in a generous amount of oil. Arrange meat and vegetables in layers in a dish, top with hot cheese sauce, as page 61, and serve. Prepare ahead if more convenient and heat through slowly in the oven.

Lasagna Make the mince sauce, page 36, or the mince stew above. Cook 6–8 oz. (150–200 g.)

lasagna in boiling salted water, then drain. Prepare the cheese sauce as page 61. Put layers of the pasta, the meat sauce, then cheese sauce in an ovenproof dish. Top with grated cheese and heat gently in the oven.
Instead of making cheese sauce, top each layer of pasta and meat sauce with sliced hard cheese and grated Parmesan cheese. Spoonfuls of cream cheese may also be added for a richer flavour (do not put cream cheese over top of dish, it would burn).

French Style Beef Cook the basic mince stew by either method, increasing the amount of onions to 3 or 4 and cutting these into rings. Put the cooked meat mixture into a flameproof dish, top with rounds of French bread and grated Gruyère or Cheddar cheese and brown under the grill (broiler) for a few minutes.

Scottish Mince Omit the flour (use method 1) and add to the mince 1 oz. (25 g. — 3 tablespoons) oatmeal blended with a little cold stock, about 45 minutes before the end of the cooking time. Stir once or twice to make quite sure the oatmeal mixture keeps smooth.

Ragoût à l'Italienne (choose beef or veal) Fry 1–2 crushed cloves of garlic with the onion, together with 2 skinned chopped tomatoes and 3 sliced mushrooms. Cook the mince mixture and add a diced green pepper (discard core and seeds) about 15 minutes before the end of the cooking time.

Economical Goulash (use either all beef, or a mixture of beef and veal, or beef and pork) *Version A* Blend 1–2 teaspoons paprika (this is not a hot pepper but sweet) with the flour; use a little less liquid than in the basic recipe, on previous page. Cook the mixture for about 40 minutes, then add a few skinned firm tomatoes and finish cooking. *Version B* If preferred, add potatoes to the goulash; in this case blend the paprika with the stock and *omit the flour.* Cook the goulash for about 30 minutes, then add 2–3 peeled sliced potatoes, cook for 10 minutes, then add the tomatoes as above. Serve a goulash with boiled potatoes or noodles.

Mince Stuffed Tomatoes (choose any minced meat) To fill 8 large tomatoes follow the basic mince stew recipe, but allow only 8 oz. (200 g.) beef or other meat and half quantities of all other ingredients. Cook the mince and allow this to cool and stiffen. Cut the tops off the tomatoes, scoop out the centre pulp. Chop the pulp and mix with the cold mince, together with finely chopped spring onions (scallions) or chives, and a very little mayonnaise. Pile the soft mixture back into the seasoned tomato cases, put the tops back on (see picture) and serve cold with more spring onions (scallions) and a mixed salad.
To serve the stuffed tomatoes hot, omit the mayonnaise. Blend the chopped tomato pulp into the hot or cold minced meat mixture. If this seems a little soft, cook gently in an open pan until any excess liquid has evaporated. Mix in the chopped spring onions (scallions) or chives. Pile back into the tomato cases, put the lids on top, put into a greased ovenproof dish and bake for about 12–15 minutes in the centre of a moderate oven.

Supper Loaf Make the minced beef mixture as either method, see previous page, but use just under ½ pint (3 dl. — 1¼ cups) stock, so you have a *thick* meat mixture by the end of the cooking time. You can use any other flavourings as desired, see pages 38 to 40. Take a large sandwich loaf, cut off one end (save this) and scoop out the centre crumb (use this for meat loaves, etc., see page 208, or making crisp breadcrumbs, see page 5). Pack the minced beef mixture into the centre of the loaf, together with slices of raw well seasoned tomatoes. Replace the slice cut off, then wrap the whole loaf in foil. Heat for about 30 minutes in a moderate oven, then serve hot as a meat pie, cutting thick slices off the loaf.

Mince stuffed tomatoes

Creole Mutton (choose minced (ground) mutton) Cook as either method, see previous page, but increase the onions to 3. Flavour the mince with a good pinch of chilli powder, add a can of corn and a diced fresh, or canned, red and green pepper about 10 minutes before the end of the cooking time. Discard the cores and seeds from the fresh vegetables.

Beef Mexicalli Increase the onions to 3, chop these and fry in the fat together with 3 skinned chopped tomatoes. Make the mince by either method on page 38, then add sufficient chilli sauce or chilli powder (blended with a little cold water) to make a really hot spicy flavour. Remember chilli flavourings are very hot, so use only a pinch or a few drops to begin with. Taste the mixture and adjust to suit your own personal taste. Tip a medium can of haricot (navy) beans into the mince 15 minutes before the end of the cooking time.

Beef Indienne Blend 1 teaspoon curry powder only with the flour, make the mince as the basic recipe, but flavour with a few drops Tabasco and Worcestershire sauces. Stir in 1–2 oz. (25–50 g. – 3–6 tablespoons) sultanas (seedless white raisins), 1 tablespoon desiccated (shredded) coconut and 1 tablespoon chutney about 10 minutes before the end of the cooking time. Serve with boiled rice.

Savoury Risotto (choose any minced meat) Omit the flour from the recipe on page 38. Add 2 oz. (50 g. – just over ¼ cup) long grain rice to the mixture 25 minutes before the end of the cooking time. *Check there is adequate moisture in the pan*, since the rice absorbs a considerable amount of liquid – it is advisable to use 1 pint (6 dl. – 2½ cups) liquid instead of ¾ pint (4½ dl. – just under 2 cups).

Sweet and Sour Pork (choose lean pork) Use either method of cooking the mince, see page 38, but a *little less stock*. Add about 4 tablespoons (5 tablespoons) syrup from a can of pineapple cubes, plus 1 tablespoon vinegar, then add 2 tablespoons (3 tablespoons) chopped mustard pickle and 4 tablespoons (5 tablespoons) halved pineapple cubes about 5 minutes before the end of the cooking time.

Beef Minestrone Use either method of cooking the mince, see page 38, but increase the amount of stock to 1 pint (6 dl. – 2½ cups). Fry 2–3 chopped tomatoes with the onion, together with 1 crushed clove of garlic. Add 1 oz. (25 g.) spaghetti (broken into small pieces) or short-length macaroni 15 minutes before the end of the cooking time, and a small can baked beans together with 4 tablespoons (5 tablespoons) shredded cabbage 5 minutes before the end of the cooking time. Serve each portion topped with grated Parmesan cheese.

Curried Mince Collops

Imperial/Metric	American
1 onion	1 onion
1 apple	1 apple
2 oz. (50 g.) fat or dripping	¼ cup shortening or drippings
1 tablespoon curry powder	1 tablespoon curry powder
1 oz. (25 g.) flour	¼ cup flour
1 pint (6 dl.) stock or water and 1 chicken or beef stock cube	2½ cups stock or water and 1 chicken or beef bouillon cube
1 lb. (½ kilo) minced beef	1 lb. ground beef
1–2 tablespoons raisins or sultanas	1–2 tablespoons raisins or seedless white raisins
1 tablespoon desiccated coconut	1 tablespoon shredded coconut
seasoning	seasoning

Cooking time 1 hour 10 minutes
Serves 4–6
Advance Preparations Cook and reheat as required.

Peel the onion and apple, grate or chop. Heat the fat or dripping in a good sized saucepan. Toss the onion and apple in this, then stir in the curry powder. Blend the flour with some of the liquid. Add to the pan, together with the rest of the liquid. Bring to the boil, stirring well as the mixture thickens. Add the meat and stir this carefully so you break up any lumps of meat. Add the dried fruit, coconut and seasoning. Cover the saucepan, lower the heat and cook slowly for about 1 hour. Stir once or twice during cooking.

Freezing This freezes well; use within 3 months.

Meat Balls

This recipe gives a delicious flavour but one kind of meat only also may be used, rather than mixing the meats as below.

Imperial/Metric	American
8 oz. (200 g.) finely minced veal	½ lb. finely ground veal
8 oz. (200 g.) finely minced pork	½ lb. finely ground pork
1 small finely minced onion	1 small finely ground onion
1 oz. (25 g.) flour	¼ cup flour
1 oz. (25 g.) soft breadcrumbs	½ cup soft bread crumbs
good pinch mixed herbs	good pinch mixed herbs
enough thin cream to bind the mixture	enough coffee cream to bind the mixture
seasoning	seasoning
for frying	**for frying**
oil, fat or margarine	oil, shortening or margarine

Cooking time 6–8 minutes
Serves 4–6
Advance Preparations Make balls and leave for few hours in refrigerator. Do not store for too long a period before freezing or cooking.

Put all ingredients except cream and seasoning into a bowl. Mix well, gradually add enough cream to give a soft consistency (this averages about 4 (5) tablespoons). Season well. With damp fingers form into tiny balls the size of a walnut, fry steadily in hot oil, fat or margarine. Drain on absorbent paper then serve hot with tomato or other sauce, see pages 105 and 61.

Freezing Make and freeze, or fry, drain well on absorbent paper, then freeze. Fry or reheat from frozen state. Use within 2–3 months.

Variations

Flavour the meat balls with about ¼ teaspoon mixed spice, nutmeg, cinnamon.
Omit both the flour and the breadcrumbs and add 3 tablespoons (4 tablespoons) soft smooth mashed potato.
Omit the cream and bind with an egg.
Mix 2 oz. (50 g. – ½ cup) chopped nuts (pine nuts, cashew nuts, peanuts) with the meat mixture.
Meat Balls in Cream Sauce Brown the balls in a little hot butter or margarine for a few minutes only, then add about 5 tablespoons (6 tablespoons) thin (coffee) cream and ½ pint (3 dl. – 1¼ cups) brown stock. Simmer the balls gently for 15 minutes. Lift out of the pan and keep hot. Blend the liquid in the pan with a little cornflour (cornstarch) or flour, then

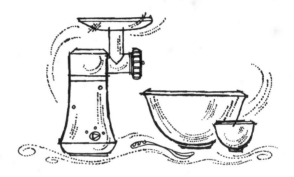

simmer gently until the liquid thickens. Replace the meat balls for 1–2 minutes; serve with the sauce.
Meat Ball Kebabs Make the mixture as the basic recipe, but roll the small meat balls in lightly floured hands to make them a little firmer in texture. Put on to metal skewers with small mushrooms, tiny tomatoes and rings of green pepper. Brush with melted butter or margarine and cook under the grill (broiler), turning once or twice, until golden brown. Serve with cooked rice. If you press the minced beef ball kebabs with oiled hands when they are on the skewers, but before cooking, they are less inclined to break.
Swiss Steaks Follow the basic recipe but use a mixture of beef and pork, or all minced (ground) beef. Form into round flat cakes. Coat with well seasoned flour and fry steadily in a little hot oil or fat (shortening).
Mock Escalopes of Veal Use the basic recipe with all veal, or a mixture of veal and pork. Form into very thin rounds and fry in hot butter until tender. Garnish with lemon slices, chopped hard-boiled (hard-cooked) egg and chopped parsley, or with anchovy fillets.

Boiled Silverside with Savoury Dumplings

Imperial/Metric	American
3–4 lb. (1½–2 kilos) salt brisket or silverside of beef*	3–4 lb. corned beef (or bottom round of beef*)
water	water
1 large onion	1 large onion
1 large carrot	1 large carrot
1 bay leaf	1 bay leaf
for the dumplings	**for the dumplings**
4 oz. (100 g.) flour (with plain flour use 1 teaspoon baking powder)	1 cup flour (with all-purpose flour use 1 teaspoon baking powder – double-acting)
good pinch salt	good pinch salt
2 oz. (50 g.) shredded suet	just under ½ cup chopped suet
½–1 tablespoon chopped herbs (optional)	½–1 tablespoon chopped herbs (optional)
water to mix	water to mix

* salted meat shrinks so allow a good 8 oz. (200 g.) per person.

Cooking time see method
Serves 6–8
Advance Preparations Soak the beef overnight in cold water to cover.

Put the beef into fresh cold water, bring to boil, add onion, carrot, bay leaf. Simmer very gently in covered pan, allowing 30 minutes to each lb. (½ kilo) and 30 minutes over. To make the dumplings sieve the flour, or flour and baking powder, and salt, add suet and herbs and mix with enough water to form a sticky dough. Roll into balls with floured hands. Add the dumplings to the stock 15–20 minutes before the end of the cooking time. Lift the meat from the stock, arrange the dumplings round. Serve a little unthickened stock in a sauceboat.

For Economy Salted meats are not quite as economical as they seem due to shrinkage in cooking.
Freezing The cooked or uncooked meat (plus dumplings) freezes well; as salted use within 6 weeks.

Variations
The dumplings may be varied by adding 1–2 teaspoons grated onion.
Add whole or sliced onions and carrots approximately 40–50 minutes before the end of the cooking time.
If wanting to serve as a cold joint, allow to cool in the stock. This helps to keep it moist.
Pressed Salt Beef The cold meat may be pressed into a neat shape. Cook the meat as above, lift out of the liquid. Put the meat into a basin or tin; it should be a fairly tight fit. Blend 2 teaspoons powdered gelatine with a little cold water, dissolve in ½ pint (3 dl. —

1¼ cups) hot stock. Strain over enough stock to cover meat. Cool, then place greaseproof (wax) paper and a weight on top, leave until firm. If any jellied stock is left it can be used as garnish.

Stewed Steak and Dumplings

Imperial/Metric	American
1—1½ lb. (½—¾ kilo) beef steak	1—1½ lb. beef, chuck or round steak
seasoning	seasoning
1½ oz. (40 g.) fat	3 tablespoons shortening
2 onions	2 onions
3 large or 6—8 small carrots	3 large or 6—8 small carrots
¾ pint (4½ dl.) water	just under 2 cups water
½—1 bay leaf	½—1 bay leaf
little nutmeg or mixed herbs	little nutmeg or mixed herbs
for the dumplings	**for the dumplings**
4 oz. (100 g.) flour (with plain flour use ¾ teaspoon baking powder)	1 cup flour (with all-purpose flour use ¾ teaspoon baking powder — double-acting)
seasoning	seasoning
2 oz. (50 g.) shredded suet	just under ⅓ cup chopped suet
water to mix	water to mix

Cooking time 2½ hours
Serves 4
Advance Preparations Stews always have a better flavour if cooked and then reheated, so this can be pre-cooked and reheated gently *but thoroughly*.

Dice the meat. Season, then brown in the hot fat. Add the sliced onions and sliced or whole carrots, water and herbs. Cover pan and simmer for 2 hours. Sieve the flour, or flour and baking powder, and seasoning, add the suet, mix to a *soft* dough with the water. Roll into balls with lightly floured hands. Check there is sufficient liquid in the stew, then drop in the dumplings and cook for 15—20 minutes. Remove bay leaf. Serve with green vegetables, etc., as soon as cooked.

Freezing The stew and dumplings freeze well. Use within 3—4 months.

Variations
Extra vegetables may be added to the stew.
Add 2 cloves and 2 teaspoons vinegar to the stew or 1—2 teaspoons paprika.
For a thicker consistency to the gravy, coat the meat in 1 oz. (25 g. — ¼ cup) seasoned flour before browning in the fat.
Dumplings may be varied by adding chopped fresh herbs, a *little* dry mustard or grated horseradish or finely chopped onion.
Stewed Steak and Kidney This is a basic beef stew which can be varied in many ways, e.g. use a mixture of stewing steak and ox (beef) kidney instead

of all beef. You can add 1—2 chopped cloves garlic to the onions for extra flavour. Use half red wine and half water instead of all water, or use beef stock or water plus 1 beef stock (bouillon) cube.
Carbonnade of Beef Omit the carrots in the basic recipe but add 1—2 cloves garlic to the onions. Cook the stew as the basic recipe (coating the meat with seasoned flour before frying) but use beer, plus 1 tablespoon vinegar, in place of water.
Beef and Orange Casserole (Illustrated) Follow directions for the basic recipe but add fine strips orange rind and green pepper to the vegetables, etc. Garnish cooked stew with pieces of orange. Omit dumplings.

Veal Niçoise

Imperial/Metric	American
1 lb. (½ kilo) stewing veal	1 lb. stewing veal
seasoning	seasoning
1 oz. (25 g.) flour	¼ cup flour
3 onions	3 onions
1 lb. (½ kilo) tomatoes	1 lb. tomatoes
4 oz. (100 g.) butter or margarine	½ cup butter or margarine
pinch thyme	pinch thyme
1 bay leaf	1 bay leaf
½ pint (3 dl.) white wine or more stock	1¼ cups white wine or more stock
8 oz. (200 g.) long grain rice	just over 1 cup long grain rice
1 pint (6 dl.) white stock or water and 1 chicken stock cube	2½ cups white stock or water and 1 chicken bouillon cube
8 oz. (200 g.) long grain rice	1½ cups frozen peas
to garnish	**to garnish**
4 tomatoes	4 tomatoes
1 clove garlic	1 clove garlic

Cooking time 1¼ *hours*
Serves 4
Advance Preparations Cook veal, etc. in pan. Collect rest of ingredients to complete cooking.

Cut veal into large chunks, coat in seasoned flour. Skin and slice the onions and tomatoes. Melt half the butter or margarine in saucepan, fry meat for approximately 10 minutes, turning frequently. Remove meat from saucepan and fry sliced onions on medium heat for 4–5 minutes. When onions are brown, replace meat, add tomatoes with seasoning, thyme, bay leaf and the wine or stock. Cover and cook at a low temperature for 1 hour. Put rice, stock or water and stock cube and seasoning into a pan. Bring to boil and stir once. Cover and simmer for 10 minutes, add peas and continue cooking for 5 minutes, or until rice is tender and liquid absorbed. Melt the remainder of the butter or margarine, fry the 4 tomatoes slowly for 5–10 minutes; cut a cross on their tops, sprinkle with crushed garlic and season. Place briefly under grill (broiler) to colour garlic. Place rice with peas in a dish, cover with meat, onions and sauce. Garnish with whole tomatoes. *Illustrated on page 34.*

Stews with Lamb and Mutton

Navarin of Lamb or Mutton Use best end or middle neck of lamb or mutton or diced meat from the shoulder. Sprinkle with salt, pepper and sugar, then fry in a little hot butter. Sprinkle a small quantity of flour over meat, then blend in enough water to cover the meat. Add a bunch of herbs and a selection of vegetables. Cover the pan and simmer for 1½ hours.
For Economy Cook extra vegetables and use these, plus extra liquid, as the basis for an economical mulligatawny soup. Sieve or emulsify the vegetables and any tiny pieces of meat, flavour with curry powder and heat.

Irish Stew This is made in a somewhat similar way to the navarin. Use the more economical scrag end of neck (neck slices). Put into a pan with water to cover, season, add plenty of sliced onions plus a few sliced potatoes (these will thicken the liquid). Simmer for about 45 minutes, then add whole potatoes and continue cooking. Top with chopped parsley.

Stewed Lamb and Caper Sauce Cook the lamb and vegetables as in the navarin, but do not fry the meat and omit any flour. Serve with caper sauce made by making a white sauce, page 61, with half milk and half lamb stock, then add 2–3 teaspoons capers and a little vinegar from the jar just before serving.

Lamb and Apple Curry

The recipe for curry sauce below is a splendid basic one that you can adapt for other foods, see variations.

Imperial/Metric	American
1¼ lb. (¾ kilo) stewing lamb	1½ lb. stewing lamb
for the curry sauce	**for the curry sauce**
1–2 onions	1–2 onions
1–2 sticks celery (optional)	1–2 stalks celery (optional)
2 oz. (50 g.) dripping or fat	¼ cup drippings or shortening
1 tablespoon curry powder*	1 tablespoon curry power*
1–2 teaspoons curry paste†	1–2 teaspoons curry paste†
1 oz. (25 g.) flour	¼ cup flour
approximately ¾ pint (4½ dl.) stock or water	approximately 2 cups stock or water
1 tablespoon chutney or seedless jam	1 tablespoon chutney or seedless jam
1–2 cooking apples	1–2 baking apples
1 tablespoon desiccated coconut	1 tablespoon shredded coconut
1–2 tablespoons sultanas (optional)	1–2 tablespoons seedless white raisins (optional)
squeeze lemon juice or few drops vinegar	squeeze lemon juice or few drops vinegar
seasoning	seasoning

* or to taste.

† gives an excellent flavour.

Cooking time 1 hour 35 minutes
Serves 4–6
Advance Preparations Cook, reheat when required.

Dice the meat. Peel and slice or chop the onions, cut the celery into small pieces. Heat the dripping or fat and toss the onions and celery in this, then stir in the curry powder, curry paste and flour. Cook gently for several minutes, stirring well. Gradually blend in the liquid (use a little more if you prefer a thinner sauce). Add the diced meat, chutney or jam and continue cooking in a tightly covered pan for 1 hour. Peel and cut the apples into fairly large pieces, add to the curry with the rest of the ingredients. Continue cooking for 30 minutes. Serve with boiled rice and accompaniments, see page 146 and below.
Illustrated on page 35.

For Economy Use less meat and add diced vegetables to the mixture, i.e. carrots, swede, beans, etc.
Freezing The curry freezes very well; you may find the sauce tends to become thinner when reheated, in which case blend a little cornflour (cornstarch) with water, stir into the sauce and thicken. Use within 3 months.

Variations

Chop the apples finely and fry with the onions, etc.
Cooked Meat Curry Make the sauce first, simmer until smooth, then add cooked meat. Leave to stand in the sauce for some hours if possible, then heat.
Fish Curry Use fish stock and rather more lemon juice. Add diced raw fish to the cooked sauce and cook gently.
Egg Curry Make the sauce and add hard-boiled (hard-cooked) eggs. Leave to stand in the sauce for some hours if possible, then heat gently.

Accompaniments for Curry

A good chutney is the most usual and pleasant accompaniment, but in addition you can serve: bananas (sprinkled with lemon juice), orange rings, sliced tomatoes and green peppers, sliced onions or pickled onions, gherkins, coconut, and dried fruit. The classic accompaniments are poppadums, parathas, chapatis — heat these Indian breads as instructed on the packet — and Bombay duck (a dried fish) which is sprinkled over the curry.
Minted Apple Relish This is shown in the picture. Peel and chop or grate dessert apples, blend with sugar, chopped mint and a little cider vinegar.

Steak and Kidney Pudding

Imperial/Metric	American
for the suet crust	**for the suet crust**
8 oz. (200 g.) flour (with plain flour use 1 teaspoon baking powder)	2 cups flour (with all-purpose flour use 1 teaspoon baking powder – double-acting)
4 oz. (100 g.) shredded suet	just under 1 cup chopped suet
seasoning	seasoning
water to mix	water to mix
for the filling	**for the filling**
1 lb. ($\frac{1}{2}$ kilo) stewing steak	1 lb. stewing steak
2–3 lamb's kidneys or 4 oz. (100 g.) ox kidney	2–3 lamb kidneys or $\frac{1}{4}$ lb. beef kidney
$\frac{1}{2}$ oz. (15 g.) flour	2 tablespoons flour
water or stock	water or stock

Cooking time   minimum of 4 hours
Serves 4–6
Advance Preparations Make the pudding. You can cook as the recipe and reheat when required.

Mix all the dry ingredients together, add enough water to make a rolling consistency. Line a greased 2-pint (1$\frac{1}{4}$-litre – 5-cup) pudding basin with three-quarters of the pastry, retain enough for the cover. Cut the meat into small pieces. Skin, core and chop the kidney. Mix the meats together and put into the lined basin, sprinkle each layer with flour and seasoning. Add enough water or stock to nearly fill the basin. Put on the pastry lid, damp the edges and seal well together. Cover with the greased greaseproof (wax) paper and foil. Leave room for the pastry to swell. Steam for a minimum of 4 hours. Serve with thickened gravy.

For Economy Use less meat and add diced carrots and onions.
Freezing This pudding freezes perfectly whether just prepared and then frozen, or cooked *lightly* and frozen (*do not over-cook*). Use within 3–4 months.

Variations

Bacon and Onion Pudding Use diced uncooked bacon or ham instead of steak and kidney. Soak the bacon or ham overnight in cold water. Add 2 chopped onions with the meat.
Chicken and Vegetable Pudding Use jointed raw chicken and vegetables instead of steak and kidney. It is better to use a less young chicken in this dish so it does not become over-cooked.
Luxury Steak and Kidney Pudding Remove the pudding from the heat when cooked, lift the lid gently and

add oysters or clams and a few mushrooms. Return to the heat for about 20 minutes only.
Vegetable Pudding Use mixed vegetables including those that provide protein (beans, peas and lentils) instead of meat. Flavour the liquid with yeast extract.

Steak and Kidney Pie

Imperial/Metric	American
1¼–1½ lb. (⅝–¾ kilo) stewing steak	1¼–1½ lb. stewing steak
4–6 oz. (100–150 g.) ox kidney	¼–⅓ lb. beef kidney
seasoning	seasoning
1 oz. (25 g.) flour	¼ cup flour
1 oz. (25 g.) fat	2 tablespoons shortening
1 pint (6 dl.) stock	2½ cups stock
2–3 tomatoes, skinned and chopped (optional)	2–3 tomatoes, skinned and chopped (optional)
short, flaky or puff pastry made with 6–8 oz. (150–200 g.) flour, etc., see recipes pages 72 and 193	basic or rich flaky pie dough, or puff paste made with 1½–2 cups flour, etc., see recipes pages 72 and 193
to glaze	**to glaze**
1 egg or little milk	1 egg or little milk

Cooking time 2 hours
Serves 4–6
Advance Preparations Prepare meat as recipe – put into pie dish, cool then cover with the pastry.

Cut the meat into 1-inch (2-cm.) cubes, roll in the seasoned flour. Fry in the hot fat for a few minutes, then gradually blend in the stock and cook until the mixture has thickened slightly. Add the tomatoes if used. Put a lid on the pan, lower the heat and simmer for approximately 1½ hours. Allow the meat to cool, put a funnel into a 1½–2-pint (⅞–1¼-litre – 4–5-cup) pie dish, lift the meat into the dish with a little of the gravy – save the rest to serve with the pie. Roll out the pastry and cover the pie. Form any scraps into leaves, etc., for decoration, brush with beaten egg or a little milk and stick into position. Brush the pie with egg or milk. Make a slit over the funnel to allow the steam to escape. Bake in the centre of a hot oven if using short crust pastry (basic pie dough), or a very hot oven if using the richer pastry, for 10 minutes, then lower the heat to moderate, 350–375°F. (180–190°C.), Gas Mark 4–5, and cook for a further 20–30 minutes.

For Economy Use less meat plus mixed vegetables.
Freezing The pie may be prepared and frozen or cooked, cooled and frozen. Use within 3 months.

Variations
Chicken and Vegetable Pie Use chicken and vegetables instead of steak and kidney. If using young chicken, the cooking time before putting the mixture into the pie dish need be only 15–20 minutes.
Luxury Steak and Kidney Pie Add button mushrooms to the meat when putting into the pie dish. Lift off

the pie crust gently when cooked and add oysters or clams and heat for about 10 minutes only.
Veal and Ham Pie Use diced stewing veal and uncooked diced ham or bacon (smoked ham) instead of steak and kidney. Soak the bacon or ham overnight in cold water. This type of pie is nicer eaten hot.

Cooking Offal (Variety Meats)

Offal (variety meats) are not always economical dishes, for some of these – calf's head, lambs' kidneys and sweetbreads – are becoming luxury dishes. It is possible, however, to make delicious and inexpensive dishes from the cheaper tripe, ox (beef) liver and ox (beef) kidney.

Many of the dishes below are ideal for invalids and older people for they are particularly easy to digest.

Here are some easy recipes to try:

Brains Prepare these carefully; wash in cold water, remove the membranes. Simmer for about 15 minutes in water with a little salt and a few drops of vinegar or lemon juice. Strain and add to a white sauce, see page 61, or fry with bacon or in butter. One of the best known dishes is the following.

Brains in Brown Butter Fry the brains in hot butter, remove from pan, allow remaining butter to turn dark brown then add lemon juice and capers and chopped parsley. Spoon over brains.

You can cut the cooked brains into neat pieces, dry well, then coat in seasoned flour or flour and egg and crumbs then fry in butter or deep fat (shortening). Drain and serve on toast or as a cocktail snack.

Brains are one of the most easily digested foods.

Feet or Trotters These are often used to make a brawn, see recipe under 'head' below, but you can simmer these in stock until tender, then remove the meat and fry this.

Head Buy calf's, lamb's or pig's head; split this. Wash in cold water with a few drops vinegar. Remove brains for sauce (below).

Head with Brain Sauce A calf's head is usually used. Simmer head in seasoned water, with herbs to flavour, for 3 hours. Remove meat from bones, dice, serve with brain sauce made by simmering brains as above. Chop and add to white sauce, page 61.

Brawn Use any meat. Cook head for $1\frac{1}{2}$ hours. Lift from liquid. Dice meat neatly. Return to liquid with a small quantity diced steak and little lemon juice. Simmer for further $1\frac{1}{2}$ hours. Pack meat in basin. Boil liquid hard to reduce slightly. Strain over meat; leave to set.

Use several trotters (feet) instead of head.

Heart The tenderest hearts to buy are lambs'. Allow one large or two small ones per person. If you buy the larger pig's or calf's (veal) heart then one should serve two people. Ox (beef) heart should be sliced and used as below.

To prepare the hearts cut away the tough parts from the outside and centre.

Roasted Hearts (suitable for the tender, smaller ones) Split the hearts and insert your chosen stuffing. Wrap each heart in plenty of well buttered foil. Cook lambs' hearts for about $1\frac{1}{4}$–$1\frac{1}{2}$ hours in a moderate oven but allow $1\frac{1}{2}$–2 hours for the larger pig's or calf's (veal) hearts. Serve with thickened gravy.

Braised Ox (Beef) Heart Slice ox heart and cook as braised kidneys on the next page, or use ox heart instead of stewing steak in the recipe on page 43, or in a curry, page 45.

Hearts are, like liver and kidneys, a good source of iron, so make a particularly important protein food.

Liver Calf's liver is the most tender and easily digested and therefore is suitable for young children or invalids; but other kinds of liver are also very important foods, for liver, like all kinds of meat, is an important protein food, but it also is rich in iron.

Ox (Beef) Liver Slice and braise this as the recipe for kidneys opposite, or use instead of steak in the recipe on page 43. If you add a little sugar to the liquid in this recipe you help to counteract the slightly bitter taste of the liver.

Fried Liver Slice liver, coat *lightly* in seasoned flour and fry for about 5–6 minutes in hot butter, dripping or fat (shortening). Do not over-cook liver, for this toughens the meat.

To give an interesting flavour to the liver make a good brown gravy in the pan in which the meat was fried; serve with fried bacon, fried tomatoes and fried rings of onion.

Sprinkle a very little sugar over the liver before coating with the seasoned flour; this gives a slightly caramel taste, which is delicious.

Orange juice can be sprinkled over the liver before frying.

Tender liver can be grilled (broiled); always keep it well basted with plenty of butter.

Use liver in pâté, e.g. rillettes, page 170, etc.; see also page 51.

Kidneys Calf's (veal), lamb's and pig's kidneys are all sufficiently tender to cook fairly quickly, whereas ox (beef) kidney must be cooked slowly; use the recipe for stewed steak on page 43, or the recipe below.

To prepare kidneys: remove the skin and any tough membranes from the outside. Cut out the cores. Small lamb's kidneys can be cooked whole, but larger kidneys should be halved or sliced.

Fried Kidneys Prepare the kidneys as above, season lightly. Fry in hot bacon fat or butter or dripping and serve on hot toast or with fried bacon and tomatoes, etc. Lamb's kidneys take about 6 minutes, calf's (veal) and pig's kidneys a little longer.

Grilled (Broiled) Kidneys As kidneys are very lean keep them well basted with melted butter or fat (shortening) during cooking. Cooking time as frying. Diced or halved or whole small kidneys are an excellent ingredient for kebabs, which can be cooked over the barbecue fire or under the grill (broiler).

Devilled Kidneys To give fried or grilled kidneys a more savoury flavour they can be dusted with cayenne pepper, a little curry powder and a few drops Worcestershire sauce before cooking.

Kidneys in Port Wine Slice lamb's kidneys, coat in seasoned flour, then fry in hot butter for several minutes. Gradually stir in port wine, or port wine and stock, to give a coating sauce. Heat for a few minutes, then serve on toast or as a filling for an omelette.

Braised Kidneys

Imperial/Metric	American
1 oz. (25 g.) flour	¼ cup flour
seasoning	seasoning
1–1¼ lb. (½–⅝ kilo) ox kidney	1–1¼ lb. beef kidney
2 oz. (50 g.) dripping or fat	¼ cup drippings or shortening
2 onions	2 onions
2 rashers streaky bacon	2 bacon slices
2–3 tomatoes	2–3 tomatoes
stock or water or wine (see method)	stock or water or wine (see method)

Cooking time 1¾ hours
Serves 4
Advance Preparations Cook and reheat as required.

Mix the flour with a generous amount of seasoning. Cut the kidney into neat fingers and coat with the seasoned flour. Fry in the hot dripping or fat for several minutes, then remove from the pan. Cut the peeled onions into rings; remove bacon rinds and dice the bacon. Fry the bacon rinds for 2–3 minutes to extract any fat, then add the diced bacon and onions and cook for several minutes. Add the thickly sliced tomatoes, with enough stock, water or wine to cover. Season this layer lightly, place the browned kidney on top. Cover the pan and cook over a low heat for 1½ hours or until the kidney is very tender. If preferred cook this dish in a *very tightly* covered casserole in a slow to very moderate oven, 300–325°F. (150–170°C.), Gas Mark 2–3. The vegetables and bacon may be sieved or emulsified to make a thick sauce, or can be served round the meat.

Variations

Braised Beef or Other Meats The above is a basic way of braising which can be adapted to cooking beef or other meats. If using prime cuts (the type generally used for frying or grilling), shorten the cooking time to 35–40 minutes; if using stewing meat then increase the cooking time to about 2–2½ hours, depending upon the thickness of the meat.

The 'mirepoix', i.e. the mixture used below the meat, can be varied — chopped celery, sliced carrots, etc., may be added. It is important not to use too much liquid though, otherwise the meat tastes as though it were stewed. Braising is a much richer form of cooking than stewing, for the meat retains much of the texture of roasting.

Burgundy Oxtail

Imperial/Metric	American
1 medium sized oxtail	1 medium sized oxtail
seasoning	seasoning
1½ oz. (40 g.) flour	6 tablespoons flour
2 oz. (50 g.) fat	¼ cup shortening
1 pint (6 dl.) beef stock or water and 1 beef stock cube	2½ cups beef stock or water and 1 beef bouillon cube
¼ pint (1½ dl.) red wine (Burgundy) or extra stock	⅔ cup red wine (Burgundy) or extra stock
1 onion	1 onion
4 cloves (optional)	4 cloves (optional)
8 oz. (200 g.) carrots	½ lb. carrots
2–3 sticks celery	2–3 stalks celery
1 clove garlic	1 clove garlic
bouquet garni	bouquet garni
4 oz. (100 g.) mushrooms	1 cup mushrooms
1 leek	1 leek
to serve	**to serve**
potatoes	potatoes
green vegetable	green vegetable
to garnish	**to garnish**
sprig parsley	sprig parsley

Cooking time minimum of 2¾ hours
Serves 4
Advance Preparations It is better to cook this the day
before required, allow it to cool then remove excess
fat and reheat.

Trim any excess fat from tail and cut into tiny pieces.
Coat in the seasoned flour. Heat the fat and fry the
oxtail in this until golden brown. Remove the oxtail
pieces from the pan and gradually stir in the stock or
water and stock cube and wine. Bring to the boil and
cook until slightly thickened, stir well. Add the onion
(stuck with the cloves), the thickly sliced carrots,
chopped celery, crushed clove of garlic, the browned
oxtail and the *bouquet garni*. Cover tightly in the pan,
or put into a casserole, cover and cook for 1¼ hours
in the centre of a very moderate oven, 325°F.
(170°C.), Gas Mark 3. Add the mushrooms, halved
if large, and the chopped leek. Cook for a further
45 minutes. Serve hot with potatoes and a green
vegetable. Top with parsley.

Variation

Add soaked haricot (navy) beans to the sauce and
cook with the meat and vegetables, or add canned
beans in tomato sauce just before serving.
For a Richer Sauce Use rather more wine and less
stock.

Tongue Ox (beef) tongue is generally salted by the butcher, so soak overnight in cold water. Lamb's and calf's tongues are rarely salted. Cover meat with fresh cold water, add pepper (and salt if not salted), bay leaf, 1–2 onions and 1–2 carrots. Bring water to boil, lower heat and simmer. Allow 40 minutes per lb. (½ kilo). When cooked remove skin and any bones from tongue.

To Serve Hot Slice and coat with Madeira or Espagnole sauce (page 61) or see recipe page 145.

To Serve Cold Put tongue or tongues into a round tin (roll to give a good shape). Boil stock until reduced to about ¼ pint (1½ dl. – ⅔ cup). Dissolve 1 teaspoon gelatine in hot stock, pour over tongue, leave with weight on top until cold.

Liver and Bacon Hot Pot

Imperial/Metric	American
1 lb. (½ kilo) leeks	1 lb. leeks
8 oz. (200 g.) tomatoes	½ lb. tomatoes
8 rashers streaky bacon	8 bacon slices
1 lb. (½ kilo) sliced lamb's liver	1 lb. sliced lamb liver
12 soaked prunes	12 soaked prunes
seasoning	seasoning
¾ pint (4½ dl.) stock or water and 1 beef stock cube	just under 2 cups stock or water and 1 beef bouillon cube
to serve	**to serve**
jacket or creamed potatoes	jacket or creamed potatoes
green vegetable	green vegetable

Cooking time 2 hours
Serves 4

Advance Preparations Cover the prunes with the stock overnight. Lift out but do not cook. Do not cook this particular casserole before required.

Clean and slice the leeks, peel and quarter the tomatoes. Remove rind from the bacon rashers and roll up tightly. Arrange sliced liver, leeks, tomatoes and prunes in casserole, seasoning each layer. Top with bacon rolls. Pour in stock or water and stock cube almost to cover contents. Cover and cook for 1½ hours in the centre of a very moderate to moderate oven, 350–375°F. (180–190°C.), Gas Mark 4–5. Remove lid and continue cooking until bacon rolls are golden brown and liver is tender. Serve hot with jacket or creamed potatoes and a green vegetable.

Variations

Use tomato purée (paste) instead of stock or water and stock cube.

Thicken stock with 1 oz. (25 g. – ¼ cup) flour, heat in pan until smooth, then add to casserole and cook as above.

Ox (beef) liver can be used in this dish. Slice it very thinly and allow approximately 2½–3 hours cooking.

More Recipes Using Offal (Variety Meats)

The recipes on this page are for meats that are suitable for invalids, as well as the rest of the family.
White stock mentioned in the recipes means stock made from veal or chicken bones.

Sweetbreads These come from the pancreas and throat of a young calf or lamb and have the advantage of being particularly easily digested. Calf sweetbreads are considered to have the better flavour.

To prepare sweetbreads: wash in plenty of cold water, then soak for 1–2 hours in cold water. Sweetbreads should be 'blanched' before being cooked. This means you put them into a pan with cold water to cover, then bring the water to boiling point and throw this away; 'blanching' whitens the meat.

Creamed Sweetbreads Put the blanched sweetbreads into a pan with a mixture of white stock and milk to cover (or use all white stock, or water with a small quantity of a chicken stock (bouillon) cube). Add a bay leaf and/or strip of lemon rind and seasoning. Cover the pan and simmer for 15–20 minutes. Lift the sweetbreads from the liquid, allow these to cool slightly then remove any tiny pieces of gristle and the skins. Meanwhile, make a coating consistency white sauce with the liquid in the pan (see page 61), add the sweetbreads plus a small quantity of cream or top of the milk. Cook gently until the sweetbreads are hot again. Serve with creamed potatoes or crisp toast and garnish with parsley and paprika pepper. This recipe can be varied by adding fried sliced mushrooms to the sauce just before serving.

Sweetbread Vol-au-Vent Sweetbreads form a popular filling for pastry cases. Prepare as for creamed sweetbreads, above, but have the sauce thicker in consistency.

Fried Sweetbreads Cook the sweetbreads in well seasoned stock or water, as for creamed sweetbreads. Drain well, cool and remove the gristle and skin. Coat in seasoned flour, then in egg and breadcrumbs. Fry in deep or shallow fat until crisp and golden brown. Drain on absorbent paper and serve with tartare sauce (see page 65) and slices of lemon.

Tripe This is both economical and nutritious, but many people dislike tripe – sometimes purely because it can look very unappetising, unless served in a colourful manner.

To prepare tripe: wash in cold water, drain then cut into neat pieces. 'Blanch' the tripe in exactly the same way as given in the instructions for preparing sweetbreads, above.

Creamed Tripe and Onions Put the 'blanched' tripe and several sliced onions into a pan. Cover with all milk, or a mixture of milk and water, or milk and white stock. Season well, add a strip of lemon rind to flavour or a pinch ground nutmeg. Cover the pan and simmer gently for about 50–60 minutes. Thicken the liquid with a little flour or cornflour (cornstarch), blended with cold milk or cream. Stir this into the sauce, add a knob of butter or margarine and cook for several minutes. Serve topped with chopped parsley, paprika and sliced hard-boiled (hard-cooked) egg (this is optional, but it does provide more colour to the dish).

Tripe au Gratin Prepare the meat as above, but stir a little grated cheese into the sauce, *after this has thickened*. Spoon into a flameproof dish, top with grated cheese, breadcrumbs and small pieces of margarine or butter. Brown under the grill (broiler).

Tripe in Brown Sauce Fry sliced onions and any other vegetables, as though making a stew, then thicken with a little flour and make a brown sauce (see page 61). Add the pieces of 'blanched' tripe and simmer for 50–60 minutes.

Freezing All uncooked offal (variety meat) freezes well, but it should be used within about 2 months. Cooked dishes such as pressed tongue, oxtail, etc., are excellent standbys in your freezer. Allow ox (beef) tongue to defrost at room temperature if you plan to serve this cold. Casserole dishes of oxtail etc., can be reheated from the frozen state. Use within 6 weeks to 2 months.

I find it better to thicken a creamy sauce (such as in tripe) after reheating, or to use cornflour, or, better still, potato flour if you thicken before freezing. Cream and wine should be added after reheating if possible.

Thickening Stews, etc. Mention is made above of using cornflour or potato flour for thickening. Use half the quantity of cornflour (cornstarch) if replacing flour in a recipe, but use exactly the same amount of potato flour as you would use ordinary flour.

Economical Poultry Dishes

Choosing Poultry

Chicken is generally the most economical poultry to buy, for as it is relatively small-boned you will have a generous amount of meat, if you buy wisely, see below. Frozen whole and jointed chickens have become some of the more economical foods, and chicken portions enable you to buy just as much as required for the meal. As chicken portions are ideal for the person living alone you will find a number of easy suggestions for using individual portions in the chapter on cooking for invalids and the elderly (see page 124).

A small spring chicken (broiler) serves 1–2 people; a medium roasting chicken weighing 4–4½ lb. (2–2¼ kilos) gives 4 good portions, and a large capon 6–8 portions.

A small duck serves 2 people, a larger one can give 4 small portions but as the breast has little meat you may find it unsatisfactory for 4 people.

When buying goose or turkey allow about 12 oz.–1 lb. (⅜–½ kilo) per person; this refers to the trussed weight of the bird.

Naturally the untrussed birds will weigh considerably more than the final weight, when the bird is prepared for the oven.

When comparing the relative prices of fresh or frozen poultry you must remember that frozen birds are 'oven-ready'.

Buying and Cooking Poultry

A young chicken, suitable for roasting, should have a plump breast, pliable wishbone and well covered legs. A small amount of fat under the skin ensures the bird will not be dry-tasting. Capons are generally much larger birds, but the same standards apply. Generally one allows 15 minutes per lb. (½ kilo) and 15 minutes over, in a moderately hot to hot oven, for roasting chickens, but details of the traditional method of roasting, plus the classic accompaniments, are on page 184. A less usual method of roasting chicken is given on page 54.

If you intend to fry or grill (broil) chicken then buy a small young bird (broiler) (or frozen portions). Cut a whole small bird into halves or 4 portions. Allow approximately 15 minutes in the frying pan (skillet) or under a pre-heated grill (broiler), and use plenty of melted butter or other form of fat to keep the flesh moist. Boiling fowls will look creamier in colour than the younger birds. If cooking these in stock or other liquid allow about 30 minutes simmering per lb. (½ kilo) unless the bird seems very old, when it is advisable to cook it very slowly for about 45 minutes per lb. (½ kilo). As boiled chicken is a very easily digested dish you will find ideas on page 128 to serve this for invalids.

While a turkey can be an economical purchase if you are entertaining a large number of people, it can be extravagant for a budget dish for the family, so I have concentrated turkey recipes in the entertaining section; see page 184 for times for roasting, etc. The points to look for when buying a turkey are similar to those given for chicken, above.

Duck and goose cannot be said to be economical poultry, unless you are fortunate enough to live in the country and can buy direct from a local farm. The main problem with these birds is that they have relatively little flesh in proportion to the size of their bones. Avoid ultra fat ducks or geese. Methods of cooking these are on pages 179 and 189.

Frozen Poultry It is important to allow whole birds sufficient time to defrost. A chicken or duck weighing about 4–4½ lb. (2–2¼ kilos) would take about 18 hours to thaw out in the refrigerator. A 12–13-lb. (6–6½-kilo) turkey or goose would need at least 24 hours and probably a little longer. If you have a really large bird for Christmas, buy this 2–3 days before you wish to cook it and allow it to thaw out gradually. Frozen chicken portions can be cooked from the frozen state.

To Use Chicken Wisely

When you buy a chicken remember you can:

1   Use the giblets to give stock, also to make an economical form of pâté (rillettes, see page 170).

2   Have a delicious hot meal with the chicken, as the recipe below, or as page 184.

3   Probably have enough cold chicken left over to serve with salad or to use in made-up dishes, e.g. curry, as page 45. Make the curry sauce, add the diced cooked chicken, heat together. Mince or chop the chicken and use it in a similar recipe to that on page 180. Remember even tiny pieces of skin can be used if minced finely. Add diced chicken to a thick sauce as a filling for pastry cases (see page 193). Add tiny pieces of chicken to scrambled egg. Use the carcass for making stock or the basis of soup, see below.

Chicken with Lemon

Imperial/Metric	American
1 chicken weighing 4–4½ lb. (2–2¼ kilos) plus giblets	1 chicken weighing 4–4½ lb. plus giblets
seasoning	seasoning
1¼ pints (7½ dl.) chicken stock (see method)	just under 3¼ cups chicken stock (see method)
4 or 5 lemons (see method)	4 or 5 lemons (see method)
pinch powdered ginger	pinch powdered ginger
4 oz. (100 g.) butter or margarine	½ cup butter or margarine
4–8 cloves (optional)	4–8 cloves (optional)
8 oz. (200 g.) long grain rice	just over 1 cup long grain rice
pinch saffron	pinch saffron
4 oz. (100 g.) raisins	⅔ cup raisins

Cooking time 2¾ *hours (including time for cooking giblets)*
Serves 4–6
Advance Preparations Cook giblets, prepare lemons, weigh out rice, etc.

Simmer chicken giblets for 1 hour in seasoned water then strain and measure out 1¼ pints (7½ dl. – just under 3¼ cups) stock. Wash and dry chicken and season well. Peel 1 lemon, sprinkle with ginger; retain peel. Stuff the chicken with the peeled lemon and ginger. Dot chicken with half the butter or margarine and roast in a moderate to moderately hot oven, 375–400°F. (190–200°C.), Gas Mark 5–6, for 1½ hours, basting frequently. Remove half peel from 2 lemons, leaving a fluted effect (see picture). Spike the 2 fluted lemons with cloves and place with chicken 15 minutes before end of cooking time. Wash and slice 1–2 other lemons. Cook the peel and lemon slices for 2 minutes in boiling water and drain. Fry peel and slices in remaining butter or margarine, over a low heat, for 1–2 minutes each side just before serving chicken. Meanwhile, place rice, 1 pint (6 dl. – 2½ cups) chicken stock, saffron, seasoning if needed and raisins in a saucepan. Bring to the boil,

stir once, cover and simmer for 15 minutes, or until the rice is tender and the liquid absorbed. When chicken is cooked remove from roasting pan. Remove lemon from body of chicken; keep the bird hot. Press out the juice from the lemon into cooking juice in the roasting pan. Add remaining chicken stock, heat thoroughly. Place rice mixture on a dish with chicken in centre. Garnish with the fluted lemons, lemon slices and peel. Serve with the lemon liquid from roasting pan. *Illustrated opposite.*

Note This dish is easier to serve if the chicken is jointed or sliced and arranged on hot rice.

For Economy Make white stock by simmering chicken carcass in seasoned water, cool and use fat for cooking and stock for soups or stews, e.g. try this:
Chicken Broth Simmer carcass with diced vegetables and 2 pints (1¼ litres – 5 cups) seasoned water. Remove pieces of meat from carcass, dice neatly and return to the pan with vegetables. 1–2 tablespoons rice can be cooked with the carcass and vegetables.

Chicken with lemon (see page 54)

Economical Chicken Dishes

All recipes are for 4 good sized fresh or frozen chicken joints, i.e. enough for 4 portions. There is no need to defrost the chicken unless stated in the recipe.

Chicken Creole Fry the well seasoned chicken joints in 1½ tablespoons (2 tablespoons) oil until golden; lift out of pan. Chop 2 onions and 2 cloves garlic. Fry in another 2 tablespoons (3 tablespoons) oil for a few minutes, then add the pulp from 1 diced red pepper; discard core and seeds. Tip a medium can of tomatoes, plus the liquid from the can, into the frying pan (skillet), season well and add few drops chilli sauce. Heat for 5 minutes then add the chicken joints. Lower the heat and simmer for 15–20 minutes. Turn the chicken in the tomato mixture several times during cooking.

Escalopes of Chicken Defrost frozen chicken. Take the bones out of the chicken joints and flatten the meat. Coat in seasoned flour, then beaten egg and crisp breadcrumbs (raspings). Fry in hot oil or oil and butter for 10–12 minutes until tender. Serve with tartare sauce (see page 65).

Orange Chicken Blend the finely grated rind of 2 oranges with 2 oz. (50 g. − ¼ cup) melted butter. Brush well seasoned chicken joints with the butter mixture. Grill (broil) until tender. Pour hot juice from 1–2 oranges over the chicken just before serving.

Parmesan Chicken Follow the recipe for escalopes of chicken but use a mixture of finely grated Parmesan cheese and breadcrumbs for coating the chicken. Serve with hot tomato purée or tomato sauce (see page 61).

Stuffings and Sauces

Making Stuffings

A stuffing adds flavour to many dishes; it also helps to keep fish, meat or poultry moist during cooking. A good stuffing helps to 'eke out' expensive foods, so it is an interesting way of saving money.

1 If you put the stuffing into the prepared fish, meat or poultry the cooking time will be the same as that required for the fish, etc. If more convenient, put the stuffing into a dish, cover, then cook for the time given in the recipe, or until all the ingredients are tender.

2 Many stuffings freeze well, see individual recipes; use within about 2 months. Where crisp ingredients, such as raw celery, are used it is better to freeze the cooked, rather than uncooked stuffing.

Apple and Onion Stuffing

Ideal for pork, duck or with pork sausages. Can be frozen.

Imperial/Metric	American
3 onions	3 onions
little water	little water
3 large dessert apples	3 large dessert apples
4 oz. (100 g.) soft breadcrumbs	2 cups soft bread crumbs
seasoning	seasoning
good pinch sugar	good pinch sugar
1 teaspoon chopped sage	1 teaspoon chopped sage
little onion stock (see method)	little onion stock (see method)

Cooking time 35 minutes or see point 1 above
Serves 6

Chop the onions, simmer for 5 minutes in water to cover, strain, keep the stock. Peel and dice the apples, blend with the par-boiled onions, breadcrumbs, seasoning, sugar and sage. Bind with a little onion stock. If cooking in a separate dish allow 30 minutes in a moderate oven.

Almond and Raisin Stuffing

Delicious with fish or chicken. Can be frozen.

Imperial/Metric	American
4 oz. (100 g.) bread (weight without crust)	$\frac{1}{4}$ lb. bread (weight without crust)
2 oz. (50 g.) butter or margarine	$\frac{1}{4}$ cup butter or margarine
4 oz. (100 g.) raisins	$\frac{2}{3}$ cup raisins
2 oz. (50 g.) blanched almonds	just under $\frac{1}{2}$ cup blanched almonds
1 egg	1 egg
seasoning	seasoning

Cooking time 25–30 minutes or see point 1 above
Serves 4

Make bread into fairly coarse crumbs. Heat butter or margarine. Toss crumbs in this until golden brown, add rest of ingredients. If cooking in a separate dish allow 20–25 minutes in a moderate oven.

Chestnut Stuffings

There are many ways of making chestnut stuffings, here are some suggestions. The quantities serve 6–7.

Chestnut and Celery Stuffing Blend canned unsweetened chestnut purée with a little lemon juice, seasoning to taste, and chopped celery. Finely diced cooked ham can also be added.

Fresh Chestnut Stuffing Slit the skins of 1 lb. (½ kilo) fresh chestnuts and simmer for 5–10 minutes, or until skins can be removed – do this while the nuts are warm. Remove outer and inner skins, simmer the chestnuts in stock or well seasoned water for 15–20 minutes. Sieve, chop or emulsify the nuts. Blend the purée with finely chopped raw bacon or cooked ham, little chopped parsley, 1 egg, seasoning.

Quick Stuffing A very quick stuffing can be made by mixing equal quantities of canned or fresh purée with sausage meat; extra ingredients may be added, as above. For a more economical stuffing add a small quantity of soft crumbs to the chestnut purée.

Crisp Herb Stuffing

Suitable to serve with fried chicken, chops and grilled (broiled) fish. Do not freeze.

Imperial/Metric	American
1 onion	1 onion
1 oz. (25 g.) butter	2 tablespoons butter
3 oz. (75 g.) crisp breadcrumbs (raspings)	¾ cup crisp bread crumbs (raspings)
2 tablespoons chopped parsley	3 tablespoons chopped parsley
1 teaspoon chopped sage	1 teaspoon chopped sage
1 teaspoon chopped thyme	1 teaspoon chopped thyme
1 teaspoon chopped chives	1 teaspoon chopped chives
2 sticks celery	2 stalks celery

Cooking time 10 minutes
Serves 6

Grate onion and fry gently in the butter. Blend the breadcrumbs with the parsley, onion, sage, thyme, chives and chopped celery. Heat together in the pan but do not cook for any long period.

Cucumber and Caper Stuffing

Excellent with fish, particularly herrings or mackerel. Do not freeze.

Imperial/Metric	American
2 oz. (50 g.) soft breadcrumbs	1 cup soft bread crumbs
¼ cucumber	¼ cucumber
1 lemon	1 lemon
seasoning	seasoning
1–2 teaspoons capers	1–2 teaspoons capers
1 egg	1 egg

Cooking time 20–25 minutes or see point 1 on
previous page
Serves 4–6

Blend the breadcrumbs with the peeled diced cucumber, grated rind of the lemon and 1 tablespoon lemon juice. Season well, add the capers and bind with the egg. If cooking in a separate dish allow 20–25 minutes in a moderate oven.

Ham and Celery Stuffing

Excellent with all meats and poultry. Can be frozen, but loses texture.

Imperial/Metric	American
3 sticks celery	3 stalks celery
few celery leaves	few celery leaves
4 oz. (100 g.) soft breadcrumbs	2 cups soft bread crumbs
4 oz. (100 g.) cooked ham	¼ lb. cooked ham
1 tablespoon chopped parsley	1 tablespoon chopped parsley
seasoning	seasoning
1 egg	1 egg

Cooking time 20 minutes or see point 1, page 56
Serves 6

Chop the celery and celery leaves finely, add breadcrumbs, chopped ham and parsley. Season well and bind with the egg. If cooking in a separate dish allow 20 minutes in a moderate oven.

Horseradish and Herb Stuffing

Excellent with herrings or mackerel. Can be frozen.

Imperial/Metric	American
2 tablespoons horseradish cream	3 tablespoons horseradish cream
4 oz. (100 g.) soft breadcrumbs	2 cups soft bread crumbs
1 tablespoon chopped parsley	1 tablespoon chopped parsley
½ teaspoon chopped thyme or little dried thyme	½ teaspoon chopped thyme or little dried thyme
2–3 tablespoons thin cream to bind	3–4 tablespoons coffee cream to bind
seasoning	seasoning

Cooking time 20–25 minutes or see point 1, page 56
Serves 4–6

Blend horseradish cream with breadcrumbs, parsley and thyme. Bind with cream to a soft spreading consistency, season. If cooking in a separate dish allow 20–25 minutes in a moderate oven.

Parsley Stuffings

These are some of the best known parsley stuffings but this herb can be added to most stuffings. These recipes freeze well and blend with most foods.

Parsley and Thyme Stuffing Blend 4 oz. (100 g. – 2 cups) soft breadcrumbs, ¾–1 tablespoon chopped parsley, 2 oz. (50 g. – generous ⅓ cup) shredded (chopped) suet, grated rind and juice ½ lemon, ¼ teaspoon dried or ½ teaspoon chopped thyme, seasoning and 1 egg. These proportions give a fairly firm texture, which makes it easy to slice neatly. For a more moist texture add enough milk or stock to give a sticky consistency.
You can use melted butter or margarine instead of the suet.

Parsley and Rice Stuffing This is used in beef olives, picture opposite (recipe page 145). Use cooked rice instead of breadcrumbs in parsley and thyme recipe.

Rolled Oat Stuffing Use half breadcrumbs and half quick cooking rolled oats in parsley and thyme recipe, above. Always make a moist texture.

Parsley Giblet Stuffing When using any of these stuffings for poultry you can add the finely chopped, lightly cooked giblets, or just the chopped liver. If using the liver only it can be chopped and used raw.

Beef olives (see page 145)

Mushroom and Tomato Stuffing

Particularly good with white (lean) fish or herrings. Can be frozen.

Imperial/Metric	American
2–3 oz. (50–75 g.) mushrooms	½–¾ cup mushrooms
8 oz. (200 g.) tomatoes	½ lb. tomatoes
1 tablespoon chopped parsley	1 tablespoon chopped parsley
3 oz. (75 g.) soft breadcrumbs	1½ cups soft bread crumbs
seasoning	seasoning

Cooking time 20 minutes or see point 1, page 56
Serves 4–6

Chop mushrooms, blend with skinned chopped tomatoes, parsley, breadcrumbs and seasoning. If cooking in a separate dish allow 20 minutes in a moderate oven.

Onion Stuffings

Onion gives such a definite flavour in a stuffing that it blends best with strongly flavoured meats – pork, duck, etc. When the onions are partly cooked first, do *not* over-cook them. These stuffings freeze well. They serve 4–6.

Sage and Onion Stuffing Peel and boil 2 large onions for 15–20 minutes in a little water. Remove, chop and blend with 2 oz. (50 g. – 1 cup) soft bread-crumbs, 1 oz. (25 g. – just under ¼ cup) shredded (chopped) suet (or use melted margarine), ½–1 teaspoon dried or ½ tablespoon chopped sage, season well and bind with 1 egg or onion stock.

Sausage and Onion Stuffing To each 1 lb. (½ kilo) sausagemeat add 2 chopped and fried onions, a little sage to flavour, and 2 tablespoons raisins. Either

this stuffing or the sage and onion may be varied by adding 2 peeled and diced dessert apples to the mixture. This saves making apple sauce to blend with pork, etc.

Whole Onion and Prune Stuffing Put whole, well seasoned uncooked onions and soaked prunes into duck or goose, and cook with the poultry. Choose fairly small onions for duck, but larger ones for goose. Whole peeled apples, tossed in a little chopped sage, may be used instead of prunes.

Pineapple Raisin Stuffing

Excellent with all meats and poultry. Can be frozen.

Imperial/Metric	American
1 medium can pineapple cubes	1 medium can pineapple cubes
4 oz. (100 g.) soft breadcrumbs	2 cups soft bread crumbs
1 lemon	1 lemon
2 oz. (50 g.) butter	¼ cup butter
3 oz. (75 g.) raisins	½ cup raisins
3 tablespoons pineapple syrup	4 tablespoons pineapple syrup
3 oz. (75 g.) chopped walnuts	¾ cup chopped walnuts

Cooking time 35 minutes or see point 1, page 56
Serves 6

Drain pineapple cubes, halve the cubes and blend with the breadcrumbs, grated rind and juice of the

lemon and melted butter. Heat the raisins with the pineapple syrup (to make them plump). Add to the mixture with the chopped walnuts. If cooking in a separate dish allow 30 minutes in a moderate oven.

Some Basic Sauces

A sauce often adds extra food value to a dish, and gives a pleasantly moist texture to the fish, meat or vegetables. Here are some points to note:

1 Stir well when adding liquid to the fat and flour (known as the 'roux'). If, in spite of stirring, the sauce is lumpy *whisk hard* or *emulsify* and reheat. *Never under-cook* a sauce, let this simmer for some time. If you detect a slight 'floury' taste the sauce is under-cooked.

2 If using cornflour (cornstarch) instead of flour in a recipe, use half the quantity given for flour. If using potato flour allow the same amount as for flour.

3 To keep sauces hot, without fear of burning, transfer to the top of a double saucepan, or a basin (bowl) over hot water.

4 To prevent a skin forming on top cover with a round of damp greaseproof (waxed) paper, or pour a little cold milk, or other liquid (stock, etc.) over the top of the thickened sauce. When ready to serve, remove the paper or blend the cold liquid into the sauce; reheat, stirring or whisking well.

Most sauces freeze well for about a month; use cornflour or potato flour to thicken if possible. A sauce made with flour tends to separate out and become thin again when reheated after freezing. The proportions given below give a coating consistency. To make a thick sauce (panada) use only half the amount of liquid. For a very thin sauce use double the amount of liquid. Quantities serve 4 people.

Brown Sauce Heat 1 oz. (25 g. − 2 tablespoons) dripping in a pan, stir in 1 oz. (25 g. − ¼ cup) flour, then cook over a low heat for 2−3 minutes. Gradually blend in ½ pint (3 dl. − 1¼ cups) brown stock (stock made from beef bones) or use water and a stock (bouillon) cube. Stir as the sauce comes to the boil and continue stirring until the mixture coats the back of the wooden spoon. Season well.
Blending Method Use proportions as recipe above, but blend the flour with the liquid, pour into the pan, add the dripping and continue as above.
Richer Brown Sauce Use twice the amount of dripping (or other fat − shortening). Fry a chopped onion and carrot in this, then continue as basic recipe. Sieve or emulsify.
Espagnole Sauce Fry chopped onion, 2 tomatoes, 2−3 mushrooms in 2 oz. (50 g. − ¼ cup) fat (shortening), then proceed as basic sauce. Sieve or emulsify, add a little sherry, reheat.
Madeira Sauce As brown sauce or richer brown sauce, but use half stock and half Madeira wine.
Tomato Sauce As brown sauce but use tomato juice in place of stock (see also page 105).

White Sauce Heat 1 oz. (25 g. − 2 tablespoons) butter or margarine in a pan, stir in 1 oz. (25 g. − ¼ cup) flour, proceed as for brown sauce, using ½ pint (3 dl. − 1¼ cups) milk instead of stock. Or use the 'blending' method.
Anchovy Sauce Flavour the white sauce with a few drops anchovy essence (extract).
Cheese Sauce Make the sauce, then stir in 3−4 oz. (75−100 g. − ¾−1 cup) grated cheese. Do not

over-cook after adding the cheese.
Parsley Sauce Make the sauce, then add about 1 tablespoon chopped parsley, heat for 2−3 minutes.
Prawn Sauce Make white sauce as above, then add a few whole or chopped prawns. Heat for 2−3 minutes only, no longer, for shell fish becomes tough with prolonged heating. Other shell fish may be used.
Mushroom Sauce Either add sliced fried mushrooms to white sauce (this gives the best colour), or simmer sliced mushrooms in milk then make the white sauce.

Vegetables and Salads

Cooking Vegetables

Vegetables contain valuable vitamins and mineral salts, these can be lost by incorrect cooking. *Always* cook green vegetables in the smallest possible amount of boiling salted water; cover the pan, cook as quickly as you can. In this way you not only retain food values, but flavour and texture. Root vegetables will need rather more water, but this should be boiling when the vegetables are added and should boil steadily.

Bacon Stuffed Peppers

Imperial/Metric	American
4 green or red peppers	4 green or red peppers
for the stuffing	**for the stuffing**
8 oz. (200 g.) streaky or back bacon	½ lb. bacon slices, or Canadian bacon
3 oz. (75 g.) margarine	generous ⅓ cup margarine
1 medium onion	1 medium onion
3 oz. (75 g.) soft breadcrumbs or cooked rice	1½ cups soft bread crumbs or generous ⅓ cup cooked rice
seasoning	seasoning
½ teaspoon powdered sage	½ teaspoon powdered sage
2 oz. (50 g.) chopped mushrooms	½ cup chopped mushrooms
to garnish	**to garnish**
4 rashers streaky or back bacon	4 bacon slices, or Canadian bacon

Cooking time 40 minutes
Serves 4
Advance Preparations Prepare peppers for baking.

Dice the 8 oz. (200 g.) bacon finely, fry for 2–3 minutes. Add 2 oz. (50 g. – ¼ cup) margarine and the finely chopped onion; continue frying until the bacon is very crisp and the onion soft. Add the rest of the ingredients for the stuffing. Cut a slice from the top of each pepper (discard cores and seeds). Cook peppers and slices removed for 5 minutes in boiling salted water. Drain carefully. Pack the stuffing into the peppers, replace lids. Melt the remaining margarine and brush over the peppers. Put into oven and bake for approximately 20–25 minutes in the centre of a moderately hot oven, 400°F. (200°C.), Gas Mark 6. While the peppers are cooking, cut the rest of the bacon rashers into smaller pieces; roll and put on skewers. Put the bacon rolls into the dish with the peppers to cook for the last 10 minutes. Remove the bacon rolls from the skewers, place on top of the peppers.

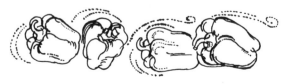

Variations

Use skinned and chopped tomatoes in place of mushrooms in the stuffing for the peppers.
Cheese Stuffed Peppers Omit the bacon and use grated cheese in the filling instead.

Pippin salad (see page 65)

Simple Ways to Cook Vegetables

Where no specific method of cooking is given, this means the vegetables are put into boiling salted water for the time given, then strained.

Artichoke, Globe Trim base of stalk. Allow 20–30 minutes. Serve hot with melted butter or pull out centre choke, serve cold with dressing, see opposite page. Dip ends of leaves in butter or dressing.

Artichoke, Jerusalem Peel or scrape. Add few drops vinegar or lemon juice to water when soaking and cooking. Allow 20–25 minutes. Serve with butter.

Asparagus Wash, trim ends of stalks, tie in small bundles. Stand upright in pan. Allow 20–25 minutes. Serve hot with butter or cold with dressing, opposite, or top with butter and cheese.

Aubergine (Eggplant) Do not peel (see page 172 for a recipe and method of counteracting bitter taste of skin). Some methods of cooking are to slice, coat in seasoned flour and fry; or halve, top with oil and seasoning, bake for 40 minutes in moderate oven; or halve, bake or boil for 15 minutes, remove pulp, mix with any stuffing then return to skins and bake for 30–35 minutes in moderate oven.

Beans, Broad (Lima) When young use pods and beans. Slice. Allow 15 minutes. When older use just beans inside. Allow 15–20 minutes. Serve with butter or parsley sauce (page 61).

Beans, Green Trim sides and ends, slice runner and large beans. Allow 15–20 minutes.

Beans, Haricot (Navy) and Other Dried Beans If A.F.D. (Accelerated Freeze Dried), cook as packet. Soak ordinary dried beans overnight then simmer in salted water for 2–3 hours. Serve with any sauces (page 61 and 105) or add to stews, etc.

Beetroot (Beets) Wash, do not peel, *simmer* in salted water until tender. Small beetroot take from 30 minutes. Buy ready cooked, slice and serve cold, or dice and heat in butter or sauces (page 61).

Broccoli and Cauliflower Keep small heads whole or divide into neat sprigs. Allow from 12 minutes according to size. Serve with white, cheese or Hollandaise sauce (pages 61 and 180), or top with fried breadcrumbs, chopped parsley and hard-boiled egg for broccoli or cauliflower polonaise.

Brussels Sprouts Remove few outer leaves, mark with cross at base of stem. Allow from 5–6 minutes.

Cabbage and Other Green Vegetables Shred just before cooking. Allow only a few minutes if young, so they retain firm texture. Red cabbage can be cooked same way then tossed in fried onions and fried apple.

Cardoons (like tall celery) Cook as celery.

Carrots, Turnips, Swedes Peel or scrape, cook whole, sliced or diced. Allow from 15 minutes depending upon tenderness. Serve with butter or sauces or mash and flavour with nutmeg.

Celeriac (celery root) Peel, slice or dice and cook as celery, or use raw.

Celery, Seakale Remove hard outer sticks, then dice or cook in portions. Allow 15–20 minutes. Can be cooked in a brown sauce.

Chicory (Endive) As celery.

Chilli Too hot to cook as a separate vegetable, use sparingly as flavouring.

Corn on the Cob (Sweetcorn) Strip away leaves. Allow 15–20 minutes, salt towards end of cooking. Serve with butter.

Courgettes (Zucchini) and Young Marrows Wipe, remove ends, cook in stock or water or slowly in butter. Slice, fry as aubergines (eggplant).

Cucumber Can be cooked as celery.

Endive (Chicory) Use as lettuce.

Fennel Serve cold in salads or cook white root as celeriac.

Kale (Greens) As cabbage.

Kohl-rabi As carrots.

Leeks Remove base and outer leaves, wash well. Allow 20–30 minutes. Serve with sauces (page 61) or with butter or use as onions.

Lentils No need to soak. Cook as dried beans.

Mushrooms Wash, trim stalks, do not peel. Simmer in milk or fry in butter. Need only a few minutes cooking. See recipe page 137.

Okra (Gumbo) Trim ends, slice or cook whole in salted water or butter. Allow from 15 minutes.

Onions Peel, slice or chop. Boil whole for 40 minutes (if small) onwards, serve with sauces (page 61) or fry in butter, oil, etc. For crisp rings dip in milk or egg white then seasoned flour and deep fry.

Parsnips As carrots, or par-boil for 10–15 minutes, then roast round joint for 40 minutes.

Peas When fresh allow 10–15 minutes, add pinch sugar and sprig mint. If dried, treat as beans.

Peppers (Capsicums – Pimientos) Dice or slice flesh, discard seeds and core. Allow 5–10 minutes, or fry in hot butter, or add raw to salads or to stews, etc.

Potatoes Many ways of cooking these, see index.

Peel or scrape when new. Put into boiling salted water, but *do not boil rapidly*. Allow from 15 minutes.
Pumpkin As courgettes or marrow, or see page 204.
Radishes Raw in salads or can be substituted for turnips in stews, etc.
Rutabaga Swedish turnip – see carrots, turnips.
Salsify (Oyster Plant) Wash and scrape well, cook as Jerusalem artichokes.
Shallots As onions. Small spring onions (scallions) are often known as shallots, these are eaten raw.

Sorrel A herb, but can be cooked as spinach.
Spinach Wash leaves well. Cook without extra water, adding seasoning only. Allow from 10 minutes. Strain well, blend with butter or cream. Chop or sieve if wished.
Sweet Potatoes, Yams As potatoes.
Tomatoes Raw or fried or grilled, or used in recipes.
Vegetable Marrow (Squash) As courgettes if very young, or peel, remove seeds and cut into pieces. Allow from 15 minutes, or steam for slightly longer.

Simple Salads

Salads need not be elaborate to be appetising. Make sure all the ingredients look fresh and introduce touches of unexpected colour and texture, see below.
Green salad ingredients, lettuce, endive (chicory), watercress, etc., should be washed in cold water then shaken in a salad container. To keep them crisp store in a covered container until ready to serve.

Green Salad This means green salad vegetables plus green pepper (optional), sliced cucumber and perhaps diced celery or white chicory.

Mixed Salad The usual mixed salad is similar to a green salad with the addition of tomatoes, radishes, sliced hard-boiled (hard-cooked) eggs, etc.

Vegetable Salads Blend cooked vegetables with mayonnaise or French dressing (see below). Top with chopped herbs. Most vegetables can be used.

Fruit Salads Most fruits blend well in salads, e.g., segments of orange (excellent with duck or pork), pineapple, peaches, bananas, sliced or halved pears and apples (toss fruit that discolours easily in lemon juice). The picture on page 63 shows:

Pippin Salad Dice 3 peeled dessert apples (toss in a little lemon juice to prevent the apples discolouring). Mix with diced celery or the base of white chicory (endive) hearts, chopped red pepper. Toss in mayonnaise or the cream dressing, recipes below. Make small balls of cream cheese, press halved walnuts against these and dust with paprika. Arrange the apple mixture on the dish with the cheese balls. Dice one or more unpeeled apples (toss in lemon juice), put on top of the dish, add chicory or celery leaves round the edge of the dish. The

picture on page 63 shows a halved red pepper for a rather eye-catching garnish.

Salad Dressings

Vinaigrette or French Dressing Blend 3 tablespoons (4 tablespoons) oil with seasoning, a pinch sugar and a little French or made mustard. Gradually work in 1½ tablespoons (2 tablespoons) lemon juice or wine or malt vinegar. This dressing can be used on most salads and can be varied by adding chopped herbs and/or crushed garlic. It is worth making a larger quantity and storing it in a screw-topped jar.

Mayonnaise Blend seasoning and a little made mustard into 1 egg yolk. *Gradually* work in up to ¼ pint (1½ dl. – ⅔ cup) salad oil and 1 tablespoon lemon juice or vinegar. If making in a liquidiser (blender) whisk the lemon juice or vinegar into the yolk, and then steadily add the oil with the machine on moderate speed.
Use the mayonnaise as the basis for:
Herb Dressing Add chopped fresh herbs.
Tartare Sauce Add chopped capers, gherkins and parsley.

Cream Dressing Add seasoning and a little sugar, lemon juice or vinegar to thick or soured cream.

65

Economical Puddings and Desserts

The recipes in this section give budget recipes such as pancakes, pies, light puddings, etc., and interesting cold desserts.

Saucer or French Pancakes

Imperial/Metric	American
2 oz. (50 g.) butter	¼ cup butter
2 oz. (50 g.) sugar	¼ cup sugar
2 eggs	2 eggs
2 oz. (50 g.) rice flour or flour	½ cup rice flour or flour
12 tablespoons milk	1 cup milk
grated rind 1 lemon	grated rind 1 lemon
for the filling and to coat	**for the filling and to coat**
jam	jam
castor sugar	granulated sugar

Cooking time 15 minutes
Serves 6
Advance Preparations Make batter but do not add egg whites until ready to cook.

Thoroughly grease 12 flat round ovenproof tins (or saucers). Cream the butter and sugar, beat in the egg yolks with a little flour, add the remainder of the flour with the milk and lemon rind. Beat this. Fold in the stiffly whisked egg whites, pour into the tins.

Bake above centre in a hot oven, 425°F. (220°C.), Gas Mark 7, until well risen, brown and firm (10–15 minutes). Turn on to a sugared paper, put a little hot jam on each and sandwich two rounds together. Pile neatly on a hot dish and dust with sugar; keep hot in low oven until ready to serve.

Variation

Orange Saucer Pancakes Use 12 tablespoons (1 cup) fresh or canned orange juice in place of the milk.

Pancakes

There is a great variety of pancakes as the following recipes show, but the important things to remember when cooking pancakes are:
1   Have a really thin layer of mixture over the bottom of the pan. A thick solid pancake is not very pleasant. Cook quickly, turn or toss to brown on both sides. Saucer pancakes are cooked in the oven, see above.
2   To keep the pancakes hot, put them on an uncovered plate over boiling water, or in a low oven.
3   Put very soft fillings in immediately before serving to prevent the pancakes becoming over-soft.
4   Hints on freezing are under strawberry pancakes (see page 71).

Pancake Batter

Imperial/Metric	American
4 oz. (100 g.) plain flour	1 cup all-purpose flour
pinch salt	pinch salt
2 eggs	2 eggs
just under ½ pint (3 dl.) milk and water	just under 1¼ cups milk and water

Cooking time as recipe, see page 71
Advance Preparations See page 71.

Sieve the flour and salt, gradually beat in the eggs and the milk and water, allow to stand.

Pancakes

Fritters

Make and serve these as quickly as possible after cooking. Like the pancake batter, the fritter batter may be left standing if wished, but do not add stiffly beaten egg whites (if included in the recipe) until just before cooking.

Always drain the fritters on crumpled tissue or kitchen paper (towels) before serving or coating with sugar.

Plain Fritter Batter

Imperial/Metric	American
4 oz. (100 g.) self-raising flour (or plain flour with 1 teaspoon baking powder)	1 cup self-rising flour (or all purpose flour with 1 teaspoon baking powder — double-acting)
pinch salt	pinch salt
1 egg	1 egg
¼ pint (1½ dl.) milk	⅔ cup milk

Cooking time as recipe
Serves 4–5
Advance Preparations Make batter and allow to stand.

Blend the sieved flour or flour and baking powder and salt with the egg and milk to give a thick batter — some fruits are better with a little extra liquid — see individual recipes.

Variations

Rich Fritter Batter Ingredients as above, but use 2 eggs, and add 1 oz. (25 g. — 2 tablespoons) melted butter or 1 tablespoon oil to the batter just before cooking.

Fluffy Fritter Batter Ingredients as plain fritter batter, but use 2 eggs. Make the batter with the yolks only, allow to stand until ready to cook then fold in the 2 stiffly whisked egg whites. This gives a deliciously light coating.

Fruit Fritters

Imperial/Metric	American
selected batter recipe	selected batter recipe
fruit, etc., see suggestions pages 69 and 70	fruit, etc., see suggestions pages 69 and 70
flour where necessary	flour where necessary
for frying	**for frying**
oil or fat	oil or shortening
to coat	**to coat**
castor sugar where necessary	granulated sugar where necessary

Cooking time 3–8 minutes, see individual recipes
Advance Preparations Make batter as individual recipe.

Make the batter, prepare the fruit as suggested on pages 69 and 70. Coat in a little flour, unless this is not mentioned (the flour helps the batter to adhere to the fruit). Fry in hot oil or fat until crisp and golden; make sure to lower heat sufficiently to cook the fruit; turn the fritters as they cook. You can choose shallow or deep oil or fat (if using the latter method the cooking time will be slightly shorter). Drain on absorbent paper, then toss in sugar unless the recipe states otherwise.

Fritters for Every Occasion

Most of the recipes that follow are based on the fritter batters on the previous page. It is, however, possible to make a fritter with choux pastry (recipe page 200) and with fine macaroon crumbs and special occasion recipes using these are given below. An interesting fritter based on cooked rice is given on page 70. All recipes on this page and page 70 serve 4–6.

Apple Fritters Use any of the batters. Peel, core and cut *good* cooking (baking) apples into ⅓-inch (nearly 1-cm.) slices and coat in flour, then in batter, fry steadily for approximately 5–6 minutes until crisp and golden brown. Drain and dust with sugar.

Apple Rum Beignets Use the fluffy fritter batter. Dip rings of peeled, sliced apple into a little rum and sugar, coat in flour then in the batter. Fry as above.

Apricot Fritters Use *well drained* canned or cooked apricots. Dip in flour, then in the fluffy batter, fry for 4–5 minutes. Drain then coat in sugar.

Banana Fritters Use the rich or fluffy batter, add 1 tablespoon water. Skin and halve large bananas, sprinkle with lemon juice for extra flavour, then dip into the batter. Fry as apple fritters.

Cherry Fritters Stone (pit) about 8–10 oz. (200–250 g.) juicy black or red cherries. Blend with the rich batter then drop spoonfuls into the oil or fat (shortening). Fry for about 4 minutes, drain then coat with sugar.

Coconut Fritters Add 3 oz. (75 g. – 1 cup) desiccated (shredded) coconut, 1 tablespoon extra water or rum and 1 oz. (25 g. – 2 tablespoons) sugar to the fluffy fritter batter, *then* fold in the egg whites. Drop in spoonfuls in the hot oil or fat (shortening), fry for 3 minutes, drain well – do not coat with sugar. Top with apricot purée or jam.

French Crullers with Strawberry Sauce Make choux pastry, page 200, and pipe into rings on aluminium foil or a tin. Lift the rings carefully, put into the hot oil or fat (shortening), fry until golden brown. Serve hot with a strawberry sauce made by heating canned or defrosted frozen strawberries.

Lemon Buns with Cherry Sauce Use the fluffy fritter batter but omit 1 tablespoon liquid. Flavour with grated lemon rind. Drop spoonfuls into the hot oil or fat (shortening) and fry until crisp and brown. Serve with hot canned cherries.

Filled 'Tops' Make the fritters as above and drain well. Cool, split and fill with vanilla flavoured cream.

Lemon Pear Fritters with Apricot Sauce Choose any of the fritter batters and flavour with a little lemon juice and finely grated lemon rind. Coat well drained halved canned pears with flour then batter and fry until golden brown. Serve with the apricot sauce made with hot apricot purée or jam.

Macaroon Fritters Use 3 oz. (75 g. – ¾ cup) flour and 1 oz. (25 g. – ¼ cup) macaroon crumbs and 1 oz. (25 g. – ¼ cup) chopped almonds. Flavour with few drops ratafia or almond essence (extract) and 1 oz. (25 g. – 2 tablespoons) sugar, add 2 egg yolks, ¼ pint (1½ dl. – ⅔ cup) milk and 2 stiffly beaten egg whites. Drop in spoonfuls in hot oil or fat (shortening), drain well. Do not coat with sugar. Top with almonds and apricot jam or purée.

Orange Fritters Add the finely grated rind of 2 oranges to the rich or fluffy fritter batter. Cut ½-inch (1-cm.) slices of orange, coat in flour then in the batter. Fry for 3–4 minutes, drain, then coat in sugar.

Peach Fritters Halve fresh peaches, remove the skins, or drain canned peaches. Dip in flour then coat in any of the batters. Fry for 4–5 minutes, drain. Dust with sugar.

Pineapple Fritters Drain rings of canned pineapple well, coat in flour then in any of the batters. Fry for 5 minutes, drain, then coat in sugar. Serve with hot syrup from the can or, as in the picture, with the syrup blended with strawberry, raspberry or apricot jam. Fresh pineapple rings may be used, but allow a slightly longer cooking time. *Illustrated on page 70.*

69

Rice and Banana Fritters Blend 2 oz. (50 g. – $\frac{1}{2}$ cup) cooked rice with 1 egg, 1$\frac{1}{2}$ oz. (40 g. – 6 tablespoons) flour, $\frac{1}{4}$ pint (1$\frac{1}{2}$ dl. – $\frac{2}{3}$ cup) milk and 3 diced bananas. Fry as the other fritters, drain and coat in sugar. Serve with heated canned mandarin oranges and syrup from the can.

Rum Flavoured Apricots with Sabayon Sauce Open a can of apricots, drain the fruit thoroughly. Add a little rum to the rich fritter batter. Coat the apricots in flour, then in batter. Fry until golden, drain, but do not coat in sugar. Serve with the sauce.
Sabayon Sauce Beat 3 egg yolks with 3 oz. (75 g. – generous $\frac{1}{3}$ cup) sugar over a pan of hot water. Gradually beat in 4 tablespoons (5 tablespoons) sherry or Madeira.

Strawberry Fritters Use the fluffy batter and coat whole large strawberries. Fry for about 3 minutes only, drain and coat in sugar.

To Reheat Pancakes
Pancakes may be made ahead, see page 71, opposite, then reheated as follows:
1   If you separate each pancake with oiled paper then wrap them all together in foil, you can reheat the 'parcel' in the oven. A 'parcel' of about 8 pancakes would take approximately 25 minutes in a moderate oven. Open the foil carefully, take out the hot pancakes, roll and serve with sugar and lemon as the picture on page 67, or fill as pages 71 or 129.
2   Unwrap the pancakes and heat in a greased frying pan (skillet) for 1–2 minutes.
3   Unwrap the pancakes, spread with filling, roll, top with a sauce, heat in the oven.

Liquids for Pancakes, etc.
While most recipes give milk for mixing batters, you can use other liquids. Dried skimmed milk gives a particularly light batter. The pancakes in the picture on page 67 were made with this milk. The Dutch housewife often uses beer and omits the egg entirely from batters. Fruit juices can be used for sweet batters. Stock or tomato juice is excellent as the basis for a savoury fritter coating or a savoury pancake.

Pineapple fritters (see page 69)

Crêpes Suzette (see opposite)

Strawberry Pancakes

Imperial/Metric	American
batter made with 4 oz. (100 g.) plain flour, etc., see page 66	batter made with 1 cup all-purpose flour, etc., see page 66
for the filling	**for the filling**
8–12 oz. (200–300 g.) fresh or defrosted frozen strawberries	½–¾ lb. fresh or defrosted frozen strawberries
little sugar	little sugar
Sauternes or other white wine	Sauterne or other white wine
for frying	**for frying**
oil or fat	oil or shortening

Cooking time few minutes for each pancake
Serves 4–6
Advance Preparations Prepare batter and the fruit, or cook the pancakes and wrap and store in the refrigerator or freezer (see under freezing).

Sieve the flour and salt, gradually beat in the eggs and the milk and water, allow to stand. Prepare the fruit some little time beforehand, slice large strawberries, sprinkle with sugar and enough wine to moisten and leave in a cool place.
To cook the pancakes: heat a little oil or fat in the pan, pour in sufficient of the batter to give a wafer-thin layer, cook until golden brown underneath, toss or turn and cook on the second side. Keep hot (see point 2, page 66) – fill with the strawberries and put on to a hot dish. Top with sugar and wine.

For Economy Use only 1 egg and the full ½ pint (3 dl. – 1¼ cups) liquid.
Freezing Pancakes freeze well. To prevent them becoming 'leathery' add 1–2 teaspoons oil to the batter *before* cooking. Separate the cooked pancakes with squares of oiled greaseproof or waxed paper and cover all pancakes with foil.

Variations

Apple and Cherry Pancakes Poach sliced apples in a little sugar, lemon juice and water. Blend with a few glacé (candied) cherries. Drain fruit, put into pancakes and fold.
Glacé Pancakes Make the pancakes and keep hot. Fill with vanilla ice cream and serve with hot chocolate sauce, see page 85.
Normandy Pancakes Cook apples in a little sugar and water until a smooth pulp. Blend with chopped nuts and sultanas (seedless white raisins) and flavour with a little lemon juice or sherry. Put into the pancakes and serve with cream flavoured with a little sherry. The apple mixture may be hot or use it cold as in the case of the other fruits.
Orange Pancakes Add the finely grated rind of 2 oranges to the flour and blend with milk and water in the usual way. Fill with pieces of fresh orange flavoured with a little curaçao and sweetened.
Pineapple Pancakes Mix the batter with syrup from a can of pineapple instead of the milk and water. Cook in the usual way, using a little more oil or fat (shortening) than usual since the batter is more inclined to stick to the pan. Fill with chopped pineapple flavoured with a little rum.

Raspberry Pancakes Use fresh or frozen raspberries instead of strawberries.
Crêpes Suzette (Illustrated on page 70) Cook the pancakes in the usual way. Spread each pancake with a filling made by creaming 3 oz. (75 g. – generous ⅓ cup) butter with the same amount of sugar and the grated rind of 2 oranges and 1 lemon. Add 4 tablespoons (5 tablespoons) orange juice, 2 tablespoons (3 tablespoons) redcurrant jelly or rose jam and the same amount of marmalade. Fold or roll the pancakes and heat in the pan in a mixture of 4 tablespoons (5 tablespoons) brandy and the same amount of Curaçao.

To Make a Good Pastry

The pastries on this and the next page are all crisp and short; for the lighter flaky and puff pastries see pages 193 and 218. It is important to keep both the ingredients and the utensils cool when making pastry and to handle this as lightly as possible.

Do not make the pastry too damp; this makes it very difficult to roll out, and also produces a slightly tough pastry. On the other hand do not make the pastry so dry it crumbles when handled. Perfect pastry should roll into a ball in the mixing bowl without too much handling, and it should not need much flour on the pastry board or rolling pin.

Biscuit Crust

Imperial/Metric	American
6 oz. (150 g.) plain flour	1½ cups all-purpose flour
2 oz. (50 g.) cornflour	⅓ cup cornstarch
1 level tablespoon castor sugar	1 level tablespoon granulated sugar
4 oz. (100 g.) butter	½ cup butter
1 egg yolk	1 egg yolk
water to mix	water to mix

Cooking time as recipe
Advance Preparations Make pastry, wrap to prevent drying; store 2–3 days in refrigerator, or freeze.

Sieve flour, cornflour and sugar together. Rub in the butter. Mix to a firm dough with egg yolk and cold water. Cooking times vary with recipes but generally

this pastry is baked at a lower temperature than short crust (basic pie dough).

Freezing The uncooked or cooked pastry keeps for several months. I prefer to bind with milk instead of water when freezing pastry.

Short Crust Pastry (Basic Pie Dough)

Imperial/Metric	American
8 oz. (200 g.) flour	2 cups flour
good pinch salt	good pinch salt
2 oz. (50 g.) margarine or butter*	¼ cup margarine or butter*
2 oz. (50 g.) cooking fat*	¼ cup shortening*
approximately 2 tablespoons cold water	approximately 3 tablespoons cold water

* or use all margarine or all butter or all cooking fat (shortening).

Cooking time as recipe
Advance Preparations Make pastry, wrap to prevent drying; store 2–3 days in refrigerator, or freeze.

Sieve flour and salt together. Rub in margarine or butter and fat until mixture looks like fine breadcrumbs. Gradually add enough cold water to make the dough into a rolling consistency, using first a knife and then the fingertips to feel the pastry. Lightly flour the rolling pin and pastry board. Roll pastry to required thickness and shape, lifting and turning to keep it light. Short crust pastry is

generally baked in a hot oven, the time and position varies with the individual recipe.

Freezing The uncooked or cooked pastry keeps for several months. I prefer to bind with milk instead of water when freezing pastry.

Variation

Sweet Short Crust Pastry (Sweet Basic Pie Dough) Add 1 tablespoon sugar to the flour, etc. in the recipe above. Mix with milk, or with yolk of an egg, as fleur pastry, see next page.

Fleur or Flan Pastry

Imperial/Metric	American
5 oz. (125 g.) butter or margarine	just under ⅔ cup butter or margarine
1–2 oz. (25–50 g.) sugar	2–4 tablespoons sugar
1 egg yolk	1 egg yolk
8 oz. (200 g.) flour (preferably plain)	2 cups flour (preferably all-purpose)
pinch salt	pinch salt
little water (or use second egg yolk)	little water (or use second egg yolk)

Cooking time as recipe
Advance Preparations Make pastry, wrap to prevent drying; store 2–3 days in refrigerator or freeze.

Cream the butter or margarine and sugar until soft and light, beat in the egg yolk, then the flour sieved with the salt, knead lightly, add the water or second egg yolk to make a rolling consistency. Knead then roll out carefully as this pastry is very 'short' and inclined to break. Times, etc. for baking are given under the recipe.

For Economy Use only 4 oz. (100 g. – ½ cup) butter or margarine.
Freezing The uncooked or cooked pastry keeps for several months.

Apple Macaroon Tart

Imperial/Metric	American
sweet short crust pastry made with 6 oz. (150 g.) flour, etc., see page 72	sweet basic pie dough made with 1½ cups flour, etc., see page 72
for the filling	**for the filling**
2 oz. (50 g.) margarine	¼ cup margarine
2 oz. (50 g.) castor sugar	¼ cup granulated sugar
few drops almond essence	few drops almond extract
1 egg	1 egg
2 oz. (50 g.) ground almonds	½ cup ground almonds
2 oz. (50 g.) soft breadcrumbs	1 cup soft bread crumbs
little apricot jam	little apricot jam
2 dessert apples	2 dessert apples
1 egg white	1 egg white
1 oz. (25 g.) castor sugar	2 tablespoons granulated sugar

Cooking time 50 minutes
Serves 4–6
Advance Preparations Cook to serve cold.

Roll out the pastry and line an 8-inch (20-cm.) flan ring or sandwich tin (layer cake pan). Bake 'blind' for 15 minutes in the centre of a hot oven, 400–425°F. (200–220°C.), Gas Mark 6–7. Meanwhile, prepare the filling. Cream margarine, sugar and almond essence, add the egg then the ground almonds and breadcrumbs. Spread the bottom of the half-baked pastry case with a little apricot jam, then with the ground almond mixture. Peel and slice the apples very thinly, put over the almond filling.

Whisk the egg white (left from the pastry). fold in the sugar, spread over the apples. Return to the oven, lower the heat to very moderate, 325°F. (170°C.), Gas Mark 3, and cook for approximately 35 minutes or until the filling is firm. Serve hot or cold.

Variation

Apricot Macaroon Tart Use halved fresh *ripe* apricots, instead of dessert apples. You will need about 6 apricots. Slice neatly then use as apples.

Date and Almond Tart

Imperial/Metric	American
short crust or flan pastry made with 6 oz. (150 g.) flour, etc., see page 72 and above	*basic pie dough or flan pastry made with 1½ cups flour, etc., see page 72 and above*
for the filling	**for the filling**
6 oz. (150 g.) stoned dates	*nearly 1 cup pitted dates*
2 tablespoons apricot jam	*3 tablespoons apricot jam*
2 tablespoons brandy	*3 tablespoons brandy*
2 egg whites	*2 egg whites*
few drops almond essence	*few drops almond extract*
4 oz. (100 g.) castor sugar	*½ cup granulated sugar*
4 oz. (100 g.) ground almonds	*1 cup ground almonds*
to decorate	**to decorate**
few stoned dates	*few pitted dates*
few blanched almonds	*few blanched almonds*

Cooking time 50 minutes
Serves 4–6
Advance Preparations Cook; reheat gently or serve cold.

Roll out pastry, line a 7–8-inch (18–20-cm.) flan ring (pie pan) and bake 'blind' for 15 minutes until pastry is just set but not brown, see directions page 77. Remove paper, etc. or foil. Meanwhile, chop dates and mix with jam and brandy. Spread over partially cooked pastry. Whisk egg whites lightly,

add essence, sugar and ground almonds. Spread over top of dates. Bake for 30–35 minutes in centre of very moderate oven, 325°F. (170°C.), Gas Mark 3, until pastry is crisp and filling pale golden. Put decorations on almond topping just before end of cooking time.

For Economy Use fine soft breadcrumbs plus extra almond essence (extract) instead of ground almonds.
Freezing This freezes well; use within 6–8 weeks.

Baked Blackberry and Apple Dumplings

Imperial/Metric	American
short crust or sweet short crust pastry made with 12 oz. (340 g.) flour etc*., see page 72	*basic or sweet basic pie dough made with 3 cups flour, etc., see page 72*
for the filling	**for the filling**
4 medium size cooking apples	*4 medium size baking apples*
4 oz. (100 g.) blackberries	*nearly 1 cup blackberries*
sugar to taste	*sugar to taste*
to decorate	**to decorate**
little sugar	*little sugar*

* the recommended conversion of 25 g. to 1 oz. may not give enough pastry for this recipe, so I suggest increasing the flour to 340 g. and the fat to 170 g.

Cooking time 40 minutes
Serves 4
Advance Preparations Prepare and cook as required.

Make the pastry as page 72, but add very slightly more water than usual, so the pastry will not break when wrapped round the apples. Roll out the pastry, cut into 4 portions. Place a peeled and cored apple

on each portion of pastry, fill centre with blackberries and sugar. Damp edges of pastry, draw up to cover apples, seal firmly. Turn apples over so the joins of pastry are underneath. Put on a lightly greased baking tray (sheet). Make 'stalks' and 'leaves'. Bake for approximately 40 minutes in the centre of a moderate to moderately hot oven, 375–400°F. (190–200°C.), Gas Mark 5–6. Dust with sugar, serve hot.

Treacle Tarts

Make the pastry, line the baking dish (pie pan), bake 'blind' (see page 77 for a definition of this) in a hot oven for approximately 15 minutes. Add the filling and continue as the recipe. To make each of these tarts use pastry made with 6 oz. (150 g. — 1½ cups) flour, etc., as page 72.

Lemon Treacle Tart Fill the half-cooked pastry with golden (light corn) syrup blended with the grated rind and juice of 1 lemon. Return tart to the oven, lower the heat to moderate, cook for a further 15—20 minutes.

The tart can be topped with a layer of soft bread-crumbs or crushed cornflakes before returning to the oven.

West Indian Treacle Tart (*Illustrated*) Cook the pastry for 15 minutes, see top of this page. Mean-while, blend 4 oz. (100 g. — ⅓ cup) black treacle (molasses) with the same amount of golden (light corn) syrup, the grated rind and juice ½ lemon and enough soft breadcrumbs to make a sticky consistency. Put into the half-cooked pastry, continue cooking for a further 15—20 minutes in a moderate oven.

To make the attractive border, shown in the picture, cut tiny circles of pastry, press round the edge before baking. Scraps of pastry left form the lattice design; these are put over the filling, then baked. As their cooking time is short, make certain the pastry is not too thick.

Cherry Fingers

Imperial/Metric	American
short crust pastry made with 8 oz. (200 g.) flour, etc., see page 72	basic pie dough made with 2 cups flour, etc., see page 72
for the topping	for the topping
3 oz. (75 g.) margarine	just over ⅓ cup margarine
3 oz. (75 g.) castor sugar	just under ⅓ cup granulated sugar
2 eggs	2 eggs
3 oz. (75 g.) self-raising flour (or plain flour with ¾ teaspoon baking powder)	¾ cup self-raising flour (or all-purpose flour with ¾ teaspoon baking powder — double-acting)
4 oz. (100 g.) soft breadcrumbs	2 cups soft bread crumbs
4 oz. (100 g.) glacé cherries	⅓ cup candied cherries
a little apricot jam	a little apricot jam

Cooking time 30—35 minutes
Makes 24
Advance Preparations Bake; reheat or serve cold.

Roll out the pastry thinly to fit a large Swiss roll tin (jelly roll pan). Prick and bake for approximately 10 minutes towards the top of a hot oven, 425°F. (220°C.), Gas Mark 7, until it is a pale golden. Meanwhile, prepare topping: cream margarine and sugar, add eggs, sieved flour or flour and baking powder, breadcrumbs and cherries. Spread the pastry with apricot jam and the cherry topping (use a damp knife for the topping). Return to the centre of the oven, lowering the heat to very moderate, 325—350°F. (170—180°C.), Gas Mark 3—4. Leave for approximately 20—25 minutes until golden. Mark into fingers while warm. Serve hot or cold.

Fruit Pies Choose pastry as pages 72, 73 or 193. Pastry made with 6 oz. (150 g. – 1½ cups) flour, etc., will serve 4–6 people in a deep pie dish.

Put 1–1½ lb. (½–¾ kilo) prepared fruit into the pie dish (baking pan). Add sugar, or other sweetening to taste, with enough water to keep the fruit moist and provide some juice. Do not add too much water, otherwise this will boil out during cooking; soft berry fruits need little, if any, liquid. If the fruit does not come well to the top of the dish, put in a pie support. Roll out the pastry to a size to cover the dish and make a long narrow strip. Damp the edges of the pie dish, press the strip round this. Top with the pastry, seal the edges, cut away any surplus, flute edges or decorate neatly. There is no need to make a slit in the top of the pastry for a sweet pie. Stand on a baking tray (sheet), cook for approximately 15–20 minutes in the centre of a hot oven (or use a very hot oven for the richer flaky or puff pastry). Lower the heat to moderate for a further 20–30 minutes. Serve hot or cold.

Fruit Tart In Britain this means the type of pie with pastry above and below the filling. Use double the amount of pastry given in the recipe above for a 9–10-inch (23–25-cm.) pie plate (pan) or pastry made with 8 oz. (200 g. – 2 cups) flour for a 7–8-inch (18–20-cm.) pie plate. Roll out half the pastry, line the dish; sprinkle lightly with cornflour (cornstarch), flour or semolina and a little sugar or brush with egg white (this prevents the pastry being softened with fruit juices). Add 1–1½ lb. (½–¾ kilo) prepared fruit, sugar, and *very little liquid*. Cover with the rest of the pastry, proceed as for a pie, but allow slightly longer cooking to crisp both layers of pastry.

Chester Fingers

Imperial/Metric	American
sweet biscuit crust pastry	**sweet biscuit crust pastry**
4 oz. (100 g.) butter	½ cup butter
2 oz. (50 g.) sieved icing sugar	½ cup sieved confectioners' sugar
8 oz. (200 g.) plain flour	2 cups all-purpose flour
1 egg yolk	1 egg yolk
water to mix	water to mix
for the topping	**for the topping**
apricot jam	apricot jam
4 oz. (100 g.) fine cake or biscuit crumbs	1 cup fine cake or cookie crumbs
4 oz. (100 g.) brown sugar	½ cup brown sugar, firmly packed
4 oz. (100 g.) mixed dried fruit	⅔ cup mixed dried fruit
1 teaspoon powdered ginger	1 teaspoon ground ginger
2 tablespoons apricot jam	3 tablespoons apricot jam
1 egg yolk	1 egg yolk
2 egg whites	2 egg whites
little castor sugar	little granulated sugar
to serve	**to serve**
cream or ice cream	cream or ice cream

Cooking time 35–40 minutes
Serves 6–8
Advance Preparations Bake and reheat when required or serve cold.

Cream butter and sugar, add flour, egg yolk and water to make a firm dough. Roll out and line a Swiss roll tin (jelly roll pan) approximately 10 inches × 8 inches (25 cm. × 20 cm.). Prick and bake for 10 minutes just above centre of moderately hot oven, 375–400°F. (190–200°C.), Gas Mark 5–6.

until firm but not coloured. Spread with jam then with the topping. To make this, mix all remaining ingredients together except egg whites and castor sugar. Whisk egg whites, stir into crumb mixture gently, spread over pastry. Return to the oven, lowering the heat to moderate, 350°F. (180°C.), Gas Mark 4, and continue cooking for another 25–30 minutes, until firm to the touch. Dust with the castor sugar before serving. Cut into slices, serve hot or cold with cream or ice cream.

To Make a Flan (Pie Shell) Make either the biscuit, flan or short crust pastry (basic pie dough) (pages 72 and 73). Put a flan ring on an upturned baking tray, this makes it easier to remove. If more convenient use a shallow cake tin or dish (pie pan). Support the pastry over a rolling pin and lower into the flan ring, tin or dish. Press down firmly. Either cut away surplus pastry or run the rolling pin over the top. Put greased greaseproof (wax) paper or foil into the pastry. Add dried beans or crusts of bread if using paper. Bake in the centre of a hot oven for short crust, but moderately hot for biscuit and flan pastry. After 15–20 minutes remove flan ring, paper, etc. Then return pastry to oven until firm. This method of baking a pastry case is described as 'baking blind'.

Uncooked Flan Case Cream 3 oz. (75 g. – 6 tablespoons) butter with the same amount of sugar. Add 6 oz. (150 g. – 3 cups) crushed cornflakes or biscuit (cracker) crumbs. Knead well, press into a flan ring. Set in the refrigerator for several hours. Fill as below.

To Make a Fruit Flan Bake the pastry case (pie shell), as above, then cool. Fill with *well drained* cooked, canned, frozen fruit or fresh fruit. Cover with a glaze:

Arrowroot Glaze To each ¼ pint (1½ dl. – ⅔ cup) sweetened fruit syrup allow 1 teaspoon arrowroot. Cornflour (cornstarch) could be used instead. Blend with the syrup. Stir over a low heat until clear and thickened. Cool slightly, then brush or spread over the fruit.

Jelly Glaze Particularly suitable for fresh fruit. Put redcurrant or apple jelly (apricot jam could be used) into a pan with water or lemon juice to dilute. Heat gently then use as above.

Rhubarb and Date Flan

Imperial/Metric	American
short crust pastry made with 6 oz. (150 g.) flour, etc., see page 72	basic pie dough made with 1½ cups flour, etc., see page 72
1 lb. (½ kilo) rhubarb	1 lb. rhubarb
3 oz. (75 g.) sugar	generous ⅓ cup sugar
3 oz. (75 g.) chopped dates	½ cup chopped dates
1 or 2 egg yolks	1 or 2 egg yolks

Cooking time 50–55 minutes
Serves 4–6
Advance Preparations Make flan case (pie shell) and store in the refrigerator for a day.

Line a 7-inch (18-cm.) flan ring (pie pan) with pastry and bake 'blind' until pale golden brown, see below. Make tiny shapes of any remaining pastry and bake at the same time. Cook rhubarb with sugar and no water in a basin (bowl) over hot water or top of a double saucepan. When soft, mash, sieve or emulsify, add the dates and egg yolks, pour into the flan case. Set for 30 minutes in centre of cool oven, 275°F. (140°C.), Gas Mark 1. Serve hot or cold, topped with pastry shapes.

Freezing Flan cases freeze well, but this filling does not freeze very well.

Variations

Apple and Sultana Flan Cook apples instead of rhubarb, add little lemon juice and 3 oz. (75 g. – ½ cup) sultanas (seedless white raisins) and the egg yolks – omit dates.

Apricot and Almond Flan Cook apricots instead of rhubarb, add 2 oz. (50 g. – ½ cup) ground or chopped almonds and the egg yolks – omit dates.

Prune and Almond Flan Soak 8 oz. (200 g. – 1⅓ cups) prunes overnight in cold water, then simmer until tender with sugar to taste. Sieve, add egg yolks and 2 oz. (50 g. – ½ cup) blanched chopped almonds – omit dates.

Deep Dish Lemon Meringue Pie

Imperial/Metric	American
short crust pastry made with 8 oz. (200 g.) flour, etc., see page 72	basic pie dough made with 2 cups flour, etc., see page 72
for the filling	**for the filling**
1½ oz. (40 g.) cornflour	6 tablespoons cornstarch
½ pint (3 dl.) water	1¼ cups water
grated rind 2 lemons	grated rind 2 lemons
juice 2 lemons	juice 2 lemons
3 oz. (75 g.) sugar	generous ⅓ cup sugar
1 oz. (25 g.) butter or margarine	2 tablespoons butter or margarine
2 egg yolks	2 egg yolks
for the meringue	**for the meringue**
2 egg whites	2 egg whites
2–4 oz. (50–100 g.) sugar	¼–½ cup sugar

Cooking time 1 hour 20 minutes
Serves 6
Advance Preparations Prepare pastry and lemon filling.

Roll out pastry and line a 1½–2-pint (⅞–1¼-litre – 4–5-cup) pie dish (baking pan) with this, use any pastry left to make an interesting edging. Bake 'blind', see page 77, for 20 minutes in the centre of a hot oven, 425°F. (220°C.), Gas Mark 7, lowering the heat to moderately hot after 10 minutes if the pastry is becoming too brown. Meanwhile, blend the cornflour with the water, lemon rind and juice and cook over a low heat, stirring well, until thickened; beat in the sugar, butter or margarine and finally the egg yolks. Put into the pastry case. Whisk the egg whites until very stiff, gradually beat in half the sugar and fold in the remainder. Pile or pipe on top of filling. Return to the oven and set for 1 hour in a very cool oven, 250°F. (130°C.), Gas Mark ½. Use the larger quantity of sugar if serving cold.

Variations

Deep Dish Orange Meringue Pie Use the grated rind of 2 oranges and 5 tablespoons (6 tablespoons) orange juice instead of lemon juice, or to give a sharper flavour use 1 tablespoon lemon juice and only 4 tablespoons (5 tablespoons) orange juice. Make the pastry case in a flan shape, as picture.
Speedy Lemon Flan Blend ¼ pint (1½ dl. – ⅔ cup) sweetened condensed milk with the grated rind of 1–2 lemons and the juice of 3 lemons. Add ¼ pint (1½ dl. – ⅔ cup) whipped cream. Top with a meringue (this is optional) as recipe, and flash for 2–3 minutes under a pre-heated grill (broiler).

Stuffed Apple Meringue

Imperial/Metric	American
4 large cooking apples	4 large baking apples
2 good tablespoons mincemeat	3 good tablespoons mincemeat
for the meringue	**for the meringue**
2 egg whites	2 egg whites
2 oz. (50 g.) castor sugar	¼ cup granulated sugar
to serve	**to serve**
custard sauce, see page 85, or cream	custard sauce, see page 85, or cream

Cooking time 1¼ hours
Serves 4
Advance Preparations Prepare apples for baking.

Core the apples and put into a baking dish, slit
round the centres to prevent apples 'bursting' during
cooking and to make it easier to remove skin. Fill
the centres with mincemeat. Bake for approximately
1 hour in the centre of a moderate oven, 350–
375°F. (180–190°C.), Gas Mark 4–5. Whisk egg
whites until very stiff, gradually beat in half the
sugar and fold in the rest. Either pile on top of
mincemeat or pipe in a ring round the top. Return
to oven for 15 minutes to brown the meringue,
lowering the heat slightly to prevent the meringue
scorching. Serve hot with custard sauce or cream,
and eat as soon as possible after cooking.

Variation
Fill the centres with brown sugar and sultanas
(seedless white raisins) or butter and brown sugar.

Put a little golden (light corn) syrup and water in
dish to make a sauce.

Mallow Topped Oranges

Imperial/Metric	American
6 large oranges	6 large oranges
2 tablespoons golden syrup	3 tablespoons light corn syrup
2 oz. (50 g.) butter	¼ cup butter
for the topping	**for the topping**
4 oz. (100 g.) white marshmallows	4 oz. white marshmallows
2 tablespoons orange peel	3 tablespoons orange peel
6 Maraschino cherries	6 Maraschino cherries

Cooking time 20 minutes
Serves 6
Advance Preparations Prepare ahead, use within a
few hours.

Grate or shred the top 'zest' of the orange peel, then
cut away remaining peel and pith. Slice the oranges,
put together again, secure with cocktail sticks, stand
in pan and cook gently in the syrup and butter for
10–15 minutes. Melt the marshmallows and orange
peel in a basin over hot water, spoon over oranges,
top with cherries. *Illustrated on page 78.*

Baked Apples Choose good sized apples and prepare and cook as the recipe on page 79. The apples may be cooked without a filling of any kind. If you remove the skin from the apples while hot you can use the pulp to make a smooth *thick* apple pulp, this is ideal for:

Fruit Fool Sweeten the pulp, blend with an equal amount of thick custard or whipped cream.

Fruit Snow Blend 1 or 2 stiffly whisked egg whites into each ½ pint (3 dl. – 1¼ cups) sweetened pulp.

Fruit Crumble Put about 1 lb. (½ kilo) prepared fruit with the minimum of water and sugar to taste into the ovenproof dish. If using hard fruit cook until half softened, but berry fruit does not need pre-cooking. Top with a crumble mixture made by rubbing 2 oz.

(50 g. – ¼ cup) margarine into 4 oz. (100 g. – 1 cup) flour. Add 3 oz. (75 g. – generous ⅓ cup) sugar. Sprinkle over the fruit, neaten with a knife and bake for approximately 35 minutes in the centre of a very moderate to moderate oven, 325–350°F. (170–180°C.), Gas Mark 3–4, until firm and golden brown. *Serves 4.*

Freezing This freezes well. Prepare and freeze, or cook lightly then freeze. Use within about 3 months.

Apple and Orange Charlotte

Imperial/Metric	American
5 oz. (125 g.) bread (weight without crust)	5 oz. bread (weight without crust)
2 oranges	2 oranges
12 oz. (300 g.) sliced apples	¾ lb. sliced apples
sugar to taste	sugar to taste
little water	little water
2 oz. (50 g.) butter or margarine	¼ cup butter or margarine
for the topping	**for the topping**
little brown sugar	little brown sugar

Cooking time 50–60 minutes
Serves 4–5
Advance Preparations Make pudding, cook as required.

Make the bread into fairly coarse crumbs. Grate the rind from the oranges, mix with the breadcrumbs. Cook the apples with sugar and water until soft, there is no need to cook the fruit until a smooth purée (stir as the fruit cooks). Put half the butter or margarine at the bottom of a pie dish (pan) and put into oven to melt. Remove hot dish carefully and sprinkle one-third of the crumbs on top of the melted butter or margarine, then add a layer of cooked apple and pieces of orange (remove as much of the pith and skin from the oranges as possible). Follow with half the crumbs left then the remainder of the fruit, and a final layer of crumbs. Put the rest of the butter or margarine on top in tiny pieces, add a sprinkling of brown sugar. Bake in the centre of a moderate oven, 350–375°F. (180–190°C.), Gas Mark 4–5, for 30–40 minutes, until crisp and brown.

Freezing This freezes well, but the luxury version, see below, is better. Use within 3–4 months.

Variations

Apple and Date Charlotte Use chopped dates in place of oranges. Flavour the crumbs with a little spice.

Apple and Lemon Charlotte Cook apples in lemon juice and water. Flavour crumbs with grated lemon rind.

Any other fruit may be used in place of apples.

Luxury Charlotte A better texture is given to the crumb layers if the crumbs are fried first. Use almost double the amount of butter or margarine. Heat this in a large frying pan, lower the heat then toss the crumbs in this until pale golden and slightly crisped. Remove pan from the heat, mix a little brown sugar with the fried crumbs together with grated fruit rind or other flavouring.

Charlotte with Suet Mix the crumbs with 2 oz. (50 g. – just under ½ cup) shredded (chopped) suet instead of using butter or margarine.

Apple Brown Betty

Imperial/Metric	American
1 lb. (½ kilo) cooking apples	1 lb. baking apples
1½ oz. (40 g.) margarine	3 tablespoons margarine
4 oz. (100 g.) soft breadcrumbs	2 cups soft bread crumbs
mincemeat or dried fruit (see method)	mincemeat or dried fruit (see method)
little mixed spice	little mixed spices
little sugar	little sugar
1 oz. (25 g.) golden syrup	1½ tablespoons light corn syrup
1 tablespoon warm water	1 tablespoon warm water

Cooking time 1½–2 hours
Serves 4–5

Slice apples. Grease a 2-pint (1¼-litre – 5-cup) pudding basin (mold) with ½ oz. (15 g. – 1 tablespoon) margarine and sprinkle some of the breadcrumbs round the inside. Fill the basin with alternate layers of uncooked apple slices topped with 1–2 oz. (25–50 g. – 3–6 tablespoons) mincemeat or dried fruit, then a dusting of mixed spice and a sprinkling of sugar, then with a layer of breadcrumbs. Continue filling the basin like this, ending with breadcrumbs. Put 1 oz. (25 g. – 2 tablespoons) margarine over the top layer of crumbs in tiny pieces. Mix golden syrup with warm water, pour over the top of the pudding. Cover with greased greaseproof (wax) paper or foil and steam for 1½–2 hours.

Variations

Use diced rhubarb instead of apples. Bake for 1 hour in a moderate oven, 350–375°F. (180–190°C.), Gas Mark 4–5. In this case, be a little more generous with the margarine on top of the pudding.
The apple brown betty may be baked instead of steaming as recipe. Allow 1 hour in a moderate oven, 350°F. (180°C.), Gas Mark 4.

Autumn Pudding

Imperial/Metric	American
10–12 oz. (250–300 g.) bread	½–¾ lb. bread
fruit (see method)	fruit (see method)
to serve	**to serve**
cream or custard	cream or custard

Cooking time depends on whether fruit is cooked
Serves 4–6
Advance Preparations Must be left at least 12 hours.

Cut bread into thin slices, or use thinly sliced bread, remove crusts. Put most of the bread into a 2-pint (1¼-litre – 5-cup) basin (mold), lining base and sides. Either open a large can of fruit and drain off the liquid, or use fruit pie filling, or cook about 1½ lb. (¾ kilo) fruit (e.g. in autumn use apples and blackberries) with the minimum of water and sugar to taste. Spoon the fruit into the bread-lined basin, cover with the remainder of the bread. Put greaseproof (wax) paper, then a flat saucer or plate and a light weight on top, leave overnight in a cool place. Serve with cream or custard.

Freezing This freezes well, defrost at room temperature. Use within 6 weeks.

Variation

You can vary the title of the pudding by the choice of fruit, e.g., a summer pudding is filled with raspberries and other berry fruit.

To Cook Steamed Puddings

When making a sponge or light type pudding allow plenty of space in the basin (mold) for the pudding to rise. Cover carefully with greased foil, or greased greaseproof (wax) paper, so the top of the pudding does not become damp. Either steam in a proper steamer over boiling water; or stand on an upturned saucer or old tin in a saucepan – this makes certain the water will not get into the pudding.

Always fill up the pan with boiling water. If you dislike a lot of steam in the kitchen you can cook the pudding in the oven. Cover the basin as above, then stand in another large container with the water halfway up the basin. Put a large sheet of foil over both the pudding basin and the outer container – this prevents evaporation of the water. Cook sponge puddings in a moderate oven, but allow about 30 minutes longer cooking time than when steaming a pudding, such as the recipe below. This makes certain the water will have time to boil and the pudding to cook.

Rich Sponge Pudding

Imperial/Metric	American
4 oz. (100 g.) butter or margarine	½ cup butter or margarine
4 oz. (100 g.) castor sugar	½ cup granulated sugar
2 eggs	2 eggs
4 oz. (100 g.) self-raising flour (or plain flour with 1 level teaspoon baking powder)	1 cup self-raising flour (or all-purpose flour with 1 level teaspoon baking powder – double-acting)

Cooking time see method
Serves 4–6
Advance Preparations Make sponge, store for up to 24 hours in the refrigerator before cooking.

Cream the butter or margarine and sugar, gradually beat in the eggs adding a little sieved flour or flour and baking powder if the mixture shows signs of curdling. Fold in the remainder of the flour. Put into a greased container, cover with greased greaseproof (wax) paper or foil. Steam for approximately 1½ hours over boiling water in 1 basin (mold); 25 minutes over boiling water in 4–6 individual moulds; nearly 20 minutes in 8–12 castle pudding tins.

For Economy Use half the amounts of butter or margarine and sugar and only 1 egg. Blend to a soft dropping consistency with milk or milk and water.
Freezing Either freeze the uncooked pudding, thaw then cook, or freeze the cooked pudding and reheat when required. If the pudding is in an ovenproof basin (mold) thaw out before reheating but if in a foil basin you can reheat from frozen state. Use within 3–4 months.

Variations

Golden Cap Pudding (Illustrated) Serve with hot golden (light corn) syrup or put some syrup into the basin, then add sponge mixture and cook as recipe.

Cherry Sponge Pudding Use 5 oz. (125 g. – 1¼ cups) flour and add 3 tablespoons (4 tablespoons) chopped Maraschino cherries. Serve with hot cherry brandy or cream.
Chocolate Chip Pudding Add 4 oz. (100 g.) chopped plain (semi-sweet) chocolate or polka dots to the flour – these remain in delicious little pieces of chocolate in the pudding. Serve with ice cream as a contrast.
Jam Pudding Serve the sponge with hot jam or put some jam into the basin, then add the sponge mixture and cook as the recipe. The name of the jam gives the name to the pudding, e.g., blackcurrant jam gives a black cap pudding.

Rainbow Pudding

Imperial/Metric	American
4 oz. (100 g.) margarine	½ cup margarine
4 oz. (100 g.) castor sugar	½ cup granulated sugar
2 large eggs	2 large eggs
5 oz. (125 g.) flour (with plain flour use 1½ teaspoons baking powder)	1¼ cups flour (with all-purpose flour use 1½ teaspoons baking powder — double-acting)
1 tablespoon milk	1 tablespoon milk
1 tablespoon coffee essence	1 tablespoon strong black coffee (sweetened)
to decorate	**to decorate**
little castor sugar	little granulated sugar
1 glacé cherry	1 candied cherry
to serve	**to serve**
coffee sauce, see page 85	coffee sauce, see page 85

Cooking time 1½ hours
Serves 4–6
Advance Preparations Make sponge, store for up to 24 hours in the refrigerator before cooking.

Cream together margarine and sugar until soft and light. Add beaten eggs and sieved flour (or flour and baking powder) alternately; put half mixture into another basin (bowl). Stir milk into one half and coffee essence into the other. Put the coffee and plain mixtures into a greased basin (mold), cover well and steam for 1½ hours. Turn out on to a hot dish. Dust with castor sugar and put a cherry on top. Serve with coffee sauce (see page 85). Make sure everyone has a slice of each flavour.

Freezing Either freeze the uncooked pudding, thaw then cook, or freeze the cooked pudding and reheat when required. If the pudding is in an ovenproof basin thaw out before reheating, but if in a foil basin you can reheat from frozen state. Use within 3–4 months.

Variations

Coffee Raisin Pudding (Illustrated) Use at least double the amount of coffee flavouring in the basic recipe above. Add 3 oz. (75 g. – ½ cup) raisins. Serve with cream and brown sugar.
Ginger Rainbow Pudding Add 1–2 teaspoons ground ginger to half the mixture, leave the other half plain. Serve with hot golden (light corn) syrup.
Mocha Pudding Blend 1 tablespoon cocoa powder with half the mixture. Flavour the remainder with coffee as the basic recipe, above. Serve with chocolate or coffee sauce (recipes on page 85).

Orange Pudding Use proportions as the basic recipe but omit both milk and coffee flavouring. Stir 2 tablespoons (3 tablespoons) marmalade into the mixture plus the finely grated rind of 1–2 oranges. Serve with hot marmalade as a sauce.
Spice Fruit Pudding Blend 1 teaspoon mixed spice or other spice with the flour, then add up to 6 oz. (150 g. – 1 cup) mixed dried fruit. Omit the coffee flavouring from the basic recipe and moisten with milk alone. Serve with hot custard sauce, page 85.

Suet Puddings

Puddings made with grated (chopped) suet instead of margarine or other fat tend to be heavier than a sponge pudding and need longer cooking.

Basic Suet Pudding To each 4 oz. (100 g. – 1 cup) self-raising flour (or use equal quantities of flour and soft breadcrumbs), allow 2 oz. (50 g. – generous $\frac{1}{3}$ cup) shredded (chopped) suet and 2 oz. (50 g. – $\frac{1}{4}$ cup) sugar. Blend to a sticky consistency with milk or egg and milk. Put into a greased basin (mold), cover well and steam for 2$\frac{1}{2}$ hours. Serve with hot jam or lemon curd or marmalade. Dried fruit can also be added to this mixture for a fruit pudding.

Fruit Pudding Make the suet crust pastry in exactly the same way as for the steak and kidney pudding on page 46. Line the basin (mold), then fill with prepared fruit and sugar to taste. Add a little water with hard fruit such as apples, firm plums, etc., but use no water with soft fruits. Cover with a lid of suet crust pastry, then paper, etc. Steam for about 2$\frac{1}{2}$ hours and serve hot with custard sauce (see next page).

Lemon Pudding Make the suet crust pastry in exactly the same way as for the steak and kidney pudding on page 46. Line the basin, then add 2–3 chopped well washed lemons and about 4 oz. (100 g. – $\frac{1}{2}$ cup) brown sugar with 2 oz. (50 g. – $\frac{1}{4}$ cup) butter. Cover with a lid of suet crust pastry, then with paper, etc. Steam for about 2$\frac{1}{2}$ hours.

Chocolate Fruit Cap Pudding

Imperial/Metric	American
2 oz. (50 g.) chopped glacé cherries	$\frac{1}{4}$ cup chopped candied cherries
1 oz. (25 g.) blanched almonds	just under $\frac{1}{4}$ cup blanched almonds
2 oz. (50 g.) sultanas or seedless raisins	$\frac{1}{3}$ cup seedless white raisins or seedless raisins
for the pudding	**for the pudding**
4 oz. (100 g.) moist brown sugar	$\frac{1}{2}$ cup moist brown sugar, firmly packed
2–3 oz. (50–75 g.) shredded suet	generous $\frac{1}{3}$–just under $\frac{2}{3}$ cup chopped suet
4 oz. (100 g.) self-raising flour (or plain flour with 1 teaspoon baking powder)	1 cup self-rising flour (or all-purpose flour with 1 teaspoon baking powder – double-acting)
1 oz. (25 g.) cocoa	$\frac{1}{4}$ cup unsweetened cocoa
1 oz. (25 g.) ground almonds	$\frac{1}{4}$ cup ground almonds
1 egg	1 egg
milk to mix	milk to mix
for the sauce	**for the sauce**
4 oz. (100 g.) plain chocolate	$\frac{1}{4}$ lb. unsweetened chocolate
$\frac{1}{4}$ pint (1$\frac{1}{2}$ dl.) water or milk	$\frac{2}{3}$ cup water or milk

Cooking time 2 hours
Serves 4–6
Advance Preparations Prepare the pudding and keep in the refrigerator for several hours before cooking.

Grease a 1$\frac{1}{2}$–2-pint ($\frac{7}{8}$–1$\frac{1}{4}$-litre – 4–5-cup) basin (mold) and put the cherries, etc., at the base. Mix the sugar and suet with the sieved flour or flour and baking powder and cocoa, add the ground almonds, egg and milk to give a soft dropping consistency. Put into the basin, cover with paper or foil and steam over boiling water for 2 hours. Turn out and coat with the sauce before serving. To make the sauce, melt the chocolate and water or milk over hot water.

For Economy Omit ground almonds and use the same amount of extra flour or use fine crumbs.
Freezing This freezes well whether cooked or uncooked. Use within 3–4 months.

Variation
Mocha Fruit Cap Pudding Use the recipe above, but mix the pudding with strong coffee instead of milk.

Sauces to Serve with Puddings

Most steamed puddings are better if served with a sauce, for this provides a moist texture to the dish. Sauces are also excellent with plain moulds, such as blancmange, ice cream, etc. Some of the easiest sauces are made as follows:

Caramel Sauce Serve with ice cream, custards, etc. To each tablespoon sugar (loaf (cube) or granulated) allow the same amount of water. Stir over a low heat until the sugar has melted, then boil steadily, without stirring, until the mixture turns golden brown. Remember the mixture continues cooking in the heat retained in the saucepan, so remove from the heat before it becomes too dark. Stir a little extra water into the caramel, then heat until this is absorbed.

Custard Sauce Serve with puddings, fruit, etc. Allow 1 egg or 1–2 egg yolks (save the whites for meringues) plus 1 tablespoon sugar to each ½ pint (3 dl. – 1¼ cups) milk. Whisk the egg or egg yolks and sugar. Whisk on the warm milk then transfer to the top of a double saucepan or stand the basin over a pan of hot, but not boiling, water. If there are small pieces of egg yolk, strain before cooking. Stir over a low heat until the mixture thickens. The custard may be flavoured with vanilla essence (extract) or a strip of lemon rind or a little sherry. Custard sauce is also made with custard powder; follow directions on the container.

Chocolate Sauce Serve with puddings, over ice cream, pears, etc. One of the easiest methods of making chocolate sauce is shown under the recipe on the previous page. Another excellent sauce is made as follows. Put 2 oz. (50 g. – ¼ cup) butter or margarine, 1½ tablespoons (2 tablespoons) sugar, 1 tablespoon golden (light corn) syrup, 1½ tablespoons (2 tablespoons) cocoa (unsweetened cocoa) and 4 tablespoons (5 tablespoons) water or milk into a saucepan. Stir over a low heat for a few minutes.

Lemon Sauce Serve with puddings, over ice cream. Grate the top 'zest', i.e. the yellow part of the rind, from 1 lemon. Put the rind plus the juice of the lemon into a saucepan. Blend 1 teaspoon cornflour (cornstarch) or arrowroot with ¼ pint (1½ dl. – ⅔ cup) water. Add to the lemon juice, etc., together with a small knob of butter or margarine and 1–2 tablespoons sugar. Stir over a low heat until thickened and clear.
Oranges, grapefruit and other citrus fruits are treated in the same way.

Coffee Sauce

Imperial/Metric	American
1 tablespoon cornflour	1 tablespoon cornstarch
¼ pint (1½ dl.) strong coffee	⅔ cup strong coffee
¼ pint (1½ dl.) milk	⅔ cup milk
1 oz. (25 g.) sugar	2 tablespoons sugar
few drops vanilla essence	few drops vanilla extract

Cooking time 10 minutes
Serves 4–6
Advance Preparations If making beforehand, cover with damp greaseproof (wax) paper or a layer of cold milk to prevent a skin forming. Whisk sharply as sauce reheats.

Blend the cornflour with the coffee. Pour over boiling milk. Return to the pan with the sugar and vanilla essence and cook until thickened and smooth; stir well as the sauce thickens.

Variation
Sweet White Sauce Use all milk in the recipe above. Add a knob of butter for extra flavour. Omit vanilla essence, add strip lemon rind.

Light Hot Puddings

Many light puddings are based upon eggs and milk. The next pages give a selection of these: more will be found on pages 131–133.

One of the most famous light desserts is the Italian zabaglione, made as follows:

Zabaglione Put 4 egg yolks and 2 tablespoons (3 tablespoons) castor (granulated) sugar into a basin over hot, but not boiling, water. Whisk until fluffy then gradually whisk in 2 tablespoons Marsala. Serve in glasses while still warm. This serves 4.

For Economy Use inexpensive white or red wine or grated orange rind and juice instead of Marsala.

Pineapple Pudding

Imperial/Metric	American
1 medium can pineapple chunks or rings	1 medium can pineapple chunks or rings
2 oz. (50 g.) butter or margarine	¼ cup butter or margarine
2 oz. (50 g.) flour, plain or self-raising	½ cup flour, all-purpose or self-rising
¼ pint (1½ dl.) milk	⅔ cup milk
4 oz. (100 g.) sugar	½ cup sugar
2 eggs	2 eggs

Cooking time   1 hour 40 minutes
Serves 4–6
Advance Preparations Make thick sauce, cover with damp greaseproof (wax) paper.

Strain the syrup from the can of pineapple, coarsely chop the fruit, put at the bottom of a pie dish (baking dish). Melt the butter or margarine in a saucepan, stir in the flour, cook over a low heat for a few minutes. Take pan off heat, gradually add the cold milk. Return to the heat, bring slowly to boil, stirring all the time to keep the sauce smooth. Cook until thickened, then add half the sugar. Cool slightly, add the pineapple syrup – this must be put in very slowly to prevent curdling – and finally the beaten egg yolks. Pour this over the fruit. Put in the centre of a very moderate oven, 325°F. (170°C.), Gas Mark 3, for about 45 minutes, until just set. Whisk the egg whites until stiff, fold in most of the remaining sugar. Pile on top of pudding, dust with the last of the sugar. Put into a very low oven, 225°F. (110°C.), Gas Mark 0–¼, for approximately 45 minutes. Serve hot.

To Save Time Brown the meringue topping for 15–20 minutes only in a very moderate oven.
To Serve Cold Use double the amount of sugar in the meringue and dry out for 1 hour at the lowest setting. Use less sugar in the pineapple base of the pudding if you dislike over-sweet desserts.

Variations
Apricots, peaches and dessert plums can all be used in this way.
Orange Pudding (Illustrated) Use canned mandarin oranges in place of pineapple. Decorate meringue with canned orange segments or pieces of fresh orange as in the picture.

Using Rice

The recipe for rice croquettes on this page uses rice in a rather unusual manner, but a rice pudding is a good way of providing milk for the family.

Rice Pudding Put 2 oz. (50 g. − just over ¼ cup) round grain rice and 1–2 tablespoons sugar into an ovenproof dish. Add 1 pint (6 dl. − 2½ cups) milk and cook very slowly in the oven for 1½–2 hours. Serve by itself, or with fruit, or with the jam sauce below. *Serves 4.*

Rice Condé Allow the rice to cool, blend with whipped cream then put into a dish, top with fruit and a glaze, such as given on page 77.

Rice Croquettes

Imperial/Metric	American
1 pint (6 dl.) milk	2½ cups milk
few drops vanilla essence or vanilla pod	few drops vanilla extract or vanilla bean
1 oz. (25 g.) butter	2 tablespoons butter
2 oz. (50 g.) sugar	¼ cup sugar
4 oz. (100 g.) round grain rice	just over ½ cup short grain rice
to coat	**to coat**
1 egg	1 egg
2 oz. (50 g.) crisp breadcrumbs (raspings) or crushed cornflakes	½ cup crisp bread crumbs (raspings) or crushed cornflakes
for frying	**for frying**
deep oil or fat	deep oil or shortening
to decorate	**to decorate**
pieces of angelica	pieces of angelica
to serve	**to serve**
jam sauce, see below	jam sauce, see below

Cooking time 40 minutes
Serves 4–6
Advance Preparations Make croquettes, fry just before serving.

Heat the milk with vanilla essence or pod. Remove pod, then add butter, sugar and rice. Cook slowly until the rice is tender and has absorbed the liquid (stir from time to time unless you use a double saucepan). Cool, then form into pear shapes. Brush with beaten egg, roll in crumbs or cornflakes and fry until crisp and brown. Decorate with angelica to look like stalks, serve with jam sauce, see below.

Jam Sauce

Imperial/Metric	American
2 level teaspoons arrowroot or cornflour	2 level teaspoons arrowroot flour or cornstarch
¼ pint (1½ dl.) water	⅔ cup water
4 tablespoons jam	5 tablespoons jam
1 oz. (25 g.) sugar	2 tablespoons sugar
little lemon juice	little lemon juice

Cooking time 10 minutes
Serves 4–6
Advance Preparations Cook and reheat before serving.

Blend arrowroot or cornflour with a little cold water, then put with all ingredients into a pan; bring to boil and cook until smooth, stir well as sauce cools.

Making a Hot Soufflé

A hot soufflé is not only a very delicious light pudding, but the high percentage of eggs makes it a nutritious one too. The basic recipe below is quite an economical one, but some of the variations are less inexpensive and suitable for special occasion meals. Adapt the vanilla soufflé by adding a little chocolate or coffee to flavour. Time the cooking of a soufflé carefully; it should be brought out of the oven and served *as soon* as it is cooked. If a hot soufflé is kept waiting it falls and is spoiled.

While it is not essential to serve a sauce with a hot soufflé the jam sauce on page 87 is a good accompaniment. The more elaborate soufflés below are better served with cream or ice cream.

Vanilla Soufflé

Imperial/Metric	American
1 level tablespoon cornflour	1 level tablespoon cornstarch
¼ pint (1½ dl.) milk	⅔ cup milk
1 oz. (25 g.) butter	2 tablespoons butter
2 oz. (50 g.) sugar	¼ cup sugar
2 tablespoons cream or extra milk	3 tablespoons cream or extra milk
½–1 teaspoon vanilla essence	½–1 teaspoon vanilla extract
3–4 eggs	3–4 eggs
for the topping	**for the topping**
little icing sugar	little confectioners' sugar

Cooking time 35–40 minutes
Serves 4
Advance Preparations Make thick sauce but never try to cook a hot soufflé in advance.

Blend the cornflour and milk and stir over a low heat until the mixture is thick. Add the butter and sugar, heat until dissolved. Blend in the cream (or extra milk), the vanilla essence and egg yolks. Finally fold in the stiffly whisked egg whites. Put into a greased 6-inch (15-cm.) soufflé dish (baker) and bake in the centre of a moderately hot oven, 375–400°F. (190–200°C.), Gas Mark 5–6, for 25–30 minutes. *Quickly* shake the sieved icing sugar on top and serve at once.

Variations

Apricot Soufflé Make a thick purée of canned or cooked dried apricots – use just *over* ¼ pint (1½ dl. – ⅔ cup) of this in place of the ¼ pint (1½ dl. – ⅔ cup) milk, add the cream or extra milk to give a slightly less thick mixture.

Crème de Menthe Soufflé Ingredients as vanilla soufflé, but omit the vanilla essence (extract) and add 2 tablespoons (3 tablespoons) crème de menthe instead of the cream or extra milk.

Lemon Soufflé Grate the rind from 1–2 lemons. Squeeze out the juice and add enough water to give

¼ pint (1½ dl. – ⅔ cup) plus 2 tablespoons (3 tablespoons). Make the sauce with this instead of milk, add the lemon rind, butter and sugar, then the egg yolks and finally the egg whites.

Orange Soufflé Use the same method as lemon soufflé.

Orléans Soufflé Ingredients as vanilla soufflé, but substitute 2 tablespoons (3 tablespoons) honey for the sugar and add 2 tablespoons (3 tablespoons) chopped glacé (candied) cherries and 1 tablespoon chopped angelica to the thick sauce before adding the egg whites.

Pineapple Soufflé Make the sauce with ¼ pint (1½ dl. – ⅔ cup) syrup from a can of pineapple instead of milk, add 4 tablespoons (5 tablespoons) finely chopped canned pineapple instead of the cream or extra milk. A little less sugar could be used.

Rum Soufflé Ingredients as vanilla soufflé, but omit the vanilla essence (extract) and add 2 tablespoons (3 tablespoons) rum instead of the cream or extra milk.

Sweets with Gelatine and Jelly

1   When using fruit-flavoured jellies (fruit-flavored gelatin) you cannot add milk and cream while the jelly is hot. The jelly should be dissolved in a small amount of very hot water, cooled, then the milk and/or cream added later to prevent curdling, see recipe page 90, and below.

2   If adding juicy fruits to the jelly use rather less water than usual to dissolve the jelly. Never add *fresh* pineapple to a jelly as this prevents it setting.

3   When adding egg whites to a jelly make certain the mixture is beginning to stiffen before folding in the egg whites. This ensures they are evenly blended. If the jelly mixture is too soft the egg whites rise to the top.

4   Always dissolve powdered gelatine thoroughly (see below). Do not use too much gelatine in a recipe otherwise the sweet will be stiff and unappetising. Generally you need ½ oz. (15 g. — 2 envelopes) to 1 pint (6 dl. — 2½ cups) of clear thin liquid, or ¼ oz. (7 g. — 1 envelope) or ½ tablespoon to thickened liquid, see mousse recipe below.

5   *To Dissolve Powdered Gelatine* It is not easy to dissolve gelatine in a small amount of water. Put the gelatine in a basin and soften in a little cold water. Either place in a pan of very hot water until dissolved or pour very hot or boiling liquid over the softened gelatine.

Family Mousse

Imperial/Metric	American
1 oz. (25 g.) cornflour or 1 envelope flavoured blancmange powder	¼ cup cornstarch or 1 envelope flavored blancmange powder
2 oz. (50 g.) sugar	¼ cup sugar
1 pint (6 dl.) milk	2½ cups milk
½ tablespoon powdered gelatine	½ tablespoon powdered gelatin
4 tablespoons water or fruit juice	5 tablespoons water or fruit juice
¼ pint (1½ dl.) evaporated milk or thick cream	⅔ cup evaporated milk or whipping cream
2 egg whites	2 egg whites

Cooking time 10 minutes

Serves 4–6

Advance Preparations Make the dessert, store in refrigerator. Use within 24 hours.

Make a blancmange in the usual way with the cornflour (cornstarch) or blancmange powder, sugar and milk. Cool, stir to prevent a skin forming. Meanwhile, soften gelatine in the cold water or fruit juice, stand over a pan of very hot water until dissolved then whisk into the cool cornflour mixture. Pour mixture into a basin to become quite cold, put a plate over the top to prevent a skin forming. When cold, but not set, fold in the whipped evaporated milk or cream. Lastly, fold in the stiffly whisked egg whites. Spoon into glasses or a serving dish.

Variations

To make an even lighter mousse increase the percentage of egg whites – using 3 to 1 pint (6 dl. – 2½ cups).

To Flavour Instead of the powdered gelatine use half a fruit-flavoured jelly (fruit-flavored gelatin). Dissolve this in ⅛ pint (¾ dl. – ⅓ cup) water. For example, for a lemon mousse use lemon-flavoured cornflour and lemon jelly. For a raspberry mousse use raspberry-flavoured cornflour and raspberry jelly. Make sure the cornflour mixture is cool before adding the jelly mixture, otherwise the mixture will curdle. Finally, add the whipped evaporated milk or cream and egg whites.

Fruit Blancmange To make a change from using milk for a blancmange use fruit juice or fruit purée. Blend the flavoured cornflour (cornstarch) with 1 pint (6 dl. – 2½ cups) fruit juice or 1¼ pints (6½ dl. – generous 3 cups) fruit purée. Add sugar to taste. Stir over a low heat until thickened. Pour into a mould (mold), rinsed out in cold water, and leave until set. Serve with cream or ice cream. If no blancmange powder is available use 1¼ oz. (35 g. – generous ¼ cup) cornflour (cornstarch).

Jelly Whip

Imperial/Metric	American
1 fruit-flavoured jelly	1 package fruit-flavored gelatin
good ½ pint (3 dl.) water	good 1¼ cups water
½ pint (3 dl.) thin cream or evaporated milk	1¼ cups coffee cream or evaporated milk

Cooking time few minutes to melt jelly
Serves 4—6

Dissolve the jelly in the very hot water, put on one side and allow it to cool and begin to stiffen slightly, then whisk in the liquid cream or evaporated milk and continue whisking until a very fluffy consistency. Put into a mould (mold) and allow to set, or spoon into individual glasses.

Variations

Jelly Banana Split Make up a raspberry jelly (gelatin) with 1 pint (6 dl. − 2½ cups) water, allow to stiffen then whisk sharply with 2 tablespoons (3 tablespoons) thick (whipping) cream to give a softer more creamy consistency. Arrange individual blocks of ice cream on 4—6 long dishes, top each portion with a whole or sliced banana. Coat with the whisked jelly. Chopped nuts or whipped cream and grated chocolate may be added for a luxury touch.

Jelly Ice Cream Sundae Make up a raspberry and a lemon jelly (gelatin) using 1 pint (6 dl. − 2½ cups) of water for each. Allow to stiffen, then whisk each jelly sharply. Arrange alternate layers of the two jellies and ice cream in tall glasses. Top with whipped cream and whisked jelly. *Serves up to 8.*

Jelly Snow Dissolve a fruit-flavoured jelly (gelatin) in ¾ pint (4½ dl. − scant 2 cups) very hot water, allow to cool and stiffen slightly, then fold in 2 stiffly beaten egg whites. Pile into glasses and top with fresh or cooked fruit and whipped cream.

Milk Jelly Dissolve a jelly (gelatin) in only ¼ pint (1½ dl. − ⅔ cup) very hot water. Cool, then add ¾ pint (4½ dl. − 2 cups) cold milk.

Jelly Cream

Imperial/Metric	American
1 fruit-flavoured jelly	1 package fruit-flavored gelatin
good ¾ pint (4½ dl.) water	good 2 cups water
¼ pint (1½ dl.) thick cream	⅔ cup whipping cream

Cooking time few minutes to melt jelly
Serves 4—6

Dissolve the jelly in the very hot water, put on one side and allow to cool and begin to stiffen slightly, then fold in the lightly whipped cream. Put into a mould (mold) and leave to set.

Variation

Honeycomb Mould (Illustrated) Dissolve the jelly (gelatin) in the same quantity of water as recipe above. Heat ¼ pint (1½ dl. − ⅔ cup) milk with the yolks of 2 eggs and 2 oz. (50 g. − ¼ cup) sugar in a double saucepan until thickened. Whisk into the liquid jelly, cool but do not allow to set. Whisk 2 egg whites until stiff, fold in 1 tablespoon sugar, stir into the jelly, pour into rinsed mould (mold) and set. If liked, make an extra jelly, whisk, spoon round mould.

A New Look to Milk Puddings

It is quite easy to make the simplest dishes look attractive, as the three recipes illustrated in the picture on this page show. All serve 4–5 people.

Orange Rice Brûlée Top a cooked rice pudding with rings of fresh orange, brown sugar and blanched almonds, and heat under the grill (broiler) for a few minutes.

Cherry Nut Mould Make a vanilla-flavoured blancmange in the usual way. When thickened and slightly cooled add chopped nuts and chopped glacé (candied) cherries. Spoon into a rinsed mould (mold), turn out and top with an apricot sauce made by adding chopped nuts and chopped cherries to apricot jam.

Ginger Creams Make a vanilla-flavoured blancmange; when cool blend in a little ginger syrup, chopped preserved ginger and whipped cream. Spoon into glasses and decorate with more cream and ginger.

Custard Brûlée

Imperial/Metric	American
¾ pint (4½ dl.) milk	just under 2 cups milk
¼ pint (1½ dl.) cream*	⅔ cup cream*
4 egg yolks	4 egg yolks
2 egg whites	2 egg whites
little vanilla flavouring	little vanilla flavoring
2 oz. (50 g.) castor sugar	¼ cup granulated sugar
approximately 1 oz. (25 g.) icing sugar	approximately ¼ cup confectioners' sugar
1 oz. (25 g.) blanched chopped almonds	¼ cup blanched chopped almonds

* thin (coffee) or thick (heavy or whipping) cream.

Cooking time 1½–2 hours
Serves 4–5
Advance Preparations Cook custard and cool.

Warm milk and cream, pour over the well beaten eggs, adding vanilla and sugar. Strain into a heat-proof dish and set very slowly in the oven, 250–275°F. (130–140°C.), Gas Mark ½–1 (see point 2 on page 131). When firm cover the custard top with sieved icing (confectioners') sugar and chopped almonds. Put under a hot grill (broiler) for 2–3 minutes, until top is brown. Serve hot or cold.

Freezing Do not freeze.

Variations
Omit almonds if nuts are found to be indigestible.
Orange Brûlée Add the finely grated rind of 2 oranges to the milk and cream. When the sweet is cooked top with sliced fresh oranges, then with icing (confectioners') sugar and almonds and put under grill (broiler).
Coffee Brûlée Add 2–3 teaspoons powdered instant coffee to the eggs in the custard brûlée.

Tea-time Specials

Home-made bread, cakes and biscuits (cookies) will save a great deal of money. If your family do not have a supper, or dinner, in the evening containing protein foods, then it is advisable to give them some of the savoury dishes (starting on page 104), so they have a well balanced diet.

Some Tea-time Menus

Sandwiches (see pages 95 and 214)	Cheese and Bacon Scones (page 98)
Honey and Cinnamon Rings (page 95)	Home-made Bread, Butter and Jam
Almond Biscuits (see below)	Orange Sponge (page 100)
Omelette (page 104) with Salad	Curried Egg Pie (page 206) with Tomatoes
Rolls and Butter	Scones (page 98), Butter and Honey
Banana Sponge Cake (page 100)	Selection of Biscuits (pages 102, 103)

Almond Biscuits

Imperial/Metric	American
4 oz. (100 g.) soft fine breadcrumbs	2 cups soft fine bread crumbs
3 oz. (75 g.) butter	generous ⅓ cup butter
4 oz. (100 g.) castor sugar	½ cup granulated sugar
¼ teaspoon almond essence	¼ teaspoon almond extract
3 oz. (75 g.) self-raising flour (or plain flour with	¾ cup self-rising flour (or all-purpose flour with
¾ teaspoon baking powder)	¾ teaspoon baking powder – double-acting)
½ teaspoon bicarbonate of soda	½ teaspoon baking soda
little warm water	little warm water
to decorate	**to decorate**
14–16 blanched almonds	14–16 blanched almonds

Cooking time 22–25 minutes
Makes 14–16
Advance Preparations Make when convenient, leave on trays until ready to cook.

Put the crumbs on a tray and crisp these in the centre of a moderate oven until a pale golden colour (this takes about 10 minutes), allow to cool. Cream the butter and sugar until soft and light, add the almond essence, flour and breadcrumbs. Blend the bicarbonate of soda with 1 tablespoon warm water and stir into the mixture. Knead firmly with your hands; if necessary add a little more warm water, but do *not* make too damp. Roll into 14–16 balls, put on to greased baking trays (sheets), allowing space to spread out, top with the almonds. Bake for 12–15 minutes in the centre of a moderate oven, 350°F. (180°C.), Gas Mark 4. Allow to cool for a few minutes on the baking trays, then lift on to a wire cooling tray (rack). Store in an airtight tin.

Home-made Bread

Do not imagine bread is difficult to make; it is simple, economical and most rewarding. If you cannot obtain fresh yeast (most Health Food Stores sell this), then use dried yeast.
Recent experiments have found a way of reducing the 'proving' (rising) time by the use of ascorbic acid (Vitamin C) tablets. Naturally any vitamin value is lost in cooking the bread, but you may find these tablets helpful if you are short of time. If you omit them then simply allow a little longer for preparation.
I have given a fairly small quantity in the recipe, but make more if you can freeze loaves, see page 93.
Use strong flour, specially milled for bread making, if possible; failing this use plain flour. If you buy fresh yeast keep this in your refrigerator for several days, or freeze. Yeast is in good condition when it crumbles easily and is not dry or hard; naturally, frozen yeast *will* be hard, but this is quite in order.

Bread

Imperial/Metric	American
1 oz. (25 g.) fresh yeast or ½ oz. (15 g.) dried yeast*	1 cake compressed yeast or 1 tablespoon active dry yeast*
barely ¾ pint (14 fl. oz. – 4½ dl.) warm water	barely 2 cups warm water
1–2 teaspoons sugar	1–2 teaspoons sugar
1 tablet (25 mg.) ascorbic acid (optional)	1 tablet (25 mg.) ascorbic acid (optional)
1–1½ level teaspoons salt	1–1½ level teaspoons salt
1½ lb. (¾ kilo) strong or plain flour	6 cups bread or all-purpose flour
1 oz. (25 g.) lard or other fat	2 tablespoons lard or shortening
to glaze (optional)	**to glaze** (optional)
1 egg, 1 level tablespoon sugar, 1 tablespoon water	1 egg, 1 level tablespoon sugar, 1 tablespoon water

*this is a generous amount of yeast for the quantity of flour, but it is specially for a recipe using ascorbic acid. You can reduce this to half if 'proving' twice in the usual manner, see recipe below. One does not increase amounts of yeast strictly in proportion to flour, for example with 3 lb. (1½ kilos – 12 cups) flour use the amounts of yeast above if allowing normal rising time; double them only if including ascorbic acid.

Advance Preparations Prepare dough, allow to rise.

First prepare the yeast liquid; there are several ways of doing this. Cream the yeast and add the water, or cream the yeast with half the sugar then add the water. If using dried yeast, blend half the sugar with the water, sprinkle the yeast on top, leave for 10 minutes, whisk or stir, then use as fresh yeast. If using the ascorbic acid tablet dissolve this in the warm yeast liquid. Mix the salt, remaining sugar and flour in a large warm bowl. Rub in the lard or other fat. Add the yeast liquid, blend with a wooden spoon or fork. Work to a firm dough, adding extra flour if necessary. The dough is the right consistency when the bowl is clean. Turn on to a floured board and knead. You can tell if kneaded sufficiently if you press with a lightly floured finger – when the dough is not kneaded enough your finger impression stays in – when it has been kneaded well the impression comes out. The correct way to knead bread dough is to fold it towards you, then to push down away from you with the heel (base of the palm) of your hand. If you use an electric mixer this can be done on a *low* speed. Do not over-knead the dough. Shape the kneaded dough into a ball, put it into the bowl and cover lightly with a cloth or polythene or put it into a large oiled polythene bag.

If Using Ascorbic Acid Leave for 5 minutes only, shape.
If Not Using Ascorbic Acid Leave until the ball of dough is nearly double its size, this would take about 1–1½ hours at room temperature, 'knock back' (i.e. knead again), then shape. This method is better if using dried yeast, even if using ascorbic acid.

Shape the dough; the amount of dough would give you the split tin loaf, the Catherine wheel loaf and about 5 rolls (see picture page 94).
Tin Loaf Use just over one-third of the dough and form this into an oblong, the same width as a 1-lb. (½-kilo) loaf tin (pan). Fold the dough in three, with the seam underneath. Smooth top, tuck in ends and put into a warmed greased 1-lb. (½-kilo) tin (pan).
Catherine Wheel Use about half the remaining dough, divide into two equal sized pieces. Roll each piece into a strand 18 inches (45 cm.) long. Twist the two strands loosely together, form into a circle, seal ends. Place in lightly greased warmed sandwich tin (layer pan). Brush with glaze, made by mixing ingredients together.
Rolls Divide the rest of the dough into small pieces and form into desired small shapes for rolls. Put on warmed greased baking tray (sheet). Some can have poppy seeds on top (as picture). Glaze if wished.
Cover all the dough lightly with oiled polythene and allow to 'prove' again. This will take 45–50 minutes for the loaves or 30–35 minutes for the rolls (they will be nearly double size).
Bake loaves in the centre of a hot oven, 450°F. (230°C.), Gas Mark 8, for 30–35 minutes. Rolls will take only 15–20 minutes. Remove from tins, cool.

Freezing Allow bread or rolls to cool, wrap and freeze. Either thaw out at room temperature or warm in the oven. Use within about 6 weeks. Fresh yeast should be divided into convenient sized pieces, wrapped and frozen. Thaw out before using or grate while hard. Keeps up to 1 year.

Tin loaf, catherine wheel loaf and rolls (see page 93)

Tea-time Sandwiches

These should be rather small and dainty for afternoon tea but would need to be more substantial for hungry children. There are many suggestions for fillings on page 214, but for tea you can offer:

Eggs Scramble or hard boil (hard cook), then chop and mix with finely chopped ham, tongue, smoked salmon (for a special occasion); moisten with mayonnaise and garnish with cress.

Cheese Mix cream cheese with chopped dates, nuts, well drained canned pineapple, grated raw apple, etc. Mix grated cheese with mayonnaise, then add chopped watercress, grated raw carrot.

Salad Ingredients A good choice for a light tea. Sliced cucumber, sliced tomato, etc.

Honey and Cinnamon Rings

Imperial/Metric	American
10 oz. (250 g.) self-raising flour (or plain flour with 2½ level teaspoons baking powder)	2½ cups self-rising flour (or all-purpose flour with 2½ level teaspoons baking powder – double-acting)
pinch salt	pinch salt
1 teaspoon ground cinnamon	1 teaspoon ground cinnamon
2 oz. (50 g.) margarine	¼ cup margarine
1 egg	1 egg
2 tablespoons honey	3 tablespoons honey
little milk	little milk
for frying	**for frying**
oil or lard or cooking fat*	oil or shortening*
to coat	**to coat**
2–3 oz. (50–75 g.) castor sugar	¼–⅓ cup granulated sugar

* have sufficient to half fill a pan, or to give a depth of 1 inch (2 cm.) if choosing shallow frying.

Cooking time 8–10 minutes
Makes about 12 rings
Advance Preparations Make rings. Keep in refrigerator for several hours or freeze, then cover, store for up to several weeks then cook from frozen state.

Sieve the flour or flour and baking powder with the salt and cinnamon. Rub in the margarine, add the egg, honey (warm this if a little stiff), then add enough milk to make a soft scone-like (biscuit-like) dough. Roll out to ½ inch (1 cm.) in thickness, cut into circles about 2½ inches (6 cm.) in diameter. Cut out the centre of the circles with a 1-inch (2-cm.) cutter. Knead the excess dough gently before rolling out and using. Put the rings on to a flat tin so they are easy to put into the fat. Heat the oil, or lard or fat, to 365°F. (185°C.): to test if the deep oil or fat is the correct temperature put in a cube of day-old bread. This should turn golden brown within 1 minute – no quicker. Lower a few rings into the pan, cook for several minutes, turn over carefully and cook until firm and golden brown. In shallow oil or fat you will need the longer cooking time. Lift out of the pan, drain on absorbent paper, then roll in sugar. The easiest way to coat these is to put the sugar in a paper bag, drop the rings in and shake.

Breads without Yeast

Many breads can be made without using yeast and the following may be taken as basic recipes that you can adjust yourself.

When making plain bread, such as Irish soda bread, below, do not make the mixture too dry, it should be even softer than a scone dough.

Irish Soda Bread

Imperial/Metric	American
1 lb. (½ kilo) plain flour	4 cups all-purpose flour
1 level teaspoon salt	1 level teaspoon salt
½ level teaspoon bicarbonate of soda	½ level teaspoon baking soda
1 level teaspoon cream of tartar	1 level teaspoon cream of tartar
milk to mix (see method)	milk to mix (see method)

Cooking time 30 minutes or about 15 minutes
Makes 1 good sized loaf or 2 smaller ones, which naturally would take a little less cooking time
Advance Preparations Weigh out ingredients but do not mix until ready to cook; or cook, cool, wrap and then freeze (see page 93).

Sieve the flour with the dry ingredients, then add enough milk to make a soft pliable dough, not too sticky. You will need just under ½ pint (3 dl. – 1¼ cups), but flours vary in the amount they absorb. Knead lightly on a floured board, then pat out until about 2 inches (5 cm.) in thickness, form into a round with floured hands. Mark into four sections (known as farls). Put on to an ungreased baking tray. Bake in the centre of a hot oven, 425–450°F. (220–230°C.), Gas Mark 7–8, for about 30 minutes; if necessary reduce the heat slightly after 20 minutes. If preferred cook the bread on a griddle. In this case make the round of dough only about ¾–1 inch (1½–2 cm.) thick. Pre-heat the griddle, to test if sufficiently hot a little flour should turn pale golden colour in 1 minute. Put the loaf on to this, cook steadily for about 7 minutes, turn and cook on the other side. It may be necessary to reduce the heat slightly towards the end of the cooking time. Wrap the oven-baked or griddle-cooked loaf in a cloth to cool, this keeps it pleasantly moist.

Variations

Using Buttermilk or Sour Milk Omit the cream of tartar in the recipe above. Increase bicarbonate of soda (baking soda) to ¾ *level* teaspoon.
Richer Bread Rub 1 oz. (25 g. – 2 tablespoons) lard or butter into the flour, etc.

Brown Bread This can be made from the recipe above, or the yeast recipe on page 93. Use equal quantities of white and wholemeal (wholewheat) flour. Wholemeal (wholewheat) bread is made by using all this type of flour. The more wholemeal flour used the more liquid is needed to mix the dough. The baking time therefore should be a little longer.
Fruit Soda Bread Increase bicarbonate of soda to 1 *level* teaspoon. Rub 2 oz. (50 g. – ¼ cup) margarine into the flour, etc. Add 2 oz. (50 g. – ¼ cup) sugar, then about 4 oz. (100 g. – ⅔ cup) dried fruit. As this is a richer bread allow about 15 minutes in the hot oven, see basic recipe, then lower the heat to moderate, 350°F. (180°C.), Gas Mark 4, and continue cooking for a further 20–25 minutes.

To Test when Bread is Cooked Bread is cooked when it has shrunk away from the sides of the tin and when it sounds quite hollow when tapped on the bottom of the loaf. If there is no hollow sound, then replace the bread in the oven. You may find it better not to return the loaf to the tin, but just to stand it on a flat baking tray (sheet) so the sides brown.

Using Yeast Dough

If you have made a fairly large quantity of the yeast dough on page 93 you can turn some into cakes for tea.

Doughnuts Take off small portions of the dough (after proving – rising), and either form into balls or roll out and cut into rings. Put on to a warmed greased baking tray (sheet) and leave to prove for about 15–20 minutes. Meanwhile heat the oil or fat as given in the recipe below. Put in the doughnuts, fry steadily for about 6–7 minutes until golden brown. Drain on absorbent paper then roll in sugar. If you require a jam doughnut this should be put into the dough before forming into the round. Make a small hole with a floured finger, put in the jam, then roll the yeast dough round this. Prove as above. Cream doughnuts are made by splitting the cooked and cooled doughnut and adding the cream.

Lardy Cake Take about 1 lb. (½ kilo) of the proven (risen) bread dough on page 93. Roll into a neat oblong about ½ inch (1 cm.) in thickness. Spread with 1 oz. (25 g. – 2 tablespoons) lard, sprinkle with the same amount of sugar and dried fruit. Fold in three (like a closed envelope) and repeat this twice, i.e. rolling, covering with lard etc. and folding. Put the dough into a greased and warmed cake tin (spring form pan) and allow to prove (rise) for 20–25 minutes. Bake for 15 minutes in the centre of a hot oven, then lower the heat to moderate for a further 20–25 minutes. Mix 1 tablespoon sugar with the same amount of water and brush over the cake when it comes from the oven.

Fruit Buns These can be made by kneading sugar and fruit into the dough. Prove and bake as rolls, page 93; see also hot cross buns, page 202.

Cinnamon Doughnuts

Imperial/Metric	American
⅓ large sandwich loaf	⅓ large sandwich loaf
¼ pint (1½ dl.) fresh or canned orange juice	⅔ cup fresh or canned orange juice
2 eggs	2 eggs
for frying	**for frying**
oil or fat	oil or shortening
to coat	**to coat**
4 oz. (100 g.) icing sugar	just under 1 cup confectioners' sugar
½ teaspoon powdered cinnamon	½ teaspoon ground cinnamon
for the apple sauce	**for the applesauce**
1½ lb. (¾ kilo) cooking apples	1½ lb. baking apples
4 tablespoons water	generous 5 tablespoons water
3 oz. (75 g.) sugar	generous ⅓ cup sugar
2 oz. (50 g.) raisins	⅓ cup raisins
1 teaspoon cinnamon	1 teaspoon cinnamon

Cooking time 15–20 minutes
Makes approximately 12
Advance Preparations Cut bread. Make sauce and reheat this when required.

First make the sauce. Simmer the peeled, cored and sliced apples in a pan with the water, until soft and pulpy, then add the sugar, raisins and cinnamon. Remove the crusts from the loaf then cut into 1¼-inch (3-cm.) cubes. Dip quickly in the orange juice and then in beaten eggs and deep fry in the hot oil or fat until golden brown. Remove from the oil or fat, drain on absorbent paper and toss in icing sugar and cinnamon while still hot. Serve with the hot apple sauce.

Variation
Use canned apple sauce, heat with the raisins and cinnamon.

Making Scones

A scone (biscuit) dough should be fairly soft. It must be sufficiently firm to roll out, but considerably softer than a pastry dough.

Most scones should be baked in a hot oven; too slow baking dries them.

Scones should be eaten when fresh, but they freeze well (see the bottom of this page), and you can freshen stale scones by heating for a short time in the oven.

Plain Scones (Biscuits) Use either self-raising flour with no raising agent, or, if you like a very well risen scone (muffin), you can sieve 1 level teaspoon bicarbonate of soda (baking soda) with each 8 oz. (200 g. – 2 cups) self-raising flour.
If using plain (all-purpose) flour sieve 3 level teaspoons baking powder (double-acting) into 8 oz. (200 g. – 2 cups) flour, or you may prefer to use ½ level teaspoon bicarbonate of soda (baking soda) and 1 level teaspoon cream of tartar to 8 oz. (200 g. – 2 cups) plain (all-purpose) flour. Do not exceed these amounts.

Basic Scones Prepare 8 oz. (200 g. – 2 cups) flour as above. Add a pinch salt, or a generous amount of seasoning, for a savoury scone. Rub 1 oz. (25 g. – 2 tablespoons) butter, margarine or other fat (shortening) into the flour, add 1–2 tablespoons sugar to the mixture, then blend with enough milk to give a soft rolling consistency. Roll out quickly and lightly on a floured board to about ¾ inch (1½ cm.) in thickness. Cut into rounds, triangles or other shapes. Put on to an ungreased baking tray (sheet). Bake for about 10 minutes towards the top of a very hot oven, 450–475°F., (230–240°C.), Gas Mark 8–9. Test to see if cooked by pressing the sides with your fingers. If no impression is left the scones are ready. Lift on to a wire cooling tray (rack). *Makes approximately 12 scones.*

Fruit Scones Add up to 3 oz. (75 g. – ½ cup) dried fruit to the flour, etc. Grease baking tray before using.

Cheese Scones Follow the directions for plain scones, but add a good pinch dry mustard to the flour with any other seasoning. Add up to 3 oz. (75 g. – ¾ cup) grated Cheddar cheese, and continue as plain scones. Grease baking tray before using.

Cheese and Bacon Scones *(Illustrated)* Fry 2–3 rashers (slices) bacon, then chop finely and cool. Continue as cheese scones above. As the bacon and cheese make the mixture fairly heavy it is advisable to add extra raising agent even to self-raising flour, see first paragraph under plain scones.

Oatmeal Scones Use half flour and half oatmeal or rolled oats in any of the above recipes. Grease baking tray before using.

Potato Scones Use half mashed potato and half flour in any of the recipes above. Grease baking tray before using.

Rusks Make any of the scone doughs above, but the plain dough is the nicest. Roll out to barely ½ inch (1 cm.) in thickness. Bake as for scones for about 6–7 minutes. Remove from the oven and split each scone through the centre. Put back on the baking tray, with the cut side downwards; continue cooking for about 20–25 minutes in a very moderate oven until crisp.

Freezing Scones freeze very well. When cold wrap or put into a polythene box. Use within 6 months. Thaw out at room temperature, or heat in the oven.

Victoria Sandwich

Imperial/Metric	American
4 oz. (100 g.) self-raising flour (or plain flour with 1 teaspoon baking powder)	1 cup self-rising flour (or all-purpose flour with 1 teaspoon baking powder – double-acting)
4 oz. (100 g.) butter or margarine	½ cup butter or margarine
4 oz. (100 g.) castor sugar	½ cup granulated sugar
2 large eggs (medium eggs for metric measures)	2 large eggs
few drops water (see method)	few drops water (see method)

Cooking time 18–20 minutes
Serves about 6
Advance Preparations Mix and leave up to 12 hours in the refrigerator or cook, cool, wrap and store in airtight tin for one or two days.

Sieve the flour, or flour and baking powder. Cream the butter or margarine and sugar until soft and light, this stage is very important. Gradually beat in the eggs, if the mixture shows signs of curdling fold in some of the flour. Add a few drops of water if necessary to make a soft dropping consistency. Divide the mixture between two greased and floured 6–7-inch (15–18-cm.) sandwich tins (layer cake pans). Bake just above the centre of a moderate oven, 350–375°F. (180–190°C.), Gas Mark 4–5 for 18–20 minutes. To test if cooked, press lightly but firmly with your finger; if no impression is left the cake is cooked. Turn out carefully and cool on a wire cooling tray (rack). Sandwich together with jam or jam and cream.

The delicious looking sponge in the picture below is based on the Victoria sandwich recipe, above, but made with butter and flavoured with orange. This cake is a Danish speciality, the details are on page 100. Biscuit recipes are on pages 102 and 103.

Variations on Victoria Sandwich

Follow directions given on page 99, but flavour as below.

Chocolate Sponge Omit 1 tablespoon flour and use this amount of sieved cocoa powder (unsweetened cocoa). Fill with butter icing made by flavouring mixture below with cocoa. Top with melted chocolate.

Orange Sponge *(Illustrated on page 99)* Add the finely grated rind of $\frac{1}{2}$–1 orange to the butter etc., in the sponge. Fill with butter icing made by creaming 2 oz. (50 g. – $\frac{1}{4}$ cup) butter and 3 oz. (75 g. – $\frac{3}{4}$ cup) sieved (sifted) icing (confectioners') sugar. Blend with $\frac{1}{2}$ tablespoon orange juice. Top the cake with glacé icing made by blending 4 oz. (100 g. – 1 cup) sieved (sifted) icing (confectioners') sugar with enough orange juice to give a flowing consistency. Spread over the cake. When nearly set top with a little more finely shredded orange rind.

Coffee Sponge Add 1 teaspoon instant coffee to the flour, use a few drops water to moisten the cake mixture. Fill and top with butter icing, see below (made with 4 oz. (100 g. – $\frac{1}{2}$ cup) butter) flavoured with strong coffee.

Banana Sponge Cake

Imperial/Metric	American
for the cake	**for the cake**
6 oz. (150 g.) margarine	$\frac{3}{4}$ cup margarine
6 oz. (150 g.) castor sugar	$\frac{3}{4}$ cup granulated sugar
3 small or 2 large eggs plus 1 egg yolk	3 small or 2 large eggs plus 1 egg yolk
2 bananas	2 bananas
6 oz. (150 g.) self-raising flour (or plain flour with $1\frac{1}{2}$ teaspoons baking powder)	$1\frac{1}{2}$ cups self-rising flour (or all-purpose flour with $1\frac{1}{2}$ teaspoons baking powder – double acting)
for the filling	**for the filling**
2–3 bananas	2–3 bananas
little lemon juice	little lemon juice
sugar to taste	sugar to taste
$\frac{1}{4}$ pint ($1\frac{1}{2}$ dl.) thick cream	$\frac{2}{3}$ cup whipping cream

Cooking time 23–25 minutes
Serves 8

Cream the margarine with the sugar. Add the eggs, or eggs and egg yolk, then stir in the mashed bananas. Finally blend in the sieved flour, or flour and baking powder. Divide between two 7-inch (18-cm.) greased and floured sandwich tins (layer cake pans). Bake for approximately 23–25 minutes just above the centre of a moderate oven, 350–375°F. (180–190°C.), Gas Mark 4–5. Turn out and allow to cool. Mash bananas with lemon juice and sugar, whip cream. Sandwich cakes with banana and cream. Serve as a dessert or for tea.

Sponge without Fat The amount of beating given to the eggs and sugar provides the aeration in this cake, so that plain (all-purpose) flour could be used without any raising agent. There is a very definite technique about mixing though, so you may care to use self-raising flour when first making this. Whisk 3 large eggs and 4 oz. (100 g. – $\frac{1}{2}$ cup) castor (granulated) sugar until thick and creamy. Sieve 3 oz. (75 g. – $\frac{3}{4}$ cup) flour twice, fold into the egg mixture with a metal spoon. Add a few drops of water to make a soft consistency (not necessary with metric measures). Divide between two well greased or lined and floured 7–8-inch (18–20-cm.) sandwich tins (layer cake pans), bake for about 12 minutes above the centre of a moderate to moderately hot oven, 375–400°F. (190–200°C.), Gas Mark 5–6. Turn out carefully. Sandwich with jam, fruit, whipped cream, etc. *Serves 6–8.*

Some Economy Cakes

These are easy cakes to make. When self-raising flour is not available use 2 teaspoons baking powder (double-acting) to each 8 oz. (200 g. − 2 cups) plain (all-purpose) flour.

Family Fruit Cake Rub 4 oz. (100 g. − ½ cup) margarine into 8 oz. (200 g. − 2 cups) self-raising flour. Add 4–6 oz. (100–150 g. − ½–¾ cup) sugar, 6 oz. (150 g. − 1 cup) dried fruit, 1 egg and enough milk, or cider, or cold strained tea, to make a sticky consistency. Put into a 7-inch (18-cm.) greased and floured cake tin (spring form pan). Bake for 1–1¼ hours in the centre of a moderate oven, 350°F. (180°C.), Gas Mark 4. Reduce the heat after 45 minutes if necessary. Eat fresh, or cool and freeze.

Potato Cakes Mash 8 oz. (200 g. − 1 cup) cooked potatoes, mix with 2 oz. (50 g. − ½ cup) self-raising flour, 1 oz. (25 g. − 2 tablespoons) melted margarine, 2 oz. (50 g. − ¼ cup) sugar, 3 oz. (75 g. − ½ cup) dried fruit and 1 egg. Pat out to ¾ inch (1½ cm.) in thickness, cut in squares. Cook on a greased and pre-heated griddle (see under Irish soda bread, page 96, for testing heat). Cook for 3–4 minutes, turn, cook for the same time on the second side. Serve hot or very fresh, topped with butter and sugar.

Vinegar Cake Ideal when short of eggs. Cream 4 oz. (100 g. − ½ cup) margarine with 4 oz. (100 g. − ½ cup) sugar. Blend 12 tablespoons (7½ fl. oz. − 2¼ dl. − 1 cup) milk with 1½ tablespoons vinegar and ¾ teaspoon bicarbonate of soda (baking soda). Add 8 oz. (200 g. − 2 cups) self-raising flour to the margarine, etc., then stir in the vinegar liquid and 6 oz. (150 g. − 1 cup) dried fruit. Put into a 7-inch (18-cm.) greased and floured cake tin (spring form pan). Bake as family fruit cake.
Freezing Cool and wrap cake. Store up to 6 months.

Rich Shortcake

Imperial/Metric	American
5 oz. (125 g.) margarine or butter	just under ⅔ cup margarine or butter
5 oz. (125 g.) castor sugar	⅔ cup granulated sugar
2 eggs	2 eggs
8 oz. (200 g.) self-raising flour (or plain flour with 2 level teaspoons baking powder)	2 cups self-rising flour (or all-purpose flour with 2 level teaspoons baking powder − double-acting)
very little milk	very little milk
for the filling	**for the filling**
see below	see below

Cooking time 20 minutes
Serves 4–6
Advance Preparations Prepare shortcake, but do not fill until ready to serve.

Cream the margarine or butter and sugar until soft and light. Gradually beat in the eggs then add the well sieved flour, or flour and baking powder, kneading the mixture well. Add just enough milk to make a soft rolling consistency. Divide into portions and press or roll to fit two well greased and floured 8-inch (20-cm.) tins. Bake above the centre of a moderately hot oven, 375–400°F. (190–200°C.), Gas Mark 5–6, for 20 minutes. Test to see if cooked, when firm to the touch and golden brown. Cool slightly in tins, turn out carefully. Fill when quite cold, see below. Store for 24 hours only − should be eaten when fresh.

Apricot Shortcake Sandwich together with drained canned or cooked apricots and whipped cream, and decorate with blanched almonds.
Peach Shortcake Sandwich together with sliced or halved fresh or drained canned peaches and whipped cream, and decorate with peaches and cream.
Pear Shortcake Sandwich together with sliced dessert or drained canned pears and whipped cream. You can flavour the cream with a little melted chocolate for an excellent combination of flavours.
Strawberry Shortcake Sandwich together with sliced or whole small sweetened strawberries and whipped cream. Top with whole fruit and cream.

Making Biscuits

Biscuits (cookies) are always a useful standby in an airtight tin. Never make a biscuit dough too moist, it should have a firm consistency. Store biscuits away from cakes, bread or pastry.
Here are some easy biscuits to make:

Afghans

Imperial/Metric	American
7 oz. (175 g.) butter	generous $\frac{3}{4}$ cup butter
2 oz. (50 g.) sugar	$\frac{1}{4}$ cup sugar
1 teaspoon vanilla essence	1 teaspoon vanilla extract
2–3 oz. (50–75 g.) chopped dates (optional)	$\frac{1}{3}$–$\frac{1}{2}$ cup chopped dates (optional)
6 oz. (150 g.) plain flour	1$\frac{1}{2}$ cups all-purpose flour
$\frac{3}{4}$ oz. (20 g.) cocoa	3 tablespoons cocoa
1 level teaspoon baking powder	1 level teaspoon baking powder
2 oz. (50 g.) cornflakes	2 cups cornflakes
for the icing	**for the icing**
4–5 oz. (100–125 g.) icing sugar	1–1$\frac{1}{4}$ cups confectioners' sugar
2 teaspoons cocoa	2 teaspoons cocoa
water to mix	water to mix
12–13 glacé cherries	12–13 candied cherries

Cooking time 20–25 minutes
Makes 25
Advance Preparations Make the biscuits, store in an airtight tin; but do not ice until ready to serve.

Cream the butter and sugar, add vanilla and dates. Sieve the flour, cocoa, baking powder, and crush the cornflakes lightly. Blend all these into the creamed butter. Knead, divide into 25 pieces, form into rounds. Place on greased baking trays, allowing room to spread out. Bake for approximately 20–25 minutes in the centre of a moderate oven, 350°F. (180°C.), Gas Mark 4. Cool slightly, then lift from the trays. When cold, top with the icing made by blending the sugar and cocoa with water to give a spreading consistency. Top each biscuit with a little icing and a halved cherry.

Variations

Reduce butter to 5 oz. (125 g. – just over $\frac{1}{2}$ cup), bind the mixture with a few drops water.
Omit the cornflakes and use rolled oats instead.

More Biscuits

Flapjacks Melt 2 oz. (50 g. – ¼ cup) margarine, 2 oz. (50 g. – ¼ cup) sugar and 2 tablespoons (3 tablespoons) golden (light corn) syrup in a pan. Stir in 6 oz. (150 g. – 1¾ cups) rolled oats or oatmeal (1 cup) and press into a very well greased 8-inch (20-cm.) sandwich tin (layer cake pan). Bake in the centre of a very moderate oven, 325°F. (170°C.), Gas Mark 3, for about 35 minutes until firm and golden. Mark in sections while warm, remove from the tin when half set. The mixture can be flavoured with a little chocolate powder, ground ginger, etc. *Makes 10–12.*

Brandy Rings (*Illustrated on page 99*) Put 4 oz. (100 g. – ½ cup) butter, 6 oz. (150 g. – 1½ cups) plain (all-purpose) flour, 1½ oz. (40 g. – ⅓ cup) sieved icing (sifted confectioners') sugar and 1 egg yolk into a bowl. Mix well, then add 1½ tablespoons (nearly 2 tablespoons) brandy. Chill for at least 30 minutes, then roll out to ¼ inch (½ cm.) in thickness; cut in rings. Brush with the egg white then sprinkle with finely chopped walnuts and sugar. Bake in centre of moderate to moderately hot oven, 375–400°F. (190–200°C.), Gas Mark 5–6, for about 10 minutes. *Makes about 30.*

Optimist Cakes (*Illustrated on page 99*) Cream 3 oz. (75 g. – generous ⅓ cup) butter with 1 oz. (25 g. – ¼ cup) sieved icing (sifted confectioners') sugar. Add 4 oz. (100 g. – 1 cup) plain (all-purpose) flour. Knead well, form into about 20 small balls. Top with blanched almonds. Bake as recipe above. *Makes 20.*

Danish Cookies (*Illustrated on page 99*) Put 5 oz. (125 g. – just under ⅔ cup) butter, 3 oz. (75 g. – ¾ cup) sieved icing (sifted confectioners') sugar, 1 egg and 6 oz. (150 g. – 1½ cups) plain (all-purpose) flour

into a bowl. Mix well, then add 2 oz. (50 g. – 2 squares) chopped plain (unsweetened) chocolate or chocolate polka dots and 2 oz. (50 g. – ½ cup) chopped mixed nuts. Put small spoonfuls on to a greased baking tray (sheet) – leave room for them to spread. Top with pieces of glacé (candied) cherry, bake as brandy rings. *Makes 40.*

Brandy Raisin Cookies (*Illustrated below*) Follow directions for brandy rings but add ½ teaspoon mixed spice and 2 oz. (50 g. – ⅓ cup) seedless raisins to the flour, etc. Chill then roll out, cut in circles, do not add egg white, etc. Bake as brandy rings.

No Cooking Required

The following can be produced without cooking, as can the chocolate cake on page 156.

Sherry Squares Crumble 5 oz. (125 g.) fruit or plain cake. Heat 1 tablespoon golden (light corn) syrup, 1 oz. (25 g. – 2 tablespoons) butter, 2 oz. (50 g. – ¼ cup) sugar and 1 tablespoon cocoa powder (unsweetened cocoa). Add 1 tablespoon sherry and the crumbs. Stir until a stiff mixture; press into a buttered tin. Leave for some hours until firm enough to cut into squares. *Makes 12–15.*

Coconut Pyramids Blend ¼ pint (1½ dl. – ⅔ cup) sweetened condensed milk with approximately 4½ oz. (115 g. – 1½ cups) desiccated (shredded) coconut. Form into pyramid shapes on rice paper or a greased tin and leave to set. These could be browned for 5–10 minutes in a moderate oven. *Makes 12–15.*

Supper Savouries

In this chapter you will find a good variety of savoury dishes, containing cheese, eggs, bacon, etc. They would be equally good for a light luncheon menu. If you have high tea rather than dinner or supper, serve these with salad to make a complete meal.

When planning a late supper avoid rather indigestible foods, i.e. those that are highly spiced (such as curried dishes). Some people also find cooked cheese dishes are not a good choice late at night.

Some Supper Menus

Scotch Eggs (hot) with Tomato Sauce (opposite)	*Rice and Beef Chowder (page 16)*
Sauté Potatoes and Cauliflower	*Home-made Rolls (page 93) and Butter*
Cheese and Biscuits	*Fresh Fruit Salad (page 148)*
Cheese Omelette (see below and opposite) and Salad	*Toasted Snacks (below) or Sandwiches (page 106)*
Orange Sponge (pages 99 and 100)	*Fresh Fruit and Cream Cheese*
Cold Ham and Pippin Salad (page 65)	*Oeufs Niçoise (page 10)*
Flapjacks (page 102)	*Date and Almond Tart (page 73)*
Bacon and Bananas (page 108)	*Frankfurters Aloha (page 108)*
Salad and Potato Pancakes (page 108)	*Mixed Salad (page 65)*
Jelly Whip (page 90)	*Uncooked Chocolate Cake (page 156)*

Quick Ideas for Toasted Snacks

There are a number of more imaginative ideas for toasted snacks on page 151, but the following are easy and quick:

Scrambled Eggs with grated cheese, or diced ham or chopped chicken, or flaked canned tuna added to the eggs before cooking.

Baked (Navy) Beans mixed with crisply fried bacon, or grated cheese, or topped with a fried egg.

Sliced Cheese spread over slices of cooked ham and heated for 2–3 minutes only under the grill (broiler). The toasted cheese can be topped with rings of fried or raw apple.

To Make Omelettes

An omelette is one of the quickest and easiest savoury or sweet dishes to make. Recipes for sweet omelettes are on page 167. The golden rule when making an omelette is to cook it as quickly as possible; too slow cooking gives a toughness to the eggs. Do not use too large or too small a pan, 6 eggs, etc., can be cooked in a 7-inch (18-cm.) pan.

Allow an average of 2 eggs for each person, break into a basin, add seasoning and 1 tablespoon water.

Do not over-beat the eggs. Heat a good sized knob of butter in the omelette or frying pan (skillet). When this is hot pour in the eggs and allow these to cook for approximately 30 seconds. Loosen the egg mixture from the sides of the pan; tilt the pan, so allowing the liquid egg to run to the sides. Continue like this for about 2 minutes, moving the pan over the heat so the omelette cooks evenly and quickly. Add the filling (see below and opposite), then fold or roll the omelette *away from the handle*. Tip on to a hot serving dish or plate.

Flavourings for Omelettes

Vegetables Cooked chopped mushrooms may be added to the eggs before cooking, or the fried mushrooms can be spread over the omelette before folding. For a more moist filling use the mushroom sauce recipe on page 61. Tomatoes can be fried by themselves, or with sliced onions, or with chopped bacon, or made into a thick tomato sauce, as the recipe below. Creamed spinach is another very good filling for an omelette.

Fish Heat shell or white (lean) fish in butter, or a white sauce, and put over the omelette before folding. Chopped anchovy fillets can be added to the eggs before cooking.

Meat Add finely diced cooked ham to the eggs before cooking, or fill the omelette with diced chicken or other cooked meat. This is nicer if heated in a thick white, cheese or other savoury sauce (see page 61).

Cheese Either add a little grated cheese to the eggs before cooking or sprinkle grated cheese over the omelette when it is almost set, or fill the omelette with a thick cheese sauce (see page 61), cream or cottage cheese.

Herbs Add chopped parsley, chopped chives or other fresh herbs to eggs before cooking.

Scotch Eggs

Imperial/Metric	American
4 eggs	4 eggs
to coat	to coat
1–2 tablespoons flour	1–2 tablespoons flour
seasoning	seasoning
12 oz. (generous 300 g.) sausagemeat	$\frac{3}{4}$ lb. sausagemeat
1 egg	1 egg
2–3 oz. (50–75 g.) crisp breadcrumbs	$\frac{1}{2}$–$\frac{3}{4}$ cup crisp bread crumbs (raspings)
for frying	for frying
oil or fat	oil or shortening

Cooking time 15–20 minutes
Serves 4
Advance Preparations Make the Scotch eggs and serve cold or prepare and fry when required.

Hard boil (hard cook) the eggs for just on 10 minutes, crack the shells and plunge into cold water.

This prevents a dark line forming round the yolk. Mix the flour with a little seasoning and dust the eggs with this, then coat in sausagemeat, a little more flour then beaten egg and crumbs. Press the coating firmly against the sausagemeat. Fry steadily in the hot oil or fat and drain on absorbent paper.

Sauté Potatoes Slice boiled potatoes. Fry in a little hot fat (shortening) until golden brown on both sides, drain on absorbent paper and sprinkle with chopped parsley.

Tomato Sauce 2 If you do not plan to sieve or emulsify the sauce, skin the tomatoes first — there are two ways of doing this, a) put into a bowl of very hot water for $\frac{1}{2}$–1 minute, lift out, cool slightly and pull away the skin, or b) insert a fine skewer into the tomato and hold over a gas burner for a few

seconds until the skin breaks, then pull this away. There is another tomato sauce on page 61. Simmer 1 finely chopped onion, small piece chopped apple, 1$\frac{1}{2}$ lb. ($\frac{3}{4}$ kilo) tomatoes, $\frac{1}{4}$ pint (1$\frac{1}{2}$ dl. – $\frac{2}{3}$ cup) water or stock, and seasoning, until tender. Sieve if wished. This sauce can be varied in many ways: toss vegetables in a knob of hot margarine; thicken with a little flour; add crushed garlic to the onion or fry finely diced bacon with the vegetables. Flavour with a little sugar as well as seasoning.

Boston Baked Beans

Imperial/Metric	American
12 oz.–1 lb. (300 g.–½ kilo) dried haricot beans	1½–2 cups navy beans
cold water	cold water
2 medium onions	2 medium onions
8–12 oz. (200–300 g.) fat, salt pork (such as belly), cut in 1-inch (2-cm.) cubes	½–¾ lb. fat, salt pork, cut in 1-inch cubes
2–4 tablespoons black treacle	3–5 tablespoons black molasses
2 level teaspoons dry mustard	2 level teaspoons dry mustard
1 level teaspoon salt	1 level teaspoon salt
good shake pepper	good shake pepper

Cooking time see method, plus overnight soaking
Serves 6–8
Advance Preparations Wash beans, cover with water and leave to soak overnight.

Drain beans, reserving ½ pint (3 dl. – 1¼ cups) water. Fill ovenproof dish, with a lid, or traditional bean pot with beans, thinly sliced onions and pork. Combine reserved water with remaining ingredients, pour into dish, cover tightly. Cook in the centre of a very slow oven, 275°F. (140°C.), Gas Mark 1, for 5–6 hours, or a slow oven, 300°F. (150°C.), Gas Mark 2, for 4 hours. Stir occasionally, add little more water if the beans seem to dry slightly while cooking.

Variation
Soak beans as above, drain, reserving only ¼ pint (1½ dl. – ⅔ cup) water. Put into dish with onions, 1 lb. (½ kilo) sliced tomatoes, pinch herbs, 1½ teaspoons sugar, 2 tablespoons (3 tablespoons) tomato ketchup (catsup), 1½ teaspoons salt, ½ teaspoon pepper. Cook as recipe. Soak gammon knuckle (smoked ham shank) overnight, simmer until tender, dice, add to the bean casserole.

Toasted Sandwiches
Toasted sandwiches are most delicious, they should be served freshly made while piping hot. Toast slices of white, brown or wholemeal (wholewheat) bread.

Meat
Club Sandwich Toast 3 slices of bread, butter lightly and sandwich with:
a) sliced chicken, lettuce and mayonnaise
b) crisply grilled bacon and sliced tomato.
A single instead of double decker sandwich could be made by putting both fillings between 2 slices of toast.
Bacon and Egg Sandwich grilled or fried bacon and fried egg between buttered toast. Top with halved tomatoes if wished, and heat under the grill for a few minutes.
Savoury Tomato Grill halved tomatoes, seasoning them well. Sandwich between buttered toast and top with fried or grilled bacon.
Curried Chicken Cover 1 slice buttered toast with chopped chicken, blended with a little butter and curry powder.
Hot Meat Simmer good thick slices of cooked meat for 2–3 minutes in a good sauce or gravy. Have the buttered toast ready and sandwich the meat between the toast. Top with sliced tomatoes and serve at once.

Cheese
Tomato Cheese Toast 2 slices bread, sandwich with raw or cooked sliced tomatoes and chutney. Top with sliced cheese, brown under grill if wished.

Cheese and Banana Cover 1 slice buttered toast with sliced cheese, heat for 2–3 minutes under the grill, top with sliced banana and a slice buttered toast.

Fish

Sardine Top 1 slice buttered toast with sardines mashed with a little chopped parsley and lemon juice. Cover with a second slice of buttered toast and top with sliced tomatoes.

Anchovy Cover 1 slice buttered toast with chopped hard-boiled egg and anchovy fillets. Top with a second slice buttered toast, little grated cheese and a lattice of anchovy fillets.

Spiced Tuna Blend flaked tuna fish with grated cheese and a little butter. Cover 1 slice buttered toast with this mixture, add sliced cucumber and a second slice buttered toast.

Fried Sandwiches

Fried sandwiches are a most delicious savoury. If you coat with beaten egg you have a thicker coating, but this is not essential, the sandwiches may be fried without coating; brown on one side, then turn over.

Cheese

Ham and Cheese Sandwich slices of bread and butter with sliced cooked ham and cheese. Dip in beaten egg and fry until crisp and brown.
The traditional Italian cheese sandwich called *Cheese in a Carriage*, and pictured on this page, is made by coating sandwiches of ham and cheese with flour, then beaten egg, then soft breadcrumbs and frying them in hot oil.

Cheese and Bacon As cheese and ham, but use crisply fried bacon instead.

Shrimp and Cheese Blend grated cheese with chopped shrimps or prawns. Use as a filling for sandwiches. Dip in beaten egg and fry.

Cheese Dreams Make cheese sandwiches adding a little chutney or mustard, if wished. Dip in beaten egg (diluted with a little milk if desired) then fry.

Meat

Corned Beef and Tomato Make sandwiches of sliced meat and tomatoes. Dip in beaten egg and fry.

Tongue and Cream Cheese Make sandwiches of tongue and cream cheese. Fry (do not coat), top with a little cream cheese and tomato just before serving.

Minced Beef Mix cooked minced beef with just enough butter to bind, add grated onion, chopped parsley and seasoning. Sandwich bread (no need to use butter) with this, then fry.

Fish

Prawns and Mushrooms Fry and drain mushrooms well, put on slices of bread and butter, top with prawns (shrimp) and a second slice of bread and butter. Dip in beaten egg and fry. Top with a few mushrooms and prawns before serving.

Fish Medley Cover bread and butter with flaked smoked salmon, chopped gherkins, a very few capers and a second slice of bread, butter and cream cheese. Do not coat with egg; fry until crisp.

Cottage Cheese and Prawns Make sandwiches, dip in beaten egg and fry. Serve with wedges of lemon.

To Keep Sandwiches Hot

The sandwiches on this page and page 106 are best served as soon as they are made. If you do need to keep them hot for a short time put fried sandwiches on absorbent paper on a heatproof dish; keep hot in the oven, with the heat at the lowest setting. I find it better to toast the bread and prepare the fillings and keep these warm in a cool oven, then to butter the bread and put the sandwiches together just before serving.

Bacon and Bananas

Imperial/Metric	American
6 rashers streaky bacon	6 bacon slices
6 small bananas	6 small bananas

Cooking time 15–20 minutes
Serves 6
Advance Preparations Prepare dish, make sure bananas are completely covered with the bacon, so they do not discolour.

Remove the rind from the rashers of bacon. Stretch the bacon by running a knife along the rashers — this makes them easier to handle. Roll round each skinned banana and put into an ovenproof dish. Bake for approximately 15–20 minutes just above the centre of a moderately hot oven, 375–400°F. (190–200°C.), Gas Mark 5–6. Serve at once.

Variation

Devilled Bananas and Bacon Sprinkle bananas with lemon juice blended with a little curry powder and Worcestershire sauce.

Frankfurters Aloha

Imperial/Metric	American
4–6 rings canned pineapple, plus syrup	4–6 rings canned pineapple, plus syrup
1–2 teaspoons made mustard	1–2 teaspoons made mustard
1 teaspoon cornflour	1 teaspoon cornstarch
8–12 frankfurters	8–12 frankfurters
to serve	**to serve**
mixed salad	mixed salad

Cooking time 10 minutes
Serves 4–6
Advance Preparations Make sauce, reheat to serve.

Drain off syrup from can of pineapple, if necessary add enough water, liquid from can of frankfurters, or stock to give 12 tablespoons (1 cup). Blend with the mustard and cornflour. Pour into frying pan, stir over very low heat until thickened slightly. Add the frankfurters and pineapple rings and heat for a few minutes. Serve with mixed salad.

Quick Potato Dishes

These potato dishes can be produced quickly to serve with supper savouries. Sauté potatoes are given on page 105, these are one of the best accompaniments to bacon, fish, sausages, etc.

Duchesse Potatoes Mash cooked potatoes, add a generous amount of butter or margarine, but *no milk*. Beat in 1 or 2 egg yolks to each 1 lb. ($\frac{1}{2}$ kilo – 2 cups) of the mashed potatoes. Pipe or pile the mixture on to a greased baking tray or ovenproof serving dish, making neat pyramid or rosette shapes. Crisp and brown for a short time in the oven. These freeze well, use within 3 months.

Potato Croquettes Mash the potatoes as above, but add milk and leave out the egg. Form into finger shapes; coat in seasoned flour, then beaten egg and crumbs. Fry *steadily* in hot oil or fat (shortening). Freeze when cold, use within 3 months.

Potato Pancakes Use half mashed potato and half flour in the pancake batter, recipe on page 66, and fry in the usual way, or try this method: grate 2 large old potatoes into a basin, add 1 oz. (25 g. – $\frac{1}{4}$ cup) flour, pinch salt or sugar (for sweet pancakes). Beat in 1 egg and 2 tablespoons (3 tablespoons) milk. Fry spoonfuls in hot fat until brown on either side. Do not freeze.

Pasta Dishes

Pasta dishes of all kinds make excellent supper dishes, for they are quickly cooked and blend with all kinds of protein foods. Whichever pasta you choose there are certain 'golden rules' to follow.

1   Allow sufficient water in which to boil the pasta. To each 4 oz. (100 g.) pasta use at least 2 pints (generous 1 litre – 5 cups) water. Always bring the water to the boil before adding the pasta and with long pasta, such as spaghetti, it is advisable to add this gradually, see below.

2   Lift the pasta once or twice during cooking to separate the pieces. Use two spoons for this.

3   Do not over-cook the pasta, otherwise it loses both texture and flavour. To test if cooked, press a piece of macaroni, or other shaped pasta, against the side of the pan with the back of a fork. If it breaks with *firm* pressure it is cooked.

4   Strain the pasta as soon as it is cooked. Some people like to rinse it in boiling water, I do not find this necessary unless I am making a dish beforehand (such as macaroni cheese).

Here are some easy pasta dishes:

Noodles with Butter and Cheese Cook egg noodles until tender; strain, tip back into the saucepan, mix with a generous amount of butter and grated cheese. Serve by itself or with grilled bacon, fish, etc.

Macaroni Cheese Cook 3 oz. (75 g.) macaroni until tender, strain, rinse in boiling water if desired (see above). Make a cheese sauce using $\frac{3}{4}$–1 pint ($4\frac{1}{2}$–6 dl. – 2–2$\frac{1}{2}$ cups) milk, etc.; the amount of sauce you make depends upon how stiff you like the dish. Stir the cooked macaroni into the cheese sauce. Put into an ovenproof dish, top with grated cheese, breadcrumbs and a small amount of margarine. Bake for 30 minutes in the centre of a moderate oven. If preferred, mix the very hot macaroni with the hot sauce, tip into a flameproof dish, add topping; crisp under the grill (broiler). This can be varied by adding chopped cooked bacon or ham, or sliced fried mushrooms, or flaked cooked fish to the macaroni, etc. It is very delicious if you put a layer of creamed spinach at the bottom of the dish, then add the macaroni in the cheese sauce and proceed as above. Macaroni fish pie is on page 27.

Pasta Scramble Cook a small quantity of macaroni or spaghetti, or other pasta. Strain and chop long pasta into small short pieces. Add to beaten eggs and scramble in the usual way. Top with cheese and fried tomatoes before serving.

Spaghetti Milanaise To cook spaghetti, bring the salted water to boiling point. Hold the strands of spaghetti in your hand and lower the bottom of these into the boiling liquid. Let the ends soften then turn the spaghetti so a little more dry pasta falls into the water, continue like this until all the pasta is immersed in the water. Cook until tender; this takes about 15 minutes, unless using the quick cooking variety. Strain and serve topped with tomato sauce (page 61 or 105) and grated cheese. The equally well known spaghetti bolognese and spaghetti marinara are on pages 37 and 13.

Gnocchi This Italian savoury is quickly made. Bring 1 pint (6 dl. – 2$\frac{1}{2}$ cups) milk to the boil, add $\frac{1}{2}$ teaspoon salt and 4 oz. (100 g. – $\frac{2}{3}$ cup) semolina. Stir well, and cook steadily until very thick. Add 1 egg and 1 oz. (25 g. – 2 tablespoons) butter, together with a little grated cheese. Tip out of the pan on to a flat dish and press out to about $\frac{1}{2}$ inch (1 cm.) in thickness. Allow to cool, then cut into small rounds. Put into a well buttered ovenproof dish, top with a layer of grated cheese and a little melted butter and heat in a hot oven for about 15 minutes. Serve with salad or with tomato sauce (see page 105). *Serves 4.*

Dealing with a Glut of Fruit, etc.

There are many times when there seems to be an abundance of fruit and vegetables in the garden or in the shops. Even if you need to buy this, the price is probably low and the quality good. This is the time to make preserves, to bottle (can) and to freeze, and recipes are on pages 112 to 123.
The recipes below give other ideas for using the fruit, etc.

Using Fruit

Delicious drinks can be made with practically all fruit when it is very plentiful and inexpensive.

Raspberryade Put about 8 oz. (200 g. – 1½ cups) raspberries into a strong large jug. Add a little sugar and pour over 1 pint (6 dl. – 2½ cups) boiling water. Crush the fruit, leave until cold. Strain and use undiluted, or topped with iced water or soda water. Other soft ripe fruits can be used in the same way.

Appleade Follow the directions as in the recipe above, but since a firm fruit like this has less juice you will need about 1 lb. (½ kilo) apples. Dice fruit and press very hard to extract juice.
Other firm fruits, such as plums, rhubarb, etc. can

be used in the same way.

Fruit in Salads, etc. Make use of a glut of fruit by adding this to salads: pears, plums, apples, etc., are delicious with green salads. Always coat fruit that discolours easily in mayonnaise or salad dressing, or toss in lemon juice. Berry fruits are particularly good in summer salads.
Garnish meat and fish dishes with cooked fruits, e.g. small baked apples, lightly cooked whole plums or damsons, or pears are excellent with roast pork or pork chops; fried apple rings give extra flavour to bacon or sausages, and cooked gooseberry purée is the traditional accompaniment to mackerel, but is equally good with other oily fish.

Using Vegetables

Cabbage When you have a glut of crisp cabbage, use the outer leaves as a hot vegetable, and the heart for a salad.
Coleslaw Shred washed cabbage finely, mix with grated raw carrot, diced dessert apple, dried fruit, chopped celery, etc., bind with mayonnaise or French dressing (recipes page 65).

Lettuce Can be cooked. Quarter the lettuce and brown lightly in a generous amount of margarine. Lift out of the pan, then make a brown sauce (recipe page 61). Put the lettuce into the sauce, cover the pan and simmer for 20–25 minutes. Braised lettuce is good with most meats.

Tomatoes Make excellent jams and jellies (see pages 113 and 114) and a home-made tomato ketchup (catsup) is very easy. The recipe is on page 120. Fresh tomatoes are a good source of Vitamin C, so serve raw tomato salad with hot or cold meats, etc.

The picture opposite shows tomatoes in chutney (recipes, pages 119 and 120). In addition tomatoes form the basis of a soup, which all the family will enjoy. As this is topped with cheese I have given the recipe on page 125, for it makes a good light meal for an invalid. Tomato Gouda pie is something children will enjoy making, as well as eating; the recipe is on page 156.

Stuffed Tomatoes These make a very easy supper dish or they could be served for breakfast. Cut the tops from large tomatoes, scoop out the pulp. Break an egg into each seasoned tomato case, top with the tomato 'lid' and a knob of butter. Bake for 10–12 minutes in a hot oven. Meanwhile, toast slices of bread, butter and top with sliced Gouda cheese. Heat for 2–3 minutes under a hot grill (broiler). Serve the tomatoes on top of the cheese toast. The tomato pulp could be used in the soup, page 125, or cook this and serve as a sauce with the savoury.

Tomato gouda pie (see page 156), tomato and cheese soup (see page 125), stuffed tomatoes (see page 110) and tomato and apple chutney (see page 120)

Preserving, Bottling and Freezing

Making Jam

Fruits vary in the amount of natural setting quality (pectin) they possess; this is why you need to adjust the quantity of sugar. The more pectin contained in the fruit, the more sugar (and water sometimes) you can use. When fruits are deficient in pectin it is advisable to use the smaller quantity of sugar (see strawberry jam, etc.). It is essential to remember the following when making jams:

1   Soften the fruit by cooking fairly slowly; if a fruit has hard skin, e.g. blackcurrants, you must make *quite certain these are softened before adding the sugar.*

2   Stir in the sugar and continue stirring until you are sure it is 100 per cent dissolved; you can check this by tapping the wooden spoon on the base of the pan. Add lemon juice if recommended in recipe.

3   When once the sugar has dissolved allow the jam *to boil rapidly* and *to reach setting point as quickly as possible. Do test for setting early* (see page 116); over-boiling sometimes destroys the setting power of the fruit.

4   Pour the jam into hot jars to within $\frac{1}{4}$ inch ($\frac{1}{2}$ cm.) of the top – the less air space, the less room for moulds to develop.

5   Put the waxed paper circle on the jam at once; the final covering can either be put on then, or when the jam is cold.

6   Always store jam in a cool, dry and well ventilated cupboard.

Steps to Making Jam

The table below and right gives most of the usual fruits and ways to use these in jam making.

Column one gives the kind of fruit and weight when prepared, i.e. peeled, etc. ready for cooking.

Column two gives any specific preparations needed.

Column three shows amount of water needed; where two amounts are given, e.g. damsons, use the lower quantities for *ripe* fruit, and the higher quantities for less ripe fruit.

Column four gives amounts of sugar; where two amounts are given use higher amount with less ripe fruit.

Column five shows flavouring and amount of lemon juice, etc. needed; this is important with fruits lacking in natural pectin, for the lemon juice or alternative adds this setting quality.

Proportions for Jam

1 lb. or $\frac{1}{2}$ kilo prepared fruit	To prepare	Water	Sugar	Additives
Apple	Peel, dice, sprinkle with sugar, leave several hours, cook slowly, stirring well.	None	1 lb. ($\frac{1}{2}$ kilo – 2 cups)	A little diced ginger can be added or 1 teaspoon ground ginger.
Apple and Blackberry (use 1 lb. ($\frac{1}{2}$ kilo) of each)	Peel and dice apples.	None	2 lb. (1 kilo – 4 cups)	None
Apricot – fresh	Halve, crack some stones, add kernels when jam nearly set.	2 tablespoons (3 tablespoons)	1 lb. ($\frac{1}{2}$ kilo – 2 cups)	Juice $\frac{1}{2}$ lemon
– dried	Soak for at least 4 hours.	3 pints (1$\frac{1}{4}$ litres – 8 cups)	3 lb. (1$\frac{1}{2}$ kilos – 6 cups)	Juice 2–3 lemons
Blackcurrant	Remove stalks.	$\frac{1}{2}$–$\frac{3}{4}$ pint (3–4$\frac{1}{2}$ dl. – 1$\frac{1}{4}$–2 cups)	1$\frac{1}{4}$ lb. ($\frac{1}{2}$ kilo plus 75 g. – 2$\frac{1}{2}$ cups)	None

1 lb. or ½ kilo prepared fruit	To prepare	Water	Sugar	Additives
Cherry – *dessert*	*Stone – if stones left in allow extra 2 oz. (50 g.).*	*2 tablespoons (3 tablespoons)*	*14 oz. (½ kilo* less *75 g. – 1¾ cups)*	*None*
– *Morello*	*As above*	*4 tablespoons (5 tablespoons)*	*1 lb. (½ kilo – 2 cups)*	*None*
Damson	*Stone while cooking or see fruit cheeses, page 114.*	*¼–½ pint (1½–3 dl. – 1¼ cups)*	*1–1¼ lb. (½ kilo– ½ kilo plus 75 g. – 2–2½ cups)*	*None*
Gooseberry	*'Top and tail' (i.e. clean – remove stalks, etc.).*	*As damson*	*As damson*	*None*
Greengage – *ripe*	*Halve if large. Remove stones, crack some, add kernels when jam nearly set.*	*2 tablespoons (3 tablespoons)*	*1 lb. (½ kilo – 2 cups)*	*None*
– *firm*	*As above*	*4 tablespoons (5 tablespoons)*	*As above*	*None*
Loganberry	*Crush slightly in pan.*	*None unless very firm, then 1–2 tablespoons*	*1 lb. (½ kilo – 2 cups)*	*None*
Marrow (Summer Squash)	*Peel and dice, sprinkle with the sugar and ginger, leave up to 12 hours then cook slowly, stirring well.*	*None*	*1 lb. (½ kilo – 2 cups)*	*Juice 1 lemon 1 teaspoon ground ginger*
Peach	*As apricot*	*As apricot*	*As apricot*	*As apricot*
Plum – *ripe*	*As greengage*	*As greengage*	*As greengage*	*As greengage*
– *firm*	*As greengage*	*As greengage*	*As greengage*	*As greengage*
Quince	*Peel and dice, simmer in water.*	*12 tablespoons (2 dl. – 1 cup)*	*1 lb. (½ kilo – 2 cups)*	*None*
Raspberry	*Simmer for 2–3 minutes only then add warmed sugar.*	*None*	*1 lb. (½ kilo – 2 cups)*	*None*
Redcurrant	*Better sieved – see cheeses, page 114.*	*¼ pint (1½ dl. – ⅔ cup)*	*1 lb. (½ kilo – 2 cups)*	*None*
Rhubarb	*Dice, then proceed as marrow (squash).*	*None*	*1 lb. (½ kilo – 2 cups)*	*Juice 1 lemon 1 teaspoon ground ginger*
Strawberry	*Simmer for 2–3 minutes only, then add warmed sugar or sprinkle sugar on fruit, leave 1 hour.*	*None*	*14 oz. (½ kilo* less *75 g. – 1¾ cups)*	*Juice 1 lemon or 4 tablespoons (5 tablespoons) undiluted redcurrant juice*
Tomato	*Slice.*	*None*	*1 lb. (½ kilo – 2 cups)*	*Juice 1 lemon*

Making Fruit Cheeses

Follow the proportions in the table on pages 112–3. but as the fruit is sieved there is no need to remove stones, etc. Cook the fruit, rub through a sieve then measure the pulp. To each 1 pint (6 dl. – 2½ cups) allow 1 lb. (½ kilo – 2 cups) sugar. Heat the pulp, stir in the sugar and proceed as for jam, see page 112.

Making Jellies

Read the points given for jam (page 112). In addition remember to allow the fruit juices to drop through the jelly bag or substitute, without pressing. If you squeeze or press, the juice will be cloudy.

Steps to Making Jellies

1   Wash the fruit, but there is no need to peel apples, etc., simply cut large fruit into convenient sized pieces. Always discard any bruised pieces or flaws in the skin.
2   Cover the fruit with the recommended amount of water in the table below.
3   Simmer gently until a pulp.
4   Put through a jelly bag – if you do not possess one, put through a double thickness of muslin placed over a fine nylon sieve – stand this over a large bowl.
5   Measure the juice and to each 1 pint (6 dl. – 2½ cups) allow 1 lb. (½ kilo – 2 cups) sugar.
6   Heat the juice, add the sugar, and lemon juice if recommended in recipe. Stir until dissolved, then boil rapidly until setting point is reached (see page 116).
7   Pour into warmed jars and seal as recommended for jam, page 112.

Proportions for Jelly

To 1 lb./½ kilo fruit (there is no need to peel or stone fruit)	Water	Additives
Apple	½ pint (3 dl. – 1¼ cups)	None
Blackberry (Bramble)	⅛ pint (¾ dl. – ⅓ cup)	1 medium cooking apple or juice 1 lemon
Blackcurrant	½ pint (3 dl. – 1¼ cups)	None
Cranberry	¼ pint (1½ dl. – ⅔ cup)	None
Damson (use fairly ripe fruit)	¼ pint (1½ dl. – ⅔ cup)	None
Gooseberry (use reasonably ripe fruit)	¼ pint (1½ dl. – ⅔ cup)	None
Loganberry	¼ pint (1½ dl. – ⅔ cup)	Juice ½ lemon if very ripe
Mint	Make apple or gooseberry jelly, add 1 tablespoon white vinegar and 1–2 tablespoons chopped mint to each 1 lb. (½ kilo – 2 cups) sugar used. Stir in when jelly has almost reached setting point.	
Plum – cooking	½ pint (3 dl. – 1¼ cups)	None
– dessert	¼ pint (1½ dl. – ⅔ cup)	Juice ½ lemon
Raspberry	¼ pint (1½ dl. – ⅔ cup)	None
Redcurrant	¼ pint (1½ dl. – ⅔ cup)	None
Strawberry	4 tablespoons (5 tablespoons)	Juice 1 lemon
Tomato	4 tablespoons (5 tablespoons)	Juice 1 lemon ¼ teaspoon ground ginger

Making Marmalade

Read the points given for jam (page 112). It is particularly important to soften the peel of the fruit before adding the sugar.

When marmalade has reached setting point *do not* put into the hot jars at once. Allow the preserve to stiffen slightly in the pan, stir to distribute the pieces of peel and then spoon into the pots.

Steps to Making Marmalade

There are two basic methods of making marmalade, and the table below gives recommendations as to the most suitable method for each fruit.

Method 1 Wash the fruit; halve, squeeze out the juice and put this into a separate container. Remove the peel and mince or chop this to the desired thickness. Tie any pith and the pips in muslin. Put the peel and the bag of pith and pips into a bowl. Add the amount of water recommended in the table and soak for 12 hours. Tip into a pan, with the bag of pith and pips. Simmer the peel in the water *until tender*, this will take about 1 hour. Remove bag of pith and pips and discard. Stir in the sugar and when dissolved add the fruit juice, plus lemon juice if recommended. Boil rapidly until setting point is reached (see page 112). Cool for a time, stir to distribute the peel, spoon into hot jars and seal.

Method 2 Wash the fruit. Put into the pan with the amount of water recommended. Simmer quickly until fruit is soft. Remove fruit from liquid, halve, take out pips. Put these into the liquid in the pan and simmer for 10 minutes. Strain liquid and return to pan. Slice fruit to desired thickness. Add to liquid, then add sugar, stir until dissolved. Continue as method 1.

Proportions for Marmalade

1 lb. or ½ kilo prepared fruit	Method to Use	Water	Sugar	Additives
Grapefruit	*1*	*2½ pints (1¼ litres – 6¼ cups)*	*2½ lb. (1¼ kilo – 5 cups)*	*Juice 1 lemon*
Lemon	*1*	*2 pints (generous litre – 5 cups)*	*2 lb. (1 kilo – 4 cups)*	*None*
Orange – *sweet*	*1 or 2*	*2 pints (generous litre – 5 cups)*	*2 lb. (1 kilo – 4 cups)*	*Juice 2 lemons*
— *Seville (sweeter type marmalade)*	*1 or 2*	*3 pints (1½ litres – 7½ cups)*	*3 lb. (1½ kilo – 6 cups)*	*Juice 2 lemons*
— *Seville (more bitter – coarse)*	*2*	*2 pints (generous litre – 5 cups)*	*2 lb. (1 kilo – 4 cups)*	*None*
Seville – *Treacle (Molasses)*	*1*	*3¼ pints (2 litres – 9 cups)*	*3 lb. (1½ kilo – 6 cups)*	*1½ tablespoons black treacle (molasses) Juice 1 lemon*
Tangerine or	*1 or 2*	*2 pints (generous litre – 5 cups)*	*2 lb. (1 kilo – 4 cups)*	*Juice 2 lemons*

Testing for Setting Point

There are various ways of testing to see if jams (or other preserves) have reached setting point:

1　*Test by Temperature*　Buy a special sugar thermometer. Stir this round very gently in the boiling jam to ascertain the overall temperature. Jam is ready when it reaches 220°F. (104°C.) but no higher.

2　*Test by Weight*　When jam is completed it should consist of 60 per cent sugar. Weigh the empty preserving pan, then weigh again when the jam has boiled for a short time. For each 1 lb. (½ kilo – 2 cups) used you should have 1⅔ lb. (approximately ¾ kilo) completed jam. Only possible with metal scales.

3　*By Skin*　Put a little jam on a saucer. Cool, push with your finger, if a skin forms the jam has reached setting point.

4　*By Flake*　Turn the wooden spoon in the hot jam until well coated. Cool slightly then hold over the pan. If the jam is hanging in a distinct 'flake' the jam is ready.

Orange or Lemon Curd　The best way to remove rind from the fruit is to choose loaf (cube) sugar and rub this over the oranges or lemons until all the yellow 'zest' is removed. Failing this use a fine grater to remove the top of the rind (called the 'zest'). Remove the 'zest' from 3 large oranges or lemons, squeeze the juice from 2 oranges or lemons. Put the rind, and juice, with 8 oz. (200 g. – 1 cup) sugar and 4 oz. (100 g. – ½ cup) butter or margarine into the top of a double saucepan or a basin. Place over a pan of *hot* but not boiling water, cook steadily until the butter or margarine has melted. Add 2 beaten eggs, then continue cooking, stirring all the time, for approximately 25 minutes or until the mixture coats the back of a wooden spoon. Pour into hot jars and seal down as for jam (see page 112). Use as a filling in cakes, tarts, etc.
Makes about 1 lb. (½ kilo).

Mincemeat

Imperial/Metric	American
4 oz. (100 g.) cooking apples (weight when peeled)	4 oz. baking apples (weight when pared)
1 lb. (½ kilo) mixed dried fruit	3 cups mixed dried fruit
4 oz. (100 g.) candied peel	¾ cup candied peel
4 oz. (100 g.) blanched almonds	just under 1 cup blanched almonds
4 oz. (100 g.) brown sugar	½ cup brown sugar
4 oz. (100 g.) shredded suet	just under 1 cup chopped suet
2 oz. (50 g.) glacé cherries (optional)	¼ cup candied cherries (optional)
1 large lemon	1 large lemon
1 teaspoon mixed spice	1 teaspoon mixed spices
1 teaspoon grated nutmeg	1 teaspoon grated nutmeg
4 tablespoons brandy, whisky, sherry or rum	5 tablespoons brandy, whisky, sherry or rum

No cooking, until put in mincepies (see page 182)
Makes 2½ lb. (1¼ kilos)

Grate apple coarsely. Mix with the fruit. It is essential that the fruit used in mincemeat should be well dried if it has been washed. Put on to flat trays, dry at room temperature for 48 hours. Add the chopped peel, chopped almonds then the sugar, suet, chopped cherries and the finely grated lemon rind and juice. Mix well with the spices and the alcohol. Put into clean dry jars, seal down as for jam (see page 112). Store in a cool, dry place.

Variations

Omit alcohol, mix with orange juice – does not keep so well.

Use melted butter or margarine in place of suet.

Making Pickles

Always use good quality malt vinegar. Inferior vinegar could prevent the pickles keeping well. Never put a metal cover directly on top of the pickles; if you do, the vinegar could cause this to rust. Put a thick round of cardboard between the top of the pickles and the metal top.

Steps to Making Pickles

First prepare the vegetables as though for cooking. Onions and shallots should be peeled with a silver or stainless knife, to avoid discoloration. The vegetables are then put into a dry or wet brine. *Always use kitchen (cooking) salt*, not refined table salt.

Dry Brine Use this for cucumber or cabbage (this gives a crisper texture than wet brine). Put the vegetables into a container with a very good sprinkling of dry salt. Leave for 24 hours, shake away surplus salt, or rinse under cold water (for milder taste) then dry.

Wet Brine Dissolve 2 oz. (50 g. – 3 tablespoons) salt in each 1 pint (6 dl. – 2½ cups) cold water. Leave vegetables for 24 hours, then drain and dry. All vegetables can be put into this kind of brine, even cucumber and cabbage (although this gives a softer texture). Onions should be left in the brine for 36–48 hours.

The next stage is to put the vegetables into jars and cover with hot or cold spiced vinegar (see below). Seal down, see above. If you leave ½ inch (1 cm.) space above vinegar you help to avoid any corrosion of the lid.

Spiced Vinegar Use white or brown malt vinegar. Allow 1 level tablespoon mixed pickling spice to each 1 pint (6 dl. – 2½ cups) vinegar, or less if you like a mild flavour. The vinegar can be simmered with the spice for up to 15 minutes, then strained, (this gives a strong flavour) or the vinegar and pickling spice can be brought to boiling point, left for up to 2 hours, then strained.

Vegetables and Fruits to Pickle

Beetroot Cook raw beetroot (beets) then slice or dice. Put into boiling salted water (1 tablespoon salt to each 1 pint (6 dl. – 2½ cups)), simmer gently for 10 minutes, drain, pack into jars, cover with hot spiced vinegar.

Cabbage, red Shred. Use cold spiced vinegar.

Cauliflower Break into sprigs. Use cold spiced vinegar.

Celery Cut into neat pieces. Use cold spiced vinegar.

Cucumber Use whole, or sliced, and cold spiced vinegar.

Gherkins As cucumber.

Mixed Pickles Use a mixture of ingredients. The picture on page 119 shows a pickle made with celery, cauliflower, onions and cabbage. White spiced vinegar enables you to appreciate the various colours better than brown vinegar.

Mushrooms Wash and simmer in lightly salted water for 5 minutes only. Drain, pack into jars and cover with boiling spiced vinegar.

Onions Peel and leave whole. Cover with cold spiced vinegar.

Shallots As onions.

Walnuts Use before outer shells harden (i.e. when green). Leave in wet brine for 3 days. Remove from brine, do not rinse. Put on trays and leave in the sun for 2–3 days or until they turn black. Turn once or twice a day. Pack in jars, cover with cold spiced vinegar.

Pickled Fruits Always use white vinegar and slightly less pickling spice than recommended for vegetables. Simmer 1 lb. (½ kilo – 2 cups) sugar in each ½ pint (3 dl. – 1¼ cups) spiced vinegar until dissolved. Prepare fruit as though for cooking – choose apples (crab apples can be left whole), apricots, damsons, plums, pears, peaches, etc. Put fruit into the sweet vinegar and simmer until *just* tender. Lift out carefully, pack into jars. Boil sweet vinegar for a few minutes to thicken. Pour over fruit and seal down at once.

Sweet Pickles Dissolve up to 1 tablespoon sugar in each 1 pint (6 dl. – 2½ cups) spiced vinegar and proceed as usual.

Mustard Pickles

Choice of Vegetables

Beans, cauliflower, celery, cucumber, marrow, onions, tomatoes, etc.

Prepare the spiced vinegar as page 117.
Remove the vegetables from the wet brine and rinse very well in cold water.

To each 2 lb. (1 kilo) prepared vegetables allow the following proportions:

1 pint (6 dl. — 2½ cups) spiced vinegar
1 tablespoon dry mustard
1 tablespoon turmeric powder
2 oz. (50 g. — ¼ cup) sugar
1 tablespoon flour or ½ tablespoon cornflour (cornstarch)
2 teaspoons ground ginger

Blend a little vinegar with the dry ingredients listed.
Bring the rest of the vinegar to the boil and pour over the blended mixture.
Return to the pan and cook until thickened; stir well.
Add the prepared vegetables (see above).
Cook steadily for 5 minutes only; do not allow the vegetables to break.
Spoon into hot jars and seal down.

Variations

Piccalilli As above, but chop vegetables finely.
Curried Pickle As above, but add 1 tablespoon curry powder.

118

Apricot chutney and tomato barbecue sauce (see page 120)

Chutneys, pickles and bottled vegetables (see pages 117–120 and 122–3)

Making Chutney

See the points given under pickles (page 117). Always use the full quantities of vinegar and sugar in the recipe, for these are the ingredients that cause the chutney to keep.

Flavouring Chutney

Chutney is often flavoured with pickling spice, see under pickles on page 117. This can be tied in a piece of muslin. Other flavourings are curry powder, ginger, mixed or allspice, onions and celery. Recipes for the chutneys shown in the picture above are on this page and page 120.

Celery and Fruit Chutney Use one well washed head celery and chop neatly. Peel and dice 8 oz. ($\frac{1}{4}$ kilo) onions, 1 lb. ($\frac{1}{2}$ kilo) apples and 2 lb. (1 kilo) tomatoes – there is no need to skin the tomatoes. Put the vegetables and fruit into the pan with 1 pint (6 dl. – $2\frac{1}{2}$ cups) brown or white malt vinegar and $\frac{1}{2}$–1 tablespoon (depending upon personal taste) of mixed pickling spice tied securely in muslin. Add $\frac{1}{2}$ tablespoon salt and simmer gently, stirring once or twice, until the mixture becomes a smooth purée (this takes about 40 minutes). Stir in 1 lb. ($\frac{1}{2}$ kilo – 2 cups) brown sugar together with 8 oz. (200 g. – $1\frac{1}{3}$ cups) sultanas (seedless white raisins) and continue stirring until the sugar is thoroughly

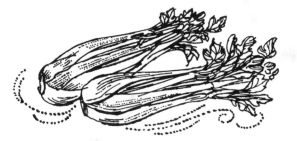

dissolved, taste and add more salt if desired. Boil steadily until the consistency of jam, remove bag of pickling spice, then put chutney into hot jars and seal down. See comments under pickles (page 117) about sealing jars. *Makes approximately 6 lb. (3 kilos).*

119

Sweet Celery Chutney Chop 1 large head of well washed celery. Peel 2 lb. (1 kilo) carrots and grate coarsely or chop finely. Peel and chop 1 lb. (½ kilo) onions. Put the vegetables into the pan with 1 pint (6 dl. – 2½ cups) white or brown malt vinegar, 1 level tablespoon salt, ¼ teaspoon ground allspice, ¼ teaspoon grated nutmeg, ½–1 teaspoon dry mustard. Simmer until the vegetables are tender (this takes about 45 minutes). Stir in ½–1 lb. (¼–½ kilo – 1–2 cups) sugar (depending upon personal taste). Continue as recipe for celery and fruit chutney. *Makes approximately 6 lb. (3 kilos).*

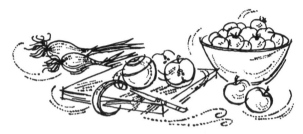

Tomato and Apple Chutney This chutney (shown in the picture on page 111) is made with ripe tomatoes, but green tomatoes may be used instead. This recipe is a good basic one that can be adapted for many other fruits, etc. The curry powder can be omitted and the same amount of mixed pickling spice used (tie this in muslin and remove before putting the chutney into jars).

Chop 2 lb. (1 kilo) tomatoes. Peel and chop 3 medium onions and 2 lb. (1 kilo) apples. Peel and crush 1 or 2 cloves garlic. Put into the pan with 1½ pints (9 dl. – 3¾ cups) brown or white malt vinegar and 1 tablespoon curry powder, ½–1 teaspoon cayenne pepper, ½ teaspoon salt. Simmer steadily, stirring now and again, until the fruit, etc., is softened, then stir in 8 oz. (200 g. – 1⅓ cups) sultanas (seedless white raisins) and 12 oz. (300 g. – 1½ cups) sugar. Stir until the sugar has dissolved then boil steadily until the consistency of jam. Put into hot jars and seal down. See comments under pickles (page 117) about sealing jars. *Makes approximately 7 lb. (3½ kilos).*
Apple Chutney Use 4 lb. (2 kilos) apples and omit the tomatoes. Alternatively, use half apples and half other fruit (plums, damsons, rhubarb, marrow, etc.).

Apricot Chutney Soak 8 oz. (200 g. – 1½ cups) dried apricots in 1½ pints (9 dl. – 3¾ cups) white malt vinegar for 12 hours. Peel and chop 2 lb. (1 kilo) apples, 3 onions, 1–2 cloves garlic, add apricots and vinegar and 2 teaspoons dry mustard. Simmer until the fruit is soft (this takes about 1½ hours), stir from time to time. Add juice of 1 lemon and 1 lb. (½ kilo – 2 cups) sugar. Continue as recipe above. *Makes about 5 lb. (2½ kilos). Illustrated on page 118.*

Tomato Ketchup It is very easy to make a home-made ketchup (catsup). Use bottles with screw-tops or proper bottling jars (see picture page 118). Make sure metal bottle tops are lined with cardboard to prevent the vinegar in the ketchup rusting the cover. It is advisable to choose well ripened, but not over-ripe tomatoes for this.

The bottles or jars should be sterilised by putting them into a pan of cold water, then bringing the water to the boil steadily. Leave the bottles or jars in the water until nearly ready to fill, then remove and allow to dry.

Boil ¾ pint (4½ dl. – just under 2 cups) white or brown malt vinegar and 1–2 teaspoons mixed pickling spice, for 5–10 minutes, then strain at once. Halve or quarter 4 lb. (2 kilos) ripe tomatoes, peel and chop 1 large onion and chop 2 large unpeeled cooking (baking) apples. Put the tomatoes, onion and apples into a pan with a very little of the spiced vinegar and cook until a smooth pulp. Stir from time to time to prevent the thick pulp from burning. Rub very thoroughly through a sieve; take care no pulp is left behind, otherwise the sauce will not thicken. Put the purée into the pan with the remainder of the vinegar, 6 oz. (150 g. – ¾ cup) sugar, ½–1 teaspoon salt and ¼ teaspoon paprika or cayenne pepper (be careful, the latter is hot). Stir until the sugar has dissolved, then boil steadily until thickened. Put a funnel into each bottle and pour in the sauce, then seal down at once. *Makes about 3 pints (1¾ litres – 7½ cups).*
Tomato Barbecue Sauce This sauce (shown in the picture on page 118) is made as the ketchup above, but the flavour is hotter and sweeter.

Proceed as above, but add 1–2 tablespoons dry mustard (depending upon personal taste) to the tomatoes, etc., and increase the amount of sugar to about 10 oz. (250 g. – 1¼ cups). The tomato purée need not be sieved for this particular sauce. Store in bottles or bottling jars.

More flavour can be given by adding a little Worcestershire sauce and increasing the pepper to ½ teaspoon.

Home Freezing

A freezer is one of the most convenient appliances in the home, for it can save money (by bulk buying and avoiding waste); it can save time by enabling you to cook or shop when convenient and pack the food away until required. You will find tips on freezing under many recipes where the result will be satisfactory.

Stress is always laid on correct wrapping before freezing; this is so the food will not dry out and lose its moist texture. Unwrapped food can be spoiled by the excessive cold in the cabinet. Specialist books give details on the types of wrapping available, but thick polythene (plastic wrap), polythene boxes and flameproof ware are all ideal.

Freezing Vegetables

Many vegetables freeze well, but in order to retain the best colour, texture and flavour and to destroy any harmful bacteria it is important to 'blanch' them; this just means boiling for a short time, then cooling them quickly.

First prepare the vegetables, as though you were going to cook them, see page 123 for more details. Put into a wire basket or in muslin, so they can be lowered into the boiling water. 'Blanch' for the times given in the table, then plunge into cold water, to which you have added some ice so the vegetables cool down quickly, drain, then pack. Freeze as the manufacturers' instructions and use within 1 year. Choose young good quality vegetables. Remember to have sufficient boiling water – you need 7–8 pints (4–4½ litres – about 5 quarts) water to each 1 lb. (½ kilo) prepared vegetables. The following is a rough guide only, full details will be found in the instruction book for your freezer.

Asparagus	for 2–3 minutes
Beans, Broad (Lima)	for 3 minutes
Beans, French or Runner (Green, Snap or Wax)	for 2 minutes (slice or chop, leave whole if small)
Broccoli or Cauliflower	divide into sprigs, allow 3 minutes
Brussels Sprouts	for 2 minutes
Carrots	for 2 minutes if diced or 5 minutes if small
Corn on the Cob (Sweetcorn)	for 4–6 minutes
Peas	for 1 minute
Spinach	for 2 minutes, 'blanch' only 8 oz. (¼ kilo) at once

Freezing Fruit

Many fruits freeze extremely well. I have given a synopsis of some ways in which fruits may be frozen. Use within 1 year, and as there is a high percentage of water in fruit never pack the containers to the very top; allow about ¾ inch (2 cm.) for expansion when the fruit is frozen.

Fruit Purées Every fruit can be used in this way and tomatoes are also excellent as a purée. Cook the fruit, or mash or emulsify in the liquidiser (blender). Use the minimum amount of water. Add sugar if wished. Either thaw out or heat from frozen state.

Raw Fruit The most successful fruits for this method are the berry fruits (except strawberries, which lose much of their flavour). Pack the clean fruit into containers; add sugar if desired. Thaw out at room temperature and serve as soon as thawed.

Poached Fruit Apples, apricots, plums, etc. are excellent in this method. Make a syrup of sugar and water as though you were cooking the fruit normally, then poach the prepared fruit until nearly soft – do not over-cook. Cool, then pack. Either thaw out or heat from the frozen state.

Bottling Fruit

It is very easy to bottle (can) fruit at home and this page gives two basic methods of doing this. Instructions for bottling vegetables are on page 123, opposite.

To Prepare Fruit for Bottling Wash and dry firm fruit – wash and drain soft fruit.

Apples and Pears Peel, core – put in cold brine – 1 *level* tablespoon kitchen salt to 2 pints (generous litre – 5 cups) water, to keep white: cook hard pears.

Peaches Put in boiling water for ½ minute, then cold water until needed – skin.

Tomatoes Skin if wished – flavour with ½ teaspoon salt, ½ teaspoon sugar to each lb. (½ kilo).

Oven Method

1 Pack fruit tightly into jars; cover with lids or thick paper.

2 Put the jars in a cool oven, 225–250°F. (110–130°C.), Gas Mark 0–½. Stand the jars on several thicknesses of paper or card to prevent the metal shelves in the oven over-cooking the bottom fruit. Sterilise for times below:

Raspberries, Loganberries 45 minutes
Rhubarb, Black or Redcurrants 50 minutes
Plums, Apples, Blackberries, Damsons, Greengages, Cherries 1 hour

Halved Peaches and Apricots, Pears, Tomatoes 1½ hours
Whole Fruit 1¼ hours
Fruit Salad Give time required by fruit needing maximum sterilising.

3 Prepare syrup. Heat 4–12 oz. (100–300 g. – ½–1½ cups) sugar to each 1 pint (6 dl. – 2½ cups) water. Lift jars from oven on to a *wooden surface*, pour over boiling syrup (boiling water only could be used) until jars *just* overflow. Put on sterilised rings and tops. Test after 24 hours, see point 8 below.

Steriliser Method

1 Prepare the fruit – see above. Pack into jars.

2 Prepare the syrup – see oven method, point 3. Allow this to *cool*, then fill jars with this – use just cold water for tomatoes and flavour as given for oven method, or bottle without liquid, see below.

3 Cover with rubber rings and tops – if screw bands, tighten, then unscrew for half a turn to allow for expansion of the glass during heating. If using a proper steriliser put in trivet; if using large pan put folded cloth or several thicknesses of paper at bottom.

4 Stand jars in the steriliser of cold water, have this as high as possible, so it comes to the neck of the jars.

5 Take 1½ hours to bring the water in the steriliser to simmering, i.e. 165–175°F. (74–79°C.) for all fruits *except pears, peaches and tomatoes*, when the water should be brought to 180–190°F. (82–88°C.).

6 Maintain the temperature for 10 minutes, except for pears, peaches and tomatoes, when it should be maintained for 30 minutes. Before lifting out the jars, bale out a little water so that it is easier and safer to lift them out.

7 Lift jars on to wooden surface, tighten screw bands.

8 Test after 24 hours. To do this, remove clips or screw bands, and the lids should be tight. If they are not, the fruit will not keep.

To Bottle without Liquid Soft fruits are better in flavour if no syrup is used: put layers of sugar between the dry fruit, or seasoning with whole or halved tomatoes. Fill jars tightly, seal as above and sterilise – the fruit shrinks down, but the flavour is excellent, even if the appearance is not ideal.

Bottling Vegetables
It is essential to bottle (can) vegetables in a pressure cooker; severe poisoning could be caused by eating bottled vegetables that have not been pressure-cooked.

To Prepare Vegetables for Bottling Prepare as if they were to be cooked; blanch as times on page 121 under freezing. Some vegetables that are not good when frozen bottle well, e.g. celery, potatoes and Jerusalem artichokes. Blanch these for 5 minutes. The picture on page 119 shows bottled celery and peppers. The pepper flesh needs 5 minutes blanching.

1   Wash vegetables well to remove all traces of soil. Prepare as though you were going to cook them.
2   Blanch – this means partially cooking – by immersing in boiling water for time given in table, on page 121, and below.
3   Cool by putting into cold water – this prevents over-cooking.
4   Pack loosely into clean bottling jars to within 1 inch (2 cm.) of the top.
5   Cover vegetables with a hot brine solution made by boiling 2–3 oz. (50–75 g. – 3 tablespoons) kitchen salt to 8 pints (4½ litres – 5 quarts) water. Tap jars to remove air bubbles.
6   Put on rubber bands and lid. Clips can be put on at once; tighten screw bands, give ½ inch (1 cm.) turn back to allow for expansion.
7   Pour 1 pint (6 dl. – 2½ cups) water into the pressure cooker: add 1 tablespoon vinegar or lemon juice, if wished, to prevent aluminium darkening.
8   Stand the jars on the rack of the cooker – make sure they do not touch each other or sides of the cooker – use paper to prevent this.
9   Fix the lid on the pressure cooker – but do not put on the pressure weight. Heat slowly and allow steam to come from the vent for 5 minutes – *this timing is most important.*

10   Put on the 10-lb. (5-kilo) weight – lower pressure does not ensure killing bacteria; higher pressure tends to over-cook the vegetables.
11   Bring to pressure slowly – and maintain for time given below. This varies with the type of vegetable being bottled.
12   Check during the processing to see that the pressure is maintained.
13   Remove pan gently from hot plate or turn off gas – reduce pressure at room temperature.
14   Open cooker as soon as pressure has dropped: put jars on to a wooden surface. Tighten screw bands.
15   Test after 24 hours – see point 8 on previous page.

Time to Allow at 10-lb. (5-kilo) pressure
Asparagus, Corn, Runner and French (Green or Wax) Beans 40 minutes
Carrots, Turnips 45 minutes
All Other Vegetables (including Peppers) 50 minutes
Broad (Lima) Beans 55 minutes

Cooking for Invalids and the Elderly

It is important to give an invalid or older person food that is easily digested, so avoid highly spiced or twice-cooked foods (such as a shepherd's pie made with cooked meat) and rather stodgy food. Remove bones and skin from poultry or fish, so it is easy to manage. Do not serve too large portions. Take away uneaten food, do not leave it in the sickroom. Some elderly people are fortunate in that their digestions are unimpaired by age and they can still 'eat anything'.

An ideal meal for an invalid would be a light soup followed by an attractive main dish of fish or poultry, then a small portion of a refreshing dessert (based on fruits, milk or egg). Make sure there are cool drinks in the sickroom and keep these in a vacuum flask or covered jug. Make the invalid tray look really inviting. If a person is very ill do not bother them by continually asking 'What would you like to eat?'. Do not put too much on the tray at one time: serve the soup, remove the soup plate or soup cup, then bring up the main course, then the dessert.

Elderly people need a reasonable amount of protein, and this can be obtained from milk as well as meats, fish, etc. They should also eat cheese, for calcium helps to prevent the formation of very brittle bones, and this is one of the problems of increasing years. Vegetables and fruit are equally important for the elderly as for younger people. It may be that they will need to be sieved to avoid pips or skin. Try to encourage older people to enjoy their meals and to take an interest in what they eat.

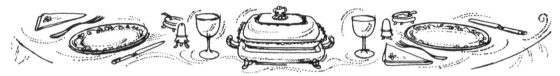

Tempting the Appetite

If a special diet has been prescribed for the invalid this must be followed and no attempt made to deviate from this. Make the food as interesting as possible within the limits of the diet.

In most cases, however, it is just necessary to encourage someone who has been ill to eat light but nutritious food. It is wiser to give small portions of food at fairly short intervals, rather than the normal three larger meals a day. The kind of meals I would suggest are as follows:

Early Morning Tea or fruit juice, then allow time for the person to freshen up.

Breakfast Egg dish or grilled bacon or poached haddock (page 29), thin bread and butter or toast, honey or marmalade, milky coffee, tea or milk. You could also include fruit or fruit juice if not served earlier. Many people of course do not like cooked breakfast.

Mid-morning Vary this. Sometimes give a milky drink or a drink made with yeast extract or beef tea (see next page) or fruit juice or coffee. Serve biscuits or, if little or no breakfast has been eaten, top plain biscuits with cheese or serve small sandwiches.

Lunch Small portion of protein food – poultry, meat, fish, eggs, etc., with vegetables (sieve or mash these if the person is very unwell). Light dessert or fresh fruit.

Tea-time Tea with small sandwiches and/or a buttered scone and/or light type of cake.

Evening Meal Same kind of foods as lunch time, but be very careful to avoid too heavy a meal. It may be wiser to serve soup, followed by an omelette or cheese, and/or a light dessert or fruit.

Late Night Drink Preferably one made with milk.

Beverages and Appetisers

Beverages

As milk is an important food use it as often as possible in drinks, etc., as well as in cooking.

Milky Drinks Mix milk with yeast or beef extracts or stock cubes. Make coffee with *all* milk, try milk shakes (page 152) or mix cold milk and soda water.

Fruit Drinks Try the recipes on page 110 or make *Lemonade* or *Orangeade*. Cut the top 'zest' from the fruit, put into a jug, add a little sugar, cover with boiling water. Leave for 10 minutes, strain, mix with the fruit juice. Dilute with hot or cold water or soda water.

Meal Starters

Choose soup only if the main course is very light. It would probably be better to omit any first course, except for the fruit suggestions below.

Grapefruit Hot or cold. Remove grapefruit segments from the halved fruit; make sure there are no pips, pieces of skin or pith on the segments. Either sweeten lightly and chill, or top with honey, or sugar and a little butter and heat for 2–3 minutes under the grill (broiler).

Melon Dice the pulp, or make into balls with a vegetable scoop. Sweeten lightly, or mix with other seasonal fruit, or flavour with ginger or sherry.

Oranges Serve as grapefruit, or mix fresh or canned juice with a little pineapple or tomato juice.

Prunes Remove stones from cooked or canned fruit. Mix prunes with orange segments, diced raw or cooked apple.

Light Nourishing Soups

The carrot milk soup on this page is an ideal recipe for someone who needs a light, but very nourishing soup. It is easily made, looks interesting and tastes appetising. Mixed root vegetables could be used instead of all carrots. The special tomato soup below is for an invalid or someone who enjoys eating tomatoes, but finds they cannot 'cope' with skins, seeds, etc. Most children would also like this soup.

Tomato and Cheese Soup Cut approximately 2 lb. (1 kilo) tomatoes into small pieces. Simmer for 15 minutes with 1 chopped onion, 1 bay leaf, 1 clove (both optional), seasoning and a few tablespoons water only. Sieve the purée (this is important if you wish to get rid of all traces of the skin) or emulsify in the liquidiser (blender); this often leaves small pieces of skin and some seeds. Meanwhile, blend 1 tablespoon cornflour (cornstarch) with 1 pint milk (6 dl. – 2½ cups). Pour into a saucepan and stir until thickened. Make sure this milk mixture is no longer boiling, then beat in the thick tomato purée. Heat slowly, without boiling. Stir in 1 tablespoon concentrated tomato purée (paste) (from a can or tube) if you like a stronger flavour. Season well.

Serve with a topping of grated Gouda cheese or with bowls of cheese. *Serves 4 as a light main meal or 6–8 as an hors d'oeuvre. Illustrated on page 111.*

Beef Tea This is an old-fashioned drink, which still has much to recommend it. While it is not possible to extract the protein from the meat by simmering it, the liquid can stimulate the appetite.

Simply simmer stewing beef in water to cover, with seasoning to taste, for several hours, then strain carefully.

Yeast extract blended with milk or water provides an equally savoury drink, and this is a good source of vitamin B.

Carrot Milk Soup

Imperial/Metric	American
1¼ pints/7 dl. milk	generous 3 cups milk
4–5 large carrots	4–5 large carrots
seasoning	seasoning
1 oz./25 g. cornflour	¼ cup cornstarch

Cooking time 20 minutes
Serves 4–6
Advance Preparations Cook lightly; reheat to serve.

Heat 1 pint (6 dl. – 2½ cups) of the milk in a pan. Peel and grate the carrots, add to the milk and season well. Blend the cornflour (cornstarch) with

remaining milk, stir into carrot mixture and continue cooking slowly, stirring all the time, until the mixture thickens.

For Economy Use half milk and half water or stock.
Note This is a good soup for a fat-free diet; use skimmed (powdered) milk.

Main Dishes

Do not imagine that everyone who is ill or elderly only enjoys bland, rather flavourless food. Many people dislike dishes lacking in strong flavour. It is, therefore, often very important that the dishes cooked are not only nourishing, but tasty as well. If you add herbs, spices, vegetables such as onion, celery, etc., to the fish, meat or chicken you will provide the desired flavours. If some of these foods, e.g. onions, are not easily digested by the patient you can easily remove them before serving the dish. Use milk, wherever possible, as part of the sauce so you provide additional protein. Often the dish will be suitable for all the family; this makes catering much easier, for it is very time-consuming if you need to plan two entirely different menus.

Plaice Fillets with Asparagus

Imperial/Metric	American
4 large plaice fillets	4 flounder fillets
12–16 cooked or canned asparagus tips	12–16 cooked or canned asparagus tips
juice ½ lemon	juice ½ lemon
seasoning	seasoning
to garnish	**to garnish**
1–2 oz. (25–50 g.) blanched almonds	¼–½ cup blanched almonds
to serve	**to serve**
½ pint (3 dl.) white or cheese sauce, see page 61	1¼ cups white or cheese sauce, see page 61

Cooking time 15 minutes
Serves 4
Advance Preparations Prepare fish, roll around the asparagus.

Skin the fillets and wrap each around several tips of well drained cooked or canned asparagus. Arrange in a shallow ovenproof dish, sprinkle with the lemon juice and season well. Cover with a lid or foil and bake above the centre of a moderate oven, 375°F. (190°C.), Gas Mark 5, until the fish is opaque (approximately 15 minutes). Meanwhile, brown the almonds. Lift fish on to a hot serving dish, garnish with the almonds. Serve with white or cheese sauce, see page 61.

Variations
Use fillets of sole or whiting.
Omit almonds if people find nuts indigestible, or too expensive; garnish with lemon or parsley.
More Fillings for the Fish Use one of the stuffing recipes given on pages 56–60, or roll the fish fillets round quartered skinned tomatoes, or cooked chopped spinach, or a little flaked canned or cooked salmon, or a little potted fish paste or home-made fish pâté (see recipes page 169).

Top Egg mousse (see page 129)   Bottom Kiwi eggs (see page 129)

More Main Dishes

Fish is an obvious choice for people who need light and easily digested foods. In addition, meat and chicken can be presented in ways that are economical and interesting too. Look at some of the recipes in the meat section, particularly those on pages 44, 52, 55, and the basic recipes below.

On this page I give a selection of easy meat and chicken dishes and in each case I have made them for one serving only, so they can be used by someone planning a quick and simple meal for themselves.

Choose meats carefully, avoid pork, which is very indigestible, and serve grilled or roasted meats or casserole dishes, rather than fried food. The creamed mince recipe below is a good basic dish, high in protein, and any minced meat, except pork, can be used. The blanquette of veal is another dish that could be adapted for tender lamb or beef.

If using a frozen chicken portion there is no need to allow time for this to defrost.

Creamed Mince Pour $\frac{1}{4}$ pint ($1\frac{1}{2}$ dl. $-\frac{2}{3}$ cup) water into a pan. Flavour this with a little chopped onion, or a pinch of dried onion, or dehydrated soup powder, or use a little yeast extract or part of a stock (bouillon) cube. Add 4–6 oz. (100–150 g. $-\frac{1}{2}-\frac{3}{4}$ cup) raw minced meat. Stir well to make a smooth mixture, add seasoning. Simmer gently for about 35–40 minutes until the meat is tender. Blend 1 tablespoon cornflour (cornstarch) with $\frac{1}{4}$ pint ($1\frac{1}{2}$ dl. $-\frac{2}{3}$ cup) milk. Stir into the minced meat mixture. Bring slowly to the boil, stirring well, then cook gently until thickened. Serve with creamed potatoes or crisp toast.

Blanquette of Veal Dice about 4 oz. (100 g. $-\frac{1}{2}$ cup) lean *tender* veal. Peel and slice 1–2 carrots and 1 small onion. Simmer the veal and vegetables in a little stock until tender (this takes about 45 minutes). Thicken with cornflour (cornstarch) and milk, as the creamed mince, above.

Chicken Fricassée Put the chicken portion into a saucepan; add 1 peeled onion or use $\frac{1}{2}$ teaspoon dehydrated onion, or 1 teaspoon dehydrated onion soup powder. Add enough cold water to cover. Season lightly, simmer gently until tender (this will take about 30 minutes). Blend 2 teaspoons cornflour (cornstarch) with a little milk, stir into the liquid in the pan and continue stirring until thickened and smooth. Remove the onion if desired, or serve this with the meal. This can be varied in many ways – add one or two strips lemon rind instead of onion; add a small knob of butter or margarine to the thickened sauce and heat for 2–3 minutes; flavour the thickened sauce with a little grated nutmeg. To save cooking separate vegetables you can add diced carrot, peas, etc., to the liquid while cooking the chicken.

Chicken à la King Cook the chicken as in the preceding recipe, thicken the sauce, then add 1–2 tablespoons cooked or well drained canned sweetcorn plus a little diced cooked ham. If you are making one chicken portion serve two people you can remove the cooked chicken joint, dice the meat, then put it back into the sauce with a generous amount of diced ham too.

Pilaff of Chicken Divide the chicken portion into 2 pieces, put into a pan, with $\frac{1}{2}$ pint (3 dl. $-1\frac{1}{4}$ cups) water, or use water plus $\frac{1}{2}$ stock (bouillon) cube. Simmer for 10 minutes, then add 1 tablespoon long grain rice and seasoning. Continue cooking until the chicken and rice are tender (approximately 15–20 minutes), and the liquid absorbed. This is a very basic recipe; you can add 1 chopped onion, 2–3 sliced mushrooms, 1 sliced tomato to the chicken and make a much more interesting dish. Instead of using water and the portion of a stock cube use tomato juice, or use water plus 2–3 teaspoons of dehydrated soup powder to give flavour to the chicken and the rice.

Supper Dishes

The pancake suggestions and egg dishes below are ideal for both an invalid and the rest of the family. Savoury soufflés, see page 149 and below, are some more excellent light dishes that are suitable for an evening meal.

Cheese Soufflé Make a thick white sauce in a large pan, using 1 oz. (25 g. — 2 tablespoons) butter, 1 oz. (25 g. — $\frac{1}{4}$ cup) flour and $\frac{1}{4}$ pint ($1\frac{1}{2}$ dl. — $\frac{2}{3}$ cup) milk. Season well. Beat in the yolks of 3—4 eggs and 3 oz. (75 g. — $\frac{3}{4}$ cup) finely grated Cheddar or Gruyère cheese. Fold in 4 stiffly beaten egg whites. Spoon into one 7-inch (18-cm.) greased soufflé dish (baker) or 4 individual soufflé dishes. Bake the larger soufflé for approximately 30 minutes and the smaller soufflés for 20 minutes in the centre of a moderate oven, 375°F. (190°C.), Gas Mark 5. Serve at once. *Serves 4.*

Note For a softer texture use 2—3 tablespoons (3—4 tablespoons) more milk, or add thin cream to the sauce.

Egg Mousse Hard boil (hard cook) 6 eggs, shell these and slice 1 egg, then chop the remainder. Make $\frac{1}{2}$ pint (3 dl. — $1\frac{1}{4}$ cups) white sauce as the recipe on page 61. Dissolve 1 tablespoon gelatine (gelatin) in 2 tablespoons (3 tablespoons) hot water. Stir most of this into the white sauce, but brush about 1 teaspoon of the dissolved gelatine inside the base of a $1\frac{1}{2}$ pint (1 litre — 4—5 cup) ring mould (mold). Arrange the sliced egg on this. Add 2 teaspoons tomato purée (paste), 1 tablespoon Worcestershire sauce, $\frac{1}{4}$ pint ($1\frac{1}{2}$ dl. — $\frac{2}{3}$ cup) thick mayonnaise, $\frac{1}{4}$ pint ($1\frac{1}{2}$ dl. — $\frac{2}{3}$ cup) whipped cream and the chopped eggs to the white sauce and gelatine mixture. Season well. Spoon into the mould, leave until firm, then turn out. Garnish with watercress and sliced tomatoes, see colour picture on page 127. *Serves 4—6.*

Kiwi Eggs Mince 1 lb. ($\frac{1}{2}$ kilo) lamb and mix with 2 oz. (50 g. — 1 cup) soft breadcrumbs, 1 finely chopped onion, 1 tablespoon Worcestershire sauce, 1 tablespoon tomato purée (paste). Season the mixture well. Hard boil (hard cook) and shell 4—5 eggs. Coat these in seasoned flour then in the lamb mixture. Brush the outside of the lamb mixture with beaten egg, then roll in soft or crisp breadcrumbs (raspings). Fry steadily (remember the lamb is not cooked) in deep oil or fat (shortening) for 15 minutes. Drain on absorbent paper and serve cold with salad or hot with vegetables, see colour picture on page 127. *Serves 4—5.*

Savoury Egg Custards Follow the instructions for making egg custards on page 131, but instead of adding sugar use a little salt and pepper instead. The custard can be given extra flavour by adding 1—2 tablespoons finely grated Cheddar, or Gruyère or Parmesan cheese, or by pouring the egg and milk over small portions of white uncooked fish, or by adding finely diced cooked bacon or ham to the egg and milk. Cook the custard as the timing for sweet custards on page 131.

Savoury Pancakes

An omelette is an ideal dish for someone who has little appetite, or a poor digestion, and the fillings can be varied to avoid monotony (see pages 104 and 105). Even so, people will tire of too many omelettes, so give small pancakes filled with savoury mixtures. The method of making the pancake batter and some sweet fillings are on pages 66 and 71; make the pancakes in exactly the same way as page 71, and fill with one of the following, or the fillings for omelettes.

Scrambled Egg By itself or mixed with a little grated cheese or diced chicken, etc.; keep the egg fairly soft.

Mashed Vegetables (carrots, spinach, etc.) Make softer by adding a small quantity of milk or cream. These could also be mixed with grated cheese, cream cheese or cottage cheese.

Cottage Cheese This is easily digested and can be mixed with a little chopped parsley. Thick cheese sauce (page 61) can also be used as a pancake filling, and cooked vegetables, or cooked fish, or cooked chicken or ham, can be mixed with the sauce.

Steamed Fish

The method of steaming fish is given on page 29, and this is a favourite way of cooking fish for an invalid. While it is an excellent method it can produce very dull looking meals. Take care therefore to garnish steamed fish in an attractive manner with slices of lemon or orange, with narrow strips of cooked carrot, etc. Fillets of white fish (free from skin) or soft roes are the best fish to steam. Season the fish well and give it additional flavour by adding a little celery salt sometimes, or a little lemon juice, or finely grated lemon rind, or freshly chopped parsley. If the diet permits using cream and butter, add a little thin cream and butter to the normal amount of milk used to keep the fish moist while steaming, or use butter and white wine over the fish to make a welcome change of flavour.

Scallops of Fish Florentine

Imperial/Metric	American
1 lb. (½ kilo) white fish	1 lb. lean fish
1 oz. (25 g.) butter	2 tablespoons butter
seasoning	seasoning
lemon juice	lemon juice
1½–2 lb. (¾–1 kilo) spinach	1½–2 lb. spinach
for the white sauce	**for the white sauce**
1 oz. (25 g.) butter	2 tablespoons butter
1 oz. (25 g.) flour	¼ cup flour
½ pint (3 dl.) milk (poor measure)	1¼ cups milk (poor measure)
for the topping	**for the topping**
few breadcrumbs	few bread crumbs
1–2 oz. (25–50 g.) cheese, grated	¼–½ cup grated cheese
little extra butter	little extra butter

Cooking time 25 minutes
Serves 4
Advance Preparations Prepare recipe and reheat when required.

Put the fish into an ovenproof dish with the butter, seasoning and lemon juice, cover and bake just above the centre of a moderately hot oven, 400°F. (200°C.), Gas Mark 6, for about 10–12 minutes. Prepare the spinach, cook, strain and sieve or chop to give a fine mixture. Place in buttered individual ovenproof dishes or scallop shells. Flake the fish into large pieces and arrange on the spinach. Make the white sauce, see recipe page 61, spoon over the fish. (Do not be too generous with the milk, otherwise the sauce tends to run to the edge of the dishes.) Sprinkle with the breadcrumbs and cheese, dot with small pieces of butter, brown under the grill (broiler) or heat in the oven.

Variations

Poach the fish instead of baking it.
Use creamed potatoes instead of spinach.

Desserts

Most of us enjoy a pleasant dessert, but this course can be particularly important for an invalid or someone who eats only a small meal. The dessert can ensure that essential foods (eggs, milk, fruit, etc.) are eaten in an easily assimilated and palatable form. Cream may be too rich for an invalid, so you can substitute unsweetened whipped evaporated milk in many recipes. To whip evaporated milk place the can in a pan of boiling water, boil steadily for 15 minutes, remove the can, chill in the refrigerator then whip. For a firmer texture, open the can *carefully* while the milk is hot, pour into a basin, add a teaspoon of gelatine dissolved in 1–2 tablespoons water (see page 89), add to the hot milk, chill then whip.

Egg Custards

When making an egg custard remember:
1   The mixture will curdle if cooked too quickly or for too long a period (in both cases the egg and milk can reach too high a temperature).
2   When cooking in the oven you will find recipes suggest standing the sweet in a dish of cold water (a bain marie). This helps to prevent curdling, and keeps the pudding moist.
3   If cooking a custard, or custard sauce, over water make certain the water *never* boils.

Basic Egg Custard

Imperial/Metric	American
2 eggs or 2–3 egg yolks*	2 eggs or 2–3 egg yolks*
1 oz. (25 g.) sugar	2 tablespoons sugar
1 pint (6 dl.) milk	2½ cups milk
for the topping (optional)	**for the topping** (optional)
little grated nutmeg	little grated nutmeg

* egg yolks alone give a richer flavoured custard.

Cooking time see method
Serves 4
Advance Preparations Prepare ahead and cook when required.

Whisk the eggs and sugar lightly; add the warm milk. Strain into the cooking container, see below. Top with nutmeg.
To bake If using one container allow about 1¼–2 hours, depending upon the depth of the mixture, in a slow to very moderate oven, 300–325°F. (150–170°C.), Gas Mark 2–3. If using small individual dishes allow about 45 minutes. Stand dish or dishes in a 'bain marie', see above.
To steam Stand the covered dish in a steamer, cook over hot, but not boiling water for time above.
To boil Cook gently – actually you must not boil – over hot, but not boiling water until thickened.

Variations

For a thicker custard that can be turned out, use 4 eggs or egg yolks to proportions above.

Bread and Butter Pudding Put thinly sliced bread and butter and a little dried fruit into a dish, cover with the custard and bake as basic recipe.
Bread and Biscuit Pudding If you run out of bread, butter cream (Graham) crackers instead, and use in a similar way to bread and butter pudding.

Apricot Pudding

Imperial/Metric	American
4–6 oz. (100–150 g.) dried apricots	⅔–1 cup dried apricots
good ½ pint (3 dl.) water	good 1¼ cups water
3 oz. (75 g.) sugar	generous ⅓ cup sugar
grated rind 1 lemon	grated rind 1 lemon
1 large macaroon biscuit	1 large macaroon cookie
4 oz. (100 g.) fine cake crumbs	2 cups fine cake crumbs
2 eggs	2 eggs
½ pint (3 dl.) milk	1¼ cups milk
to serve	to serve
cream	cream

Cooking time 2 hours
Serves 4–6
Advance Preparations Prepare and cook apricots.

Soak the apricots overnight in the water, then simmer next day with 2 oz. (50 g. – ¼ cup) sugar and the lemon rind until soft, but not pulpy. Crush the macaroon biscuit. Grease a 1½–2 pint (⅞–1¼ litre – 4–5 cup) basin (pudding mold) and coat with some of the mixed macaroon and cake crumbs. Drain the apricots, put half the fruit at the bottom of the basin, cover with half the remaining crumbs.

Add the rest of the apricots and finally the last of the crumbs. Beat the eggs with the milk and remaining sugar, strain slowly over the fruit and crumbs. Cover with greased paper or foil and steam over hot, but not boiling, water for approximately 50 minutes to 1 hour, until firm. Turn out and serve hot with cream, and any apricot syrup left.

Variation
Use dried prunes instead of apricots, but stone the prunes and stuff with chopped almonds.

Cream Diplomat Pudding

Imperial/Metric	American
vanilla pod or few drops vanilla essence	vanilla bean or few drops vanilla extract
1 pint (6 dl.) milk	2½ cups milk
1–2 oz. (25–50 g.) sugar	2–4 tablespoons sugar
2–3 heaped tablespoons fine cake crumbs	3–4 heaped tablespoons fine cake crumbs
4 egg yolks	4 egg yolks
2 egg whites	2 egg whites
custard cream sauce, see opposite	custard cream sauce, see opposite

Cooking time 45 minutes–2 hours (see method)
Serves 4–6
Advance Preparations Make crumbs; but do not allow custard to stand longer than 30 minutes.

Put the vanilla pod or vanilla essence into the milk, add the sugar and bring to the boil. Pour over the cake crumbs. Stand for 30 minutes, then pour over the beaten egg yolks and whites. If a more 'fluffy' texture is required, fold in the stiffly beaten egg whites separately, *just before cooking*. Grease 1 large or several smaller moulds (molds), cups or basins, and pour in the mixture. Steam gently for about 2 hours (in the large mould) or 45 minutes to 1 hour for the smaller moulds. Make sure that neither the mixture nor the water in the pan under the steamer is allowed to boil. Serve hot or cold with the custard cream sauce. If serving hot, allow the pudding to set for several minutes in the mould before turning out on to a dish.

Freezing Do not freeze.

Custard Cream Sauce

Imperial/Metric	American
$\frac{1}{2}$ pint (3 dl.) milk	*$1\frac{1}{4}$ cups milk*
vanilla pod or few drops vanilla essence	*vanilla bean or few drops vanilla extract*
1–2 tablespoons sugar	*1–2 tablespoons sugar*
1 teaspoon cornflour	*1 teaspoon cornstarch*
1 egg yolk	*1 egg yolk*
$\frac{1}{4}$ pint ($1\frac{1}{2}$ dl.) thick cream	*$\frac{2}{3}$ cup whipping cream*

Cooking time *approximately 20 minutes*
Serves 4–6
Advance Preparations This sauce keeps well for 24–36 hours in a refrigerator.

Put most of the milk into a saucepan with the vanilla pod or essence and sugar. Bring to the boil, then remove vanilla pod. Blend the rest of the milk with the cornflour and egg yolk, add the hot, but not boiling, milk. Pour mixture into the top of a double saucepan, or into a basin (bowl) over hot water; cook the custard slowly until thickened. Cool custard, stir well to prevent a skin forming then add the *liquid* cream and whisk or beat hard to give a very smooth sauce.

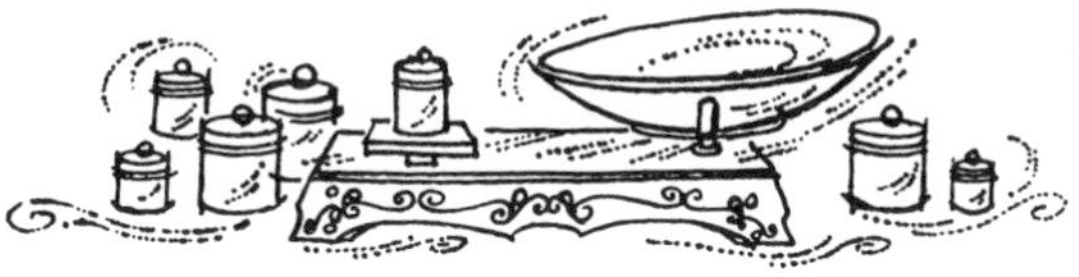

Mocha Meringue Pudding

Imperial/Metric	American
2 oz. (50 g.) fine cake or breadcrumbs	*1 cup fine cake or bread crumbs*
1 oz. (25 g.) chocolate powder	*$\frac{1}{4}$ cup chocolate powder*
$\frac{3}{4}$ pint ($4\frac{1}{2}$ dl.) milk	*scant 2 cups milk*
1 tablespoon coffee essence	*1 tablespoon strong black coffee – sweetened*
2 egg yolks	*2 egg yolks*
2 oz. (50 g.) sugar (little less if using cake crumbs)	*$\frac{1}{4}$ cup sugar (little less if using cake crumbs)*
for the meringue	**for the meringue**
2 egg whites	*2 egg whites*
2 tablespoons castor sugar	*3 tablespoons granulated sugar*
to decorate	**to decorate**
little grated chocolate	*little grated chocolate*

Cooking time *$1\frac{1}{2}$–$1\frac{3}{4}$ hours*
Serves 4
Advance Preparations Prepare ingredients.

Put the cake or breadcrumbs and chocolate powder into a basin (bowl). Warm the milk. Blend the coffee essence and egg yolks, gradually beat in milk.
Stir over the crumbs, chocolate powder and sugar, allow to stand for 10 minutes. Pour into an oven-proof dish, set for 1–$1\frac{1}{4}$ hours in the centre of a slow oven, 275°F. (140°C.), Gas Mark 1, until firm. Whisk the egg whites stiffly, fold in sugar, pile or pipe on top of the chocolate base. Brown in the slow oven for 30 minutes. Cover with the grated chocolate and serve hot.

Variations
Chocolate Meringue Pudding Omit coffee essence (strong black coffee), use 2 oz. (50 g. – $\frac{1}{2}$ cup) chocolate powder or 1 oz. (25 g. – $\frac{1}{4}$ cup) cocoa.
Coffee Meringue Pudding Omit chocolate powder, use 3 oz. (75 g. – $1\frac{1}{2}$ cups) cake or breadcrumbs and 2 tablespoons (3 tablespoons) coffee essence (strong black coffee).
To Serve the Above Puddings Cold Use 4 oz. (100 g. – $\frac{1}{2}$ cup) sugar to the 2 egg whites, and set the meringue for 1 hour in a very slow oven. In this way the meringue will remain crisp when the dessert is served cold.

Cookery for Men

In this section I have concentrated upon recipes that men will like to cook, and to eat too. It may be that the 'man of the house' cooks because it is his interest, in which case he will also find many recipes in other sections of this book that he may care to try. On the other hand, it could be that he is cooking due to necessity — illness, etc. I have rather assumed the latter is the case, and have concentrated on good straight-forward basic cooking methods in this chapter — roasting, frying, grilling meat, etc., as well as some interestingly flavoured casseroles, together with easy savouries and desserts.

Main Dishes

Methods of Cooking

Never try to roast, grill (broil) or fry cuts of meat that are not of good quality, for you will be very disappointed in the result. You can, however, make a delicious stew or casserole dish with the cheaper cuts.

Grilled Cod Steaks with Almonds and Mushrooms

Imperial/Metric	American
3–4 oz. (75–100 g.) butter	⅜–½ cup butter
4 cod steaks (preferably from tail)	4 cod steaks (preferably from tail)
seasoning	seasoning
2 tablespoons grated Parmesan cheese	3 tablespoons grated Parmesan cheese
2–4 oz. (50–100 g.) blanched almonds	½–1 cup blanched almonds
4 oz. (100 g.) small button mushrooms	1 cup small button mushrooms
to garnish	**to garnish**
2–3 small tomatoes	2–3 small tomatoes
sprigs parsley	sprig parsley

Cooking time 15 minutes
Serves 4
Advance Preparations Blanch almonds. Wash but do not skin mushrooms.

Melt all the butter in a frying pan and brush the cod steaks on one side with a little of this butter, season lightly. Put the fish on the grid of the grill (broiler) pan, cook until golden brown, then turn. Season the second side, brush with more melted butter, sprinkle with the cheese. Continue cooking the fish until golden brown and tender. Meanwhile, fry the almonds and mushrooms in the butter remaining in the pan. Place the fish on the serving dish, add the nuts and mushrooms. Garnish with halved tomatoes and parsley.

Variations

Use turbot or other white (lean) fish, or whole trout. Fry the fish in half the butter, lift on to a hot dish, sprinkle with cheese and keep warm in the oven while cooking the nuts and mushrooms in the remaining butter.

Pork steaks with mustard sauce (see page 140)

Grilled Steak

Choose cuts of beef given on page 32. Light or switch on the grill (broiler) several minutes before cooking the steak. Put the steak on the grid of the grill pan and brush with melted butter or oil. Cook on one side, then turn with tongs – do not put the prongs of a fork into the meat (it allows the juices to run out) – brush the second side with butter and cook to taste.

Minute Steak One minute cooking each side.

Under-done Steak ('rare') About ¾ inch (1½ cm.) thick, 3–4 minutes each side.

Medium-done Steak Cook as under-done steak, then lower heat for further 3 minutes.

Well-done Steak Cook as under-done steak, then lower heat for further 5–6 minutes.

Serve with grilled (broiled) tomatoes, mushrooms and parsley (maître d'hôtel) butter.

Parsley Butter Work chopped parsley and lemon juice into butter, chill, cut into squares or rounds. Put on the meat just before serving.

Note Frozen steaks do not need defrosting, cook from the frozen state. Never cook steaks until immediately before serving.

Fried Steak

Choose cuts of beef given on page 32. Heat the fat in the pan, do not allow it to become too hot. Put in the steak, it can be seasoned lightly if wished, and fry for times given below: turn with tongs or fish slice, do not put prongs of fork into meat. Use butter, oil, or good dripping (drippings) for frying.

Minute Steak One minute cooking each side.

Under-done Steak ('rare') About ¾ inch (1½ cm.), 3 minutes on each side.

Medium-done Steak Cook as under-done, then lower heat and cook for further 2–3 minutes.

Well-done Steak Cook as under-done, then lower heat and cook for further 4–6 minutes.

Serve with fried tomatoes, mushrooms, fried potatoes and parsley (maître d'hôtel) butter – see above.

Steak Trinidad

Imperial/Metric	American
seasoning	seasoning
4 steaks	4 steaks
1 tablespoon Angostura Bitters	1 tablespoon Angostura Bitters
2 onions	2 onions
1 clove garlic	1 clove garlic
3 tomatoes	3 tomatoes
2 oz. (50 g.) mushrooms	½ cup mushrooms
3–4 oz. (75–100 g.) butter or dripping*	⅜–½ cup butter or drippings*
5 tablespoons brown stock or water and ½ beef stock cube	6 tablespoons brown stock or water and ½ beef bouillon cube
to garnish	**to garnish**
watercress	watercress
fried potatoes, see opposite	fried potatoes, see opposite

* depending upon amount of fat on the steaks.

Cooking time 15–20 minutes

Serves 4

Advance Preparations Cook vegetables but not meat, just season and sprinkle with Angostura Bitters.

Season the steaks, sprinkle with the Angostura Bitters, leave for 1 hour. Peel and slice the vegetables.

Heat half the butter or dripping, fry the vegetables until soft. Lift on to hot dish. Heat the remaining butter or dripping, fry the steaks to personal taste, see timing above. Add the stock, or water and stock cube, and vegetables a few minutes before the end of the cooking time. Top the steaks with the moist vegetables, garnish with watercress, fried potatoes.

Grilling and Frying Meats

The details of grilling (broiling) steak and frying steak on page 136 can be followed for other meats. The amount of fat used will depend upon the natural fat in the meat, i.e.:

Lamb Needs little if any fat for grilling, and the minimum amount for frying.

Pork Should not require fat for grilling, and only a lightly greased pan for frying.

Veal Must be kept well basted with fat when grilling, and should be cooked in a generous amount of fat when frying, see escalopes of veal, on page 138.

Lamb Cutlets and Chops (about $\frac{3}{4}$ inch ($1\frac{1}{2}$ cm.) in thickness)   Require a total cooking time of 12–14 minutes. Cook quickly on either side, then lower the heat.

Pork Slightly longer than lamb, i.e. total 15–16 minutes.

Veal See recipe on page 138, or allow about same time as pork for cutlets and chops.

To Grill or Fry Vegetables

Prepare and season *whole mushrooms* and *halved tomatoes*. Heat a little extra fat in the pan of the grill (broiler), toss the vegetables in this, or brush with the melted fat. Cook for 2–3 minutes, then place meat on the pan above the vegetables. Either fry the vegetables first in a little fat, then keep hot while cooking the meat, or fry in a separate pan. If cooking only 1 or 2 portions of meat you may be able to fry the vegetables in the same frying pan (skillet).

To Fry Potatoes Peel and slice the potatoes or cut into chip shapes (French fries). While you can fry these in shallow oil or fat it is always better to use deep oil or fat. Dry the potatoes. Heat the oil or fat until one slice or chip of potato rises to the top of the bubbling fat, or until a cube of day-old bread turns golden-coloured, within 1 minute. Fry the potatoes steadily until tender. Lift out of pan, reheat the fat or oil and fry potatoes quickly for 1–2 minutes until crisp and brown. Drain on absorbent paper.

Beef Fondue

The colour picture on page 139 shows one of the most popular ways of cooking and serving tender beef. The dish consists of prime diced beef, fried in hot oil, then dipped in one of the cold sauces. The dish has several accepted titles, i.e. it can be called just beef fondue or beef fondue bourguignonne, or simply beef à la bourguignonne (this is a little confusing since there is a well known beef stew with a similar name).

Cut the lean beef – choose the best quality steak – into neat dice. Keep covered until ready to cook, so the beef does not become dry. Prepare the various sauces, see below. Heat the oil in a proper fondue pot, see picture, keep this hot over a burner. *Make sure the table, etc., is well protected from the high heat.* Dip metal fondue forks into the meat, then hold the cubes in the hot oil until cooked to personal taste. Transfer to ordinary *cold* forks, so you cannot burn your mouth. Dip into one of the sauces. Serve with French bread, green salad and a good wine.

Some Sauces to Serve with Beef Fondue

Sour Cream Sauce Blend $\frac{1}{2}$ pint (3 dl. – $1\frac{1}{4}$ cups) dairy soured cream or thick (whipping) cream and 1 tablespoon lemon juice with 3–4 tablespoons thick mayonnaise. Season well.

Curry Cream Sauce Make the sauce above, blend 2 teaspoons curry paste with the mixture. Add a shake cayenne pepper and a shake Worcestershire sauce.

Spiced Tomato Sauce Blend 2 tablespoons (3 tablespoons) tomato purée (paste) into $\frac{1}{4}$ pint ($1\frac{1}{2}$ dl. – $\frac{2}{3}$ cup) mayonnaise. Add 1 tablespoon sherry, few drops Tabasco sauce, pinch grated nutmeg and 3 tablespoons (4 tablespoons) whipped cream.

Tartare Sauce Follow the recipe on page 61, or make the sour cream sauce and add finely chopped parsley, gherkins and capers to taste.

The sauces above (shown in picture page 139), plus 2–2$\frac{1}{2}$ lb. (1–1$\frac{1}{4}$ kilo) diced beef will serve 6–7 people.

Escalopes of Veal

Imperial/Metric	American
4 fillets of veal*	4 veal fillets*
1 tablespoon flour	1 tablespoon flour
seasoning	seasoning
1 egg	1 egg
approximately 2 oz. (50 g.) crisp breadcrumbs (raspings)	approximately $\frac{1}{2}$ cup crisp bread crumbs (raspings)
for frying	**for frying**
2–3 oz. (50–75 g.) butter or fat	$\frac{1}{4}$–$\frac{3}{8}$ cup butter or shortening
to garnish	**to garnish**
1 lemon	1 lemon
1 hard-boiled egg (optional)	1 hard-cooked egg (optional)
small sprig parsley	small sprig parsley

*these are thin slices cut from the leg of veal.

Cooking time 10 minutes
Serves 4
Advance Preparations Coat veal slices, chill in refrigerator. Boil the egg and prepare garnish.

The veal slices should be very thin; if too thick flatten with a rolling pin. Mix flour and seasoning. Coat the meat in seasoned flour then in the beaten egg and breadcrumbs. Heat the butter or fat (always be as generous as possible with this as veal is such a lean meat). Fry the meat fairly quickly until golden brown on both sides. Lower the heat and cook the meat for several minutes to make certain the veal is tender. Drain on absorbent paper, lift on to a hot dish. Meanwhile, slice lemon and chop the egg and parsley. Garnish each escalope with a lemon slice and top these slices with the egg and parsley mixture if liked, or just a sprig of parsley.

Note The veal fillets may be lightly fried in a pan, then finished in the oven. This makes it an easier dish to serve when entertaining – do not cover in the oven so the escalopes remain crisp.

Variations
Add 1 or 2 anchovy fillets to the garnish above.
Top with lemon slices, omit chopped egg and parsley.
Veal Holstein Top each escalope with a fried egg instead of the classic garnish given in the recipe.
Veal Cordon Bleu Make sure the thin slices of meat are *very* thin. Fold each escalope over thin slices of cooked ham and Gruyère cheese. Coat and fry as the basic recipe, but allow about 5 minutes longer cooking time to make sure the meat is cooked.

Beef fondue (see page 137)

Pork Steaks with Mustard Sauce

Imperial/Metric	American
1 can figs (size immaterial)	1 can figs (size immaterial)
8 oz. (200 g.) long grain rice	just over 1 cup long grain rice
1 pint (6 dl.) stock or water and 1 chicken stock cube	2½ cups stock or water and 1 chicken bouillon cube
seasoning	seasoning
4–6 fillets lean pork (cut from leg)	4–6 slices lean pork (cut from leg)
1–2 teaspoons dry mustard	1–2 teaspoons dry mustard
3 oz. (75 g.) butter or margarine	generous ⅓ cup butter or margarine
2 tablespoons dry white wine	3 tablespoons dry white wine
¼ pint (1½ dl.) thick cream	⅔ cup whipping cream

Cooking time 20–25 minutes
Serves 4–6
Advance Preparations Collect ingredients. measure syrup from figs. This is better when freshly cooked.

Drain 4 tablespoons (5 tablespoons) syrup from the figs, put on one side. Put rice, stock, or water and stock cube, and seasoning in a saucepan with drained syrup from the figs. Bring to boil, stir once. Cover and simmer for 15 minutes, or until rice is tender and liquid absorbed. Rub pork fillets with half the mustard, season well. Fry quickly in half the butter or margarine for 1–2 minutes on either side, then lower the heat and cook slowly for 10 minutes, or until meat is tender. Lift meat out of the pan and keep hot. Add the remainder of the butter or margarine to the pan, heat gently. Blend the rest of the mustard with the wine, pour this, plus the cream, into the frying pan and stir over a very low heat for 1–2 minutes, do not allow mixture to boil. Meanwhile, heat figs in remaining syrup. To serve, spoon the rice on to a dish, top with the pork and well drained figs. Spoon the mustard sauce over the pork just before serving. *Illustrated on page 135.*

For Economy Do not waste remaining fig syrup. use this as part of liquid to make a lemon jelly (gelatin).
Freezing Frozen fillets pork may be cooked unthawed.

Beef and Olives

Imperial/Metric	American
1¼–1½ lb. (⅝–¾ kilo) chuck steak	1¼–1½ lb. beef shoulder
1 oz. (25 g.) flour	¼ cup flour
seasoning	seasoning
pinch chilli powder	pinch chili powder
2 onions	2 onions
1 clove garlic	1 clove garlic
2 oz. (50 g.) fat	¼ cup shortening
1 pint (6 dl.) water, or use stock if available	2½ cups water, or use stock if available
about 18 stuffed olives	about 18 stuffed olives

Cooking time 2¾ hours
Serves 4–6
Advance Preparations Cook ahead; reheat to serve.

Cut the steak into neat fingers. then roll in flour mixed with seasoning and chilli powder (use this sparingly, it is very hot). Peel the onions. cut into rings and crush the clove of garlic. Toss the meat. onions and garlic in the hot fat for several minutes then blend in the liquid, bring just to boiling point, lower the heat. cover the pan and simmer gently for 2½ hours. Add olives 5–10 minutes before serving.

For Economy Use less meat; add canned haricot beans towards end of cooking time. Use 2 tablespoons chopped vinegar pickles instead of olives.
Freezing Freezes well; may need extra thickening when reheated. Use within 4 months.

Roasting Meat

The method of roasting beef, given below on this page, shows the basic way of cooking this, and any meat, by roasting. Many people will argue that our accepted method of roasting, i.e. in a tin in the oven, is *not* true roasting and that the only correct method is on a turning spit. Perhaps you have such an attachment on your cooker, in which case use this and follow the timings for fast roasting. Accompaniments for roast meat are on page 142. The table below gives roasting times; choose meat cuts as table pages 32 and 33.

Times for Roasting Meat

Meat	Fast Roasting	Slow Roasting	Fat Required	To Serve
Beef	*See below*	*See below*	*See below*	*Yorkshire pudding, horseradish sauce or mustard, thin gravy.*
Lamb	*20 minutes per lb. ($\frac{1}{2}$ kilo) 20 minutes over.*	*35 minutes per lb. ($\frac{1}{2}$ kilo) 35 minutes over.*	*Minimum — see beef*	*Mint sauce, thin gravy.*
Mutton	*20 minutes per lb. ($\frac{1}{2}$ kilo) 20 minutes over.*	*Recommended for mutton. 35 minutes per lb. ($\frac{1}{2}$ kilo) 35 minutes over.*	*None*	*Onion sauce or redcurrant jelly, thick gravy.*
Pork	*Recommended for pork. 25 minutes per lb. ($\frac{1}{2}$ kilo) 25 minutes over.*	*35–40 minutes per lb. ($\frac{1}{2}$ kilo) 35–40 minutes over.*	*Brush fat with oil or melted lard, salt lightly if desired.*	*Apple sauce. Sage and onion stuffing (page 60). Thick gravy.*
Veal	*As pork*	*As pork*	*Cover with plenty of fat. Keep well basted during cooking.*	*Parsley stuffing (page 58), bacon rolls. Sausages. Thick gravy.*
Venison	*As pork*	*As pork*	*As veal or page 207*	*As veal*

Roast Beef

Choose cuts of beef given on page 32. Weigh the meat — cooking time depends on this. Put the meat into the roasting tin (pan). Spread only the minimum of fat on the meat (about 1 oz. (25 g. — 2 tablespoons); sirloin or rib with a reasonable amount of natural fat needs no extra fat. If preparing in advance, wipe meat, put ready to cook, or place in oven if using automatic cooker. *Allow frozen joints to defrost.*

Fast Roasting Use a moderately hot to hot oven, 400–425°F. (200–220°C.), Gas Mark 6–7. After 30 minutes you can reduce the heat slightly.

Slower Roasting This is suitable for frozen meat, meat you feel may not be quite as tender as you would wish, or when it is more convenient to use this method. The advantage is that you tend to make tougher meat more tender; the disadvantage (in my opinion) is that the meat does not retain quite as much flavour. Use a very moderate oven, 325–350°F. (170–180°C.), Gas Mark 3–4.

Under-done ('rare') Fast roasting allow 15 minutes cooking time per lb. ($\frac{1}{2}$ kilo) and 15 minutes over. Slow roasting 25 minutes per lb. ($\frac{1}{2}$ kilo) and 25 minutes over.

Medium-done (i.e. well-done on outside, less well-done in centre) Fast roasting allow nearly 20 minutes per lb. ($\frac{1}{2}$ kilo) and 20 minutes over. Slow roasting 30 minutes per lb. ($\frac{1}{2}$ kilo) and 30 minutes over.

Well-done Good 20 minutes or even 25 minutes per lb. ($\frac{1}{2}$ kilo) and 20 minutes over; this longer cooking is not really recommended for beef, the time given for slow roasting (medium-done) should be sufficient for most people.

If Using a Covered Roasting Tin or Foil Allow extra 20 minutes cooking time or 25°F. (14°C.) higher temperature, or one mark higher in a gas cooker.

Accompaniments for Beef

Yorkshire Pudding Make a batter in exactly the same way as when making pancakes, see the recipe page 66. Heat a knob of fat in one oblong tin or thickly grease deep patty tins (muffin pans). Heat the tin or tins very thoroughly in a very hot oven. Pour in the batter. Bake for 10–15 minutes towards the top of a very hot oven, then lower the heat for a further 15–20 minutes when cooking a large pudding, or for 5 minutes when cooking smaller puddings. Serve at once.

Horseradish Cream While one can buy excellent prepared horseradish cream the home-made variety is delicious. Mix grated fresh horseradish with whipped cream, then flavour with a small amount of made mustard, seasoning, lemon juice or vinegar. Horseradish may be added to a white sauce (page 61).

Accompaniments for Lamb and Mutton

Mint Sauce Chop fresh mint finely, mix with sugar and vinegar to taste, or prepare this in the blender.

Onion Sauce Cook several onions in seasoned water until just tender. Make a white sauce as page 61, but use half milk and half onion stock. Add the chopped onions and serve.

Stuffing for Breast of Lamb (*Illustrated above*) Blend 8 oz. ($\frac{1}{4}$ kilo) sausagemeat with 2 tablespoons (3 tablespoons) dry packet sage and onion stuffing, or use breadcrumbs and chopped fresh or dried sage to taste. Add 1 teaspoon mixed herbs and 1 tablespoon chutney. Season the mixture well, then spread over boned breast of lamb and roast as the tables on page 141.

Accompaniments for Pork and Veal

Apple Sauce Cook apples with sugar to taste until a smooth purée, sieve or emulsify in the blender. Spice or dried fruit can be added to make a change.

Bacon Rolls to Serve with Veal Halve rashers (slices) bacon, form into rolls, put on to metal skewers and cook for a short time in the oven, when roasting the veal.

Veal stuffings and sage and onion stuffing (parsley and thyme) are on pages 58 and 60.

Marinated roast pork (see page 144)

Marinated Roast Pork

Imperial/Metric	American
4–4¼ lb. (2–2¼ kilos) loin pork*	4–4¼ lb. pork loin*
seasoning	seasoning
4 oz. (100 g.) butter or dripping	½ cup butter or drippings
4 onions	4 onions
8 oz. (200 g.) streaky bacon rashers	½ lb. bacon slices
4 oz. (100 g.) mushrooms	1 cup mushrooms
12 oz. (300 g.) long grain rice	just over 1½ cups long grain rice
1½ pints (9 dl.) stock	4 cups stock
2 oz. (50 g.) flour	½ cup flour
1 liqueur glass brandy (optional)	1 liqueur glass brandy (optional)
for the marinade	**for the marinade**
1 onion	1 onion
4 cloves (optional)	4 cloves (optional)
shake pepper or few peppercorns	shake pepper or few peppercorns
1–2 bay leaves	1–2 bay leaves
1 carrot	1 carrot
small sprig sage	small sprig sage
½ head celery	½ bunch celery
1–2 leeks	1–2 leeks
1 bottle cheap red wine	1 bottle cheap red wine
1 tablespoon vinegar	1 tablespoon vinegar

* ask butcher to remove bones or do this yourself, but save bones to make stock.

Cooking time 2–2¼ hours
Serves 8
Advance Preparations Marinate meat, simmer bones
and prepare ingredients.

Put the pork into a deep casserole. Add all the
ingredients for the marinade. *Do not chop vegetables
too finely.* Leave for 2 days if possible. Turn the pork
2 or 3 times daily as it absorbs some of the liquid.
Simmer the bones in well seasoned water, make
about 2 pints (1¼ litres – 5 cups) stock as you may
need extra for the sauce.
Lift the pork from the marinade, let it drain over the
container, then pat dry with absorbent paper.
Spread half the butter or dripping over the pork
before cooking, unless very fat, then omit *most* of
this. To roast, allow 25 minutes per lb. (½ kilo) and
25 minutes over, above centre of a moderately hot
oven, 375–400°F. (190–200°C.), Gas Mark 5–6.
Slice the 4 onions and put in the tin with seasoning
about 45 minutes before the meat is cooked.
Cut the bacon into fairly large pieces, fry in a large
pan, add the thickly sliced mushrooms, rice and
1½ pints (9 dl. – 4 cups) stock. Bring to the boil, stir
briskly, season if necessary, cover pan, lower heat
and cook for 15 minutes. Lift the marinated
vegetables from the wine. Toss in the remaining
butter or dripping, then blend in the flour. Add the
strained liquid from the marinade and stir over a
low heat until thickened. If the sauce is too thick
stir in a small quantity of stock. Season well.
Lift the pork from the roasting tin, put on to a hot
dish, sprinkle with the warmed brandy, ignite this.
Spoon a little fat from the tin into the wine sauce.
Arrange the sliced pork, or the whole joint, on the
rice mixture, top with the well drained onion rings
and the sage from the marinade, see picture page
143. Serve the sauce separately.

For Economy The recipe above is an ideal way of
making an average joint serve a good number.
Freezing If using a frozen joint, thaw out *before*
putting into marinade.

Easy Stews

Do not imagine that every stew has to be cooked for a long time. The following recipe, using cooked tongue, is ready within minutes.

Tongue in Raisin Sauce

Imperial/Metric	American
medium can tongue or 12 oz. (300 g.) sliced cooked tongue	medium can tongue or $\frac{3}{4}$ lb. sliced cooked tongue
for the sauce	for the sauce
2 oz. (50 g.) butter or margarine	$\frac{1}{4}$ cup butter or margarine
1 oz. (25 g.) blanched almonds	just under $\frac{1}{4}$ cup blanched almonds
$\frac{1}{4}$ pint (1$\frac{1}{2}$ dl.) red wine plus 3 tablespoons	$\frac{2}{3}$ cup red wine plus 4 tablespoons
$\frac{1}{4}$ pint (1$\frac{1}{2}$ dl.) stock or water	$\frac{2}{3}$ cup stock or water
4 oz. (100 g.) seedless raisins	$\frac{2}{3}$ cup seedless raisins
1 tablespoon cornflour	1 tablespoon cornstarch
1–2 tablespoons vinegar	1–2 tablespoons vinegar
1 oz. (25 g.) sugar or 1 tablespoon honey	2 tablespoons sugar or 1 tablespoon honey

Cooking time 15–20 minutes
Serves 4
Advance Preparations Make sauce for reheating.

Heat the butter or margarine in a pan and brown the almonds. Lift out of the pan. Blend in the $\frac{1}{4}$ pint (1$\frac{1}{2}$ dl. – $\frac{2}{3}$ cup) wine and stock or water. Bring to the boil, add the raisins. Blend the cornflour with the remaining wine, stir into the liquid and bring to the boil, stir until thickened. Add the rest of the sauce ingredients (except nuts). Put the sliced tongue into the mixture, heat for a few minutes then add the nuts.

For Economy Omit wine, use all water with a very little brown vinegar to flavour.

Beef Olives This well known stew (or casserole) is shown in the picture on page 59. It may be cooked in advance and reheated when required.
Buy 4–6 thin slices of topside (round) of beef or stewing steak (allow 1 large slice or 2 smaller ones per person). Make a stuffing; the recipes on page 58 give parsley stuffings, and one of these is the usual choice; but use any other you prefer. Spread the stuffing over the slices of meat and tie or skewer firmly. Toss the rolls of meat in well seasoned flour and fry in a little hot fat (shortening). Lift out of the pan, toss any vegetables required in the fat, the picture shows small onions and mushrooms, but other vegetables could be used. Stir in about $\frac{3}{4}$ pint (4$\frac{1}{2}$ dl. – 2 cups) brown stock or water and 1 stock (bouillon) cube. Bring the sauce to the boil, stir until thickened. Replace the beef rolls in the sauce, cover the pan and simmer gently for 1$\frac{1}{2}$–2$\frac{1}{2}$ hours, depending upon the tenderness of the beef – topside would need the shorter cooking time. If more convenient transfer to a casserole, cover tightly and cook for the same time in a slow to very moderate oven, 300–325°F. (150–170°C.), Gas Mark 2–3. Serve with cooked rice (recipe for cooking long grain rice is on page 146). Remember to remove the cotton or skewers before lifting the meat rolls and vegetables on to the hot serving dish. *Serves 4–6.*

For Economy Use stewing steak and the longer cooking time.
Freezing This dish freezes well, reheat from the frozen state; use within 3 months.
Veal Birds Use thin slices of stewing veal instead of beef and roll round a stuffing.

To Serve with Stews

Noodles or boiled rice, see recipe below, are ideal accompaniments to this and other casseroles. Instructions for cooking pasta are on page 109.

Boiled Rice Choose long grain type rice. Either cook the rice in plenty of boiling salted water until tender, strain, rinse in cold or boiling water, spread out on flat dishes and heat gently; or put the rice with twice the amount of water (if pre-fluffed rice) and salt to taste, or $2\frac{1}{2}$ times the amount of water if ordinary long grain rice (i.e. 1 cup rice to $2-2\frac{1}{2}$ cups water) in a pan, bring the water to boiling, stir, cover the pan and simmer for 15 minutes. No stirring or straining is necessary, the rice absorbs all the water.

Beef Casserole

Imperial/Metric	American
1–1½ lb. (½–¾ kilo) stewing beef*	*1–1½ lb. stewing beef**
2 rashers streaky bacon	*2 bacon slices*
seasoning	*seasoning*
1 oz. (25 g.) flour	*¼ cup flour*
1 oz. (25 g.) lard or dripping	*2 tablespoons shortening or drippings*
4 small carrots	*4 small carrots*
4 medium potatoes	*4 medium potatoes*
1 level teaspoon made mustard	*1 level teaspoon made mustard*
¾ pint (4½ dl.) stock or water and 1 beef stock cube	*just under 2 cups stock or water and 1 beef bouillon cube*
3–4 oz. (75–100 g.) cooked peas or sweetcorn	*about ¾ cup cooked peas or sweetcorn*
4–8 pickled onions	*4–8 pickled onions*
to serve	**to serve**
creamed spinach	*creamed spinach*

* choosing beef for a casserole dish: use skirt, chuck, 'leg of mutton' cut, bladebone, brisket, flank (shoulder, chuck, round, brisket, flank). For more luxurious dish, choose rump steak.

Cooking time   2 hours 10 minutes
Serves 4
Advance Preparations Cook casserole beforehand and reheat thoroughly when required.

Dice the meat neatly and chop the bacon. Roll the meat in the seasoned flour. Heat the lard or dripping and toss the meat and bacon in this for several minutes. Transfer to a casserole, then add the peeled quartered carrots and potatoes, the mustard blended with the stock, or water and stock cube. Cover the casserole tightly and cook for $1\frac{1}{2}$ hours in the centre of a very moderate oven, 325–350°F. (170–180°C.), Gas Mark 3–4. Add the peas or sweetcorn and the pickled onions and cook for a further 30 minutes, or until the meat is very tender. Serve hot with creamed spinach and mustard.

Variation

Diced green pepper can be added with the carrots.

Cooking Bacon

Bacon (smoked ham) whether cut into rashers (slices) or as a joint is an ideal meat for easy cooking.
To Fry Bacon Rashers Cut away the rinds, but fry these in the pan, either before, or with the rashers, to provide extra fat. It is a good idea to lay the rashers in the pan so the fat of one rasher is under the lean of the next. In this way you should require little, if any, fat in the pan for cooking. Put the bacon into an *unheated* pan then fry fairly quickly.
To Grill (Broil) Bacon It is a mistake to preheat the grill first. The bacon should be put under a cold grill, *then* the grill heated. In this way you prevent the fat from curling and burning at the edges. When grilling thick bacon rashers or slices of gammon (Canadian bacon or ham butt) snip the fat at regular intervals, so it does not curl. Slices of pineapple and other canned or fresh fruit can be heated towards the end of the cooking time and these make a pleasant change from tomatoes, mushrooms, etc.
The recipe that follows is for a joint of prime bacon, i.e. gammon (smoked ham – shank half or butt half). Cheaper cuts can be used if the cooking time is lengthened to 35–40 minutes per lb. gentle simmering.

Treacle Glazed Gammon

Imperial/Metric	American
5 lb. (2½ kilos) middle gammon	5 lb. smoked ham, butt half
4 tablespoons black treacle	5 tablespoons molasses
12 peppercorns	12 peppercorns
1 bay leaf	1 bay leaf
¼ pint (1½ dl.) dry cider	⅔ cup dry cider
to garnish	**to garnish**
cloves	cloves

Cooking time 2½ hours
Serves 8–10
Advance Preparations Soak the gammon overnight.

If using a mild or sweet cure, rinse the gammon in cold running water, place in a saucepan and cover with fresh cold water. If using well salted gammon soak overnight in cold water. Add 2 tablespoons (3 tablespoons) black treacle (molasses), the peppercorns and the bay leaf; bring slowly to the boil and *simmer* for 1½ hours (water must never continue boiling). Drain the joint, strip off the skin and score the fat into diamonds with a sharp knife. Warm the remaining 2 tablespoons (3 tablespoons) black treacle and pour over the fat surface. Place the joint in a roasting tin and pour the cider over the top. Cook for approximately 1 hour in the centre of a very moderate oven, 350–375°F. (180–190°C.). Gas Mark 4–5, basting frequently with the cider. Decorate with cloves and serve hot with vegetables. This is also delicious served cold with salad. If serving cold, allow to cool in the cider.

Variation
Use half treacle, half golden (corn) syrup or honey.

Desserts and Savouries

Easy Desserts

Most men are not particularly fond of making desserts, but the following are simple yet very delicious.

Rings of Fresh Pineapple Sprinkle with a little Kirsch; other fresh fruits can be served in the same way. To prepare the pineapple cut fairly thick slices; then cut away the skin with kitchen scissors or a knife. Remove the centre hard core.

Fresh Fruit Salad Peel apples, pears, bananas and cut into neat slices; sprinkle with lemon juice to keep a good colour. Cut away the peel from oranges and cut the segments away from the skin. Mix together and moisten with orange juice or Kirsch, or use a small can of fruit (pineapple, peaches, etc.), which will provide syrup and additional fruit; slice the canned fruit neatly.

Ice Cream With hot sauces, e.g. melted chocolate (melt plain chocolate in a basin over hot, but not boiling water), or melt fudge or peppermint creams.

Spiced Bananas

Imperial/Metric	American
½ pint (3 dl.) cheap red wine	1¼ cups cheap red wine
2 tablespoons redcurrant jelly	3 tablespoons red currant jelly
½–1 teaspoon mixed spice	½–1 teaspoon mixed spice
4–6 firm bananas	4–6 firm bananas
to decorate	**to decorate**
1 oz. (25 g.) blanched almonds	just under ¼ cup blanched almonds
to serve	**to serve**
cream or ice cream	cream or ice cream

Cooking time *few minutes*
Serves 4–6
Advance Preparations Prepare earlier in day.

Heat the wine, jelly and spice together for a few minutes; stir to blend in the jelly. Cool slightly. Pour over whole or sliced bananas. Top with almonds. Serve warm or cold with cream or ice cream.

Lemon and Port Wine Jelly

Imperial/Metric	American
1 lemon-flavoured jelly	1 package lemon-flavored gelatin
just over ½ pint (3 dl.) water	just over 1¼ cups water
¼ pint (1½ dl.) cheap port wine	⅔ cup cheap port wine
¼ pint (1½ dl.) thick cream	⅔ cup whipping cream
to decorate	**to decorate**
2 oz. (50 g.) blanched almonds, split	just under ½ cup blanched almonds, split

Cooking time *few minutes to melt jelly*
Serves 4
Advance Preparations Make jelly, allow to set.

Dissolve the jelly in the very hot water, cool slightly then add the port wine. Allow to cool and stiffen slightly, then blend in the lightly whipped cream.

Put into a mould; when set decorate with almonds.

Variations
Omit cream, add extra ¼ pint (1½ dl. – ⅔ cup) water.
Marshmallow Jelly Make up a fruit-flavoured jelly – lemon, orange, lime – and when it is cool add 2–3 chopped marshmallows. Put into a mould to set.

Savouries

A savoury is an excellent alternative to a dessert at the end of a meal; or rather more generous portions can be served for a light supper or luncheon dish. The recipes on this page serve 4 people as a light main dish, or 6–8 for after-dinner savouries.

Welsh Rarebit There are many recipes for this classic dish, but the following is simple and very good. Grate 12–14 oz. (300–350 g.) Cheddar or Gruyère or Double Gloucester cheese. Blend this with 2 oz. (50 g. – ¼ cup) butter, 1–2 teaspoons made-mustard, a shake salt and pinch cayenne pepper. Add either 1 tablespoon milk and 1 tablespoon beer, or 2 tablespoons beer, or 1 egg yolk and 1 tablespoon beer, or milk and a few drops of Worcestershire sauce. Toast and butter 4 good size or 6–8 small slices of bread, spread with the rarebit mixture and brown under the grill (broiler). For a softer mixture use a little more liquid.

Hawaiian Rarebit Top the rarebit mixture with rings of pineapple and heat under the grill.
York Rarebit Put slices of cooked ham on the buttered toast, top with the rarebit and brown under the grill.

Devils on Horseback Wrap cooked and stoned prunes in small rashers (slices) of bacon. Grill until the bacon is crisp. Serve on buttered toast.

Angels on Horseback Wrap large oysters in the bacon instead of prunes; season lightly and sprinkle with lemon juice. Grill until the bacon is crisp. Serve on buttered toast.

Making Soufflés

A soufflé is an ideal savoury with which to end a meal, as well as a complete light luncheon dish. A cheese soufflé recipe is on page 129. Cheese may be added to the mushroom mixture in the recipe below.

Mushroom Soufflé

Imperial/Metric	American
4 oz. (100 g.) mushrooms	1 cup mushrooms
¼ pint (1½ dl.) milk	⅔ cup milk
1 oz. (25 g.) butter or margarine	2 tablespoons butter or margarine
1 oz. (25 g.) flour	¼ cup flour
4 tablespoons thin or thick cream	5 tablespoons coffee or whipping cream
4 eggs	4 eggs
seasoning	seasoning

Cooking time 50 minutes
Serves 4
Advance Preparations Cook mushrooms, weigh out rest of ingredients; do not separate eggs until ready to cook dish.

Chop the mushrooms and simmer for 5 minutes in the milk. Heat butter or margarine, stir in flour and cook for 2–3 minutes over low heat. Gradually blend in the mushrooms and liquid, then the cream. Bring to the boil, stir until thickened. Add egg yolks, seasoning, and fold in the stiffly whisked egg whites. Put into a buttered 6–7-inch (15–18-cm.) soufflé dish and bake for 30–35 minutes in the centre of a moderate oven, 375°F. (190°C.), Gas Mark 5.

For Economy Use mushroom stalks or try:
Speedy Mushroom Soufflé Heat a can of condensed mushroom soup. Blend 1 tablespoon cornflour (cornstarch) with 3 tablespoons (4 tablespoons) milk, stir into soup, cook until thickened. Add 3 egg yolks, then 3 stiffly whisked egg whites. Cook as above.

Pears Stuffed with Iced Cheese and Pimento

Imperial/Metric	American
lettuce	lettuce
1 lemon	1 lemon
4 large dessert pears	4 large dessert pears
for the filling	for the filling
4–6 oz. (100–150 g.) Cheddar or Cheshire cheese	$\frac{1}{4}$– $\frac{3}{8}$ lb. Cheddar or Cheshire cheese
1 canned or fresh red pepper	1 canned pimiento or fresh red pepper
1$\frac{1}{2}$–2 tablespoons mayonnaise	2–3 tablespoons mayonnaise
3 tablespoons thick cream	4 tablespoons whipping cream
seasoning (optional)	seasoning (optional)

No cooking
Serves 4 or gives 8 small portions
Advance Preparations Freeze cheese mixture, do not prepare pears until ready to serve.

This dish is equally good as an hors d'oeuvre or an original savoury for the end of the meal.
Grate the cheese very finely. Chop the well drained canned or fresh red pepper: discard the core and seeds from a fresh pepper. Mix the cheese, pepper, mayonnaise and cream. Add a little seasoning, if desired, and mix briskly until a fairly firm mixture. Form into 8 balls. Frost these in the freezing compartment of the refrigerator for 1–1$\frac{1}{2}$ hours. Wash and dry the lettuce and arrange on the serving dish. Squeeze the juice from the lemon. Halve the pears lengthways; do not peel. Scoop out the cores and sprinkle the pears with lemon juice and place the dish over a bed of ice. Put the iced cheese balls into the centre of each halved pear.

Speedy Savouries

The picture above shows a very simple, but appetising sandwich that could be served as a savoury; other quick and easy suggestions are below.

Olive Pin Wheels Cut thin slices of bread from a fresh loaf; it is more effective if you cut the slices down the length of the loaf. Spread the slices with butter and soft liver pâté. There is a recipe for chicken liver pâté on page 170. If using bought liver pâté, you may find this a little stiff for spreading, in which case blend with a small quantity of butter or thick (whipping) cream.

Arrange a line of Spanish stuffed olives along one long end of each slice, then roll up, as if making a Swiss roll, with the olives in the centre. Keep covered with damp paper, or a damp cloth or foil, until almost ready to serve. Cut into neat slices with a sharp knife.

Note Fresh bread should roll easily, but bread becomes even more pliable if you press each slice with a rolling pin before spreading.

To vary this sandwich, use soft cream cheese or cheese spread instead of liver pâté.

Mushrooms on Toast Wash, but do not peel, small mushrooms. Fry for 5–6 minutes in hot butter or dripping (drippings) and serve on hot buttered toast.

The mushrooms can be topped with grated cheese and put for 1–2 minutes under a hot grill (broiler).

Roes on Toast Wash and dry fresh soft herring roes. Either heat slowly in a little well seasoned milk for 6–8 minutes, or put the roes on to a large plate. Add a little milk or thin (coffee) cream, butter and seasoning. Cover with a second plate or a saucepan lid. Steam over a pan of boiling water for 10–12 minutes until tender. Spoon carefully on to hot buttered toast and garnish with parsley and paprika or cayenne pepper.

Sardines on Toast Put well drained canned sardines on to hot buttered toast. Garnish with twists of lemon and tomatoes. The sardines can be sprinkled with grated Parmesan cheese and put for 1–2 minutes under a hot grill (broiler).

Scotch Woodcock Scramble eggs lightly, spoon on to buttered toast. Top with well drained canned anchovy fillets and capers; or I like sliced olives for a garnish.

151

Cookery for Children

This chapter is meant to suggest some of the dishes that children will enjoy, but also ideas that children may cook for themselves. The tips for children to read are on this page, below.

If you plan meals for a small child try and combine these with family cooking. As soon as the baby starts mixed feeding you can take out a small portion of the family meal and sieve this or put it into your liquidiser (blender) and emulsify the ingredients, so they are a smooth purée. Never give a baby or young toddler pips, skin, small bones or highly spiced foods. As the child gets older introduce as many new flavours as possible. Many adults are very conservative about food and will not try new ideas; often this is because their diet was very restricted and monotonous when they were young, so they never developed the habit of experimenting with new dishes.

Children need adequate amounts of protein, fats, vitamins and minerals. They also must have some carbohydrates (starchy foods and sugars), but they should be limited. A child who 'fills up' on too many buns, iced lollies, etc., is often overweight and has dental problems.

Make meal times enjoyable times for all the family and try and introduce interesting ways of presenting foods; for example, try kebabs, see picture page 155, which give meat, etc., a new look. Let the children help you with the cooking, so they have a good reason for eating the dishes afterwards.

The Importance of Milk

Many children enjoy milk and will drink it without trouble. Other children dislike this important food and it has to be 'disguised' in a palatable fashion.

Milk Shakes These are one of the most attractive and appetising milk drinks. Use special flavoured syrups or fresh fruit or a little chocolate powder or coffee. Add ice or ice cream for *really* cold milk shakes. Put the flavouring with cold milk and a small amount of crushed ice or ice cream into the liquidiser (blender); switch on to high speed for about 30–50 seconds, then serve. If you have no electric liquidiser, whisk the ingredients in a basin or tall jug. Use hot milk for cold weather milk shakes; in which case avoid acid fruits which could cause the milk to curdle.

Other ways of serving milk are in junkets (page 157), as a milky sauce (see recipes page 61) over vegetables, fish, etc., or in meat or chicken dishes (see page 128). Milk and eggs are used in the home-made ice cream recipe on the opposite page.

Tips for Children

It is fun to be left to cook for your family or friends, but there are many things to consider before starting.

Safety This means care when handling knives (always ask an adult to show you the right way to cut or chop foods).

Check you know how to ignite a gas cooker or switch on an electric one; it is often wiser to get an adult to do this.

Make certain the handles of pans full of hot food are turned towards the centre of the cooker.

Always get an adult to bring hot food from the oven, or lift heavy pans from the cooker.

Method Check the recipe ingredients carefully to make certain you have everything required.

You will find cooking easier if you weigh out or measure all the ingredients for the recipe before you begin. Clear up as you go; nothing looks worse than an untidy kitchen.

Easy Menus

An Italian Menu

There are many easy and interesting dishes that come from Italian kitchens. On this page is a typical menu, which is not too difficult. Make the ice cream in plenty of time, so it will set. Prepare all the ingredients for the risotto and you can start to cook this before the meal, and reheat at the last minute. Do not over-cook the rice though, otherwise it will become sticky and unappetising. If you enjoy Italian food look up the spaghetti recipes in the index, for they provide cheap and very varied meals.

Liver Risotto

Imperial/Metric	American
1 onion	1 onion
2 tablespoons olive oil or 2 oz. (50 g.) margarine	3 tablespoons olive oil or ¼ cup margarine
6 oz. (150 g.) long grain rice	just under 1 cup long grain rice
¾ pint (4½ dl.) water and ½ chicken stock cube	2 cups water and ½ chicken bouillon cube
8 oz. (200 g.) lambs' or calves' liver, sliced	½ lb. lamb or calf liver, sliced
small can tomatoes	small can tomatoes
good pinch salt	good pinch salt
shake pepper	shake pepper
small can peas or packet frozen peas	small can peas or packet frozen peas
3–4 tablespoons grated cheese*	4–5 tablespoons grated cheese*

* this can be Cheddar, Gruyère, Parmesan or any other cheese you like.

Cooking time 30 minutes
Serves 4
Advance Preparations Prepare all the ingredients. If you want to cook this dish beforehand, use a little extra water so the mixture does not become too stiff when reheated.

First peel and chop or slice the onion. Heat the oil or margarine in a good size saucepan. Add the onion and cook for 2–3 minutes only. Move the saucepan away from the heat and tip in the rice. Stir this round in the oil or margarine until all the grains look greasy. Add the water and stock (bouillon) cube and heat steadily, then simmer gently for 10 minutes. Stir once or twice to make sure the rice is moving round in the liquid. Meanwhile, cut the liver into ½–1-inch (1–2-cm.) pieces. Put the liver, the tomatoes and any liquid from the can, together with the salt and pepper and the peas, into the rice mixture. Continue cooking for another 15 minutes until the rice is tender. A risotto should be stiff enough to spoon out of the saucepan on to hot plates or a hot dish and to pile quite neatly. Top each serving with grated cheese and eat at once.

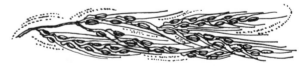

Economical Ice Cream Most people enjoy ice cream and this is a very economical way of making it. Separate the yolks from the whites of 2 eggs. Beat the yolks with 2 oz. (50 g. – ¼ cup) sugar. Add ½ pint (3 dl. – 1¼ cups) warm milk. Cook this mixture in the top of a double saucepan over hot, but not boiling, water until the custard coats the back of a wooden spoon. Stir as the mixture cools, then blend in a little flavouring: this can be ½ teaspoon vanilla essence (extract), 1 oz. (25 g. – ¼ cup) chocolate powder, or 3–4 oz. (75–100 g. – ½ cup) mashed fruit. Whip ½ pint (3 dl. – 1¼ cups) full cream unsweetened evaporated milk (page 131 tells you about this) while the custard cools. Fold the whipped evaporated milk into the custard. Spoon into 1 or 2 freezing trays and freeze as quickly as possible until the ice cream begins to stiffen, this will take about 45 minutes. Whisk 2 egg whites until very stiff. Spoon the ice cream out of the freezing trays into a mixing bowl. Beat until frothy then fold in the two stiffly whisked egg whites. Put back again into the freezing trays and continue freezing.

Party Loaf

Imperial/Metric	American
1 large loaf	1 large loaf
choose one of these fillings	**choose one of these fillings**
a) 8 oz. (200 g.) cream cheese	**a)** 1 cup cream cheese
seasoning	seasoning
4 oz. (100 g.) margarine	½ cup margarine
b) 8 oz. (200 g.) liver sausage	**b)** ½ lb. liver sausage
seasoning	seasoning
4 oz. (100 g.) margarine	½ cup margarine
c) can sardines	**c)** can sardines
2 level teaspoons curry paste or powder	2 level teaspoons curry paste or powder
seasoning	seasoning
4 oz. (100 g.) margarine	½ cup margarine
d) 8 oz. (200 g.) cottage cheese	**d)** 1 cup cottage cheese
seasoning	seasoning
squeeze lemon juice	squeeze lemon juice
4 oz. (100 g.) margarine	½ cup margarine
to decorate	**to decorate**
6 oz. (150 g.) salted peanuts	just under 1 cup salted peanuts
to garnish	**to garnish**
pineapple	pineapple
parsley or watercress	parsley or watercress
radish rose	radish rose

No cooking
Serves 6—8
Advance Preparations Prepare loaf, do not decorate or garnish, wrap in foil or polythene. Store in refrigerator for up to 24 hours.

Choose the selected filling, in each case blend the flavouring with the margarine – you can use all one filling, or half quantity of two different ones, or a quarter quantity of the four fillings. Remove all the crusts from the loaf, then slice this lengthways to give 4 long slices. Spread one slice with the filling, then put on second slice and cover – continue like this until the loaf is put together again. Save about one-third of the filling for coating the loaf. Coat the top and sides, not the ends, with the remaining filling. Press the chopped salted peanuts against this. Garnish with pineapple, parsley or watercress and radish rose before serving. Slice fairly thickly to serve.

Note To cut fairly fresh bread: dip bread knife in hot water, shake fairly dry and use while warm.
Freezing This filled loaf freezes very well with any of the fillings listed. Use within 1 month.

Cheese Kebabs Most of the countries round the Mediterranean, Greece, Turkey, etc., serve various kinds of kebab. In the picture above, cheese and meat together make a delicious meal. Make small meat balls as the recipe on page 41, flour these, then fry until golden. coloured. If you feel these are too difficult then use tender rump or fillet steak, or other tender meat, or sausages instead. Grill (broil) the meat or sausages until tender, then cut into neat pieces. Put the meat balls, or pieces of meat, or sliced sausages and cubes of Cheddar cheese and quartered tomato, or pieces of red and green pepper on to metal skewers. Cook these kebabs under a hot grill, turning them *carefully*, for several minutes. Serve with boiled rice (see page 146) or with mashed potatoes or crisp rolls and butter.

A refreshing dessert to follow the kebabs is given below.

Grape and Orange Snow

Imperial/Metric	American
1 orange-flavoured jelly	1 package orange-flavored gelatin
$\frac{1}{2}$ pint (3 dl.) water, very hot or boiling	1$\frac{1}{4}$ cups water, very hot or boiling
$\frac{1}{4}$ pint (1$\frac{1}{2}$ dl.) fresh or canned orange juice	$\frac{2}{3}$ cup fresh or canned orange juice
2 egg whites	2 egg whites
6 oz. (150 g.) grapes	$\frac{1}{3}$ lb. grapes
to decorate	**to decorate**
little thick cream	little whipping cream
grapes	grapes

No cooking
Serves 4—6

Make up the jelly, but use only the $\frac{1}{2}$ pint (3 dl. — 1$\frac{1}{4}$ cups) water. Cool, then add the orange juice.

Allow to begin to stiffen, whisk sharply, adding the stiffly whisked egg whites and the skinned and de-seeded grapes. Spoon into 4—6 sundae glasses and top with whipped cream and whole grapes (not skinned).

155

Menu for a Snack Meal

This would be a good meal for your friends when they come in to spend an evening with you. A salad could be served with the tomato gouda pie. If everyone is very hungry have cups of canned or home-made soup to start the meal (there are many recipes for soup in this book). As puff pastry is quite difficult to make I suggest you buy frozen puff pastry, let it thaw out sufficiently to roll it out. Make the chocolate cake some time beforehand, so it has time to harden. Serve fresh fruit to end the meal.

Tomato Gouda Pie

Imperial/Metric	American
12 oz. (340 g.) frozen puff pastry*	¾ lb. frozen puff paste*
8–10 oz. (200–250 g.) Gouda cheese	about ½ lb. Gouda cheese
4–5 tomatoes	4–5 tomatoes
2–3 oz. (50–75 g.) mushrooms	2–3 oz. mushrooms
seasoning	seasoning
1 oz. (25 g.) butter (melted)	2 tablespoons melted butter

* or home-made puff pastry with 6 oz. (150 g. — 1½ cups) flour, etc. (see page 218).

Cooking time 25–30 minutes
Serves 4 as a main dish, 6–8 as a snack
Advance Preparations Prepare pastry case and topping.

Roll out the pastry until it is large enough to line a Swiss roll tin (jelly roll pan) measuring approximately 10 inches (25 cm.) × 8 inches (20 cm.). Put the pastry into the tin, cut away any untidy edges. Prick the base of the pastry. Cut the cheese into thin slices and put over the pastry. Slice the tomatoes and mushrooms and arrange on top of the cheese (see the picture on page 111). Add a very little seasoning and brush the butter over the top of the vegetables. Bake for 15–20 minutes in the centre of a hot to very hot oven, 425–450°F. (220–230°C.), Gas Mark 7–8, until the pastry has turned golden coloured, then lower the heat to moderate, 350–375°F. (180–190°C.), Gas Mark 4–5, and allow another 10 minutes cooking. Cut into slices and serve hot. *Illustrated on page 111.*

Uncooked Chocolate Cake

Imperial/Metric	American
2 oz. (50 g.) butter	¼ cup butter
2 tablespoons golden syrup	3 tablespoons light corn syrup
3 oz. (75 g.) sugar	6 tablespoons sugar
2 oz. (50 g.) cocoa or chocolate powder	½ cup unsweetened cocoa or chocolate powder
few drops vanilla essence	few drops vanilla extract
6 oz. (150 g.) crisp breadcrumbs (raspings)	1½ cups crisp bread crumbs (raspings)
to decorate (optional)	**to decorate** (optional)
halved nuts, or 4 oz. (100 g.) plain chocolate	halved nuts, or ¼ lb. semi-sweet chocolate

No cooking
Serves 10
Advance Preparations Can be made several days ahead.

Melt the butter, syrup and sugar in a saucepan, remove from heat, stir in the sieved cocoa or chocolate powder and vanilla essence and continue stirring until smooth. Lastly add the breadcrumbs. Grease a 7-inch (18-cm.) square or round sandwich tin (layer cake pan), press the mixture into the tin and allow to stand for several hours.

To decorate, this cake may either be dotted with halved nuts before it is set, or covered with melted chocolate.

Desserts and Baking

Some Desserts
When you require an easy light dessert and you have plenty of milk make this:
Junket Heat 1 pint (6 dl. – 2½ cups) milk to blood heat (it should feel just warm to the touch). Stir in 1 tablespoon sugar, and then the amount of rennet recommended on the bottle (generally 1 teaspoon). Pour into 4 dishes and leave to clot at room temperature, *then* put into the refrigerator.

Fruit 'Tartlets'

Imperial/Metric	American
12 slices thin fresh bread	12 slices thin fresh bread
2 oz. (50 g.) butter	¼ cup butter
little sugar	little sugar
about 1 lb. (½ kilo) fruit	about 1 lb. fruit
¼ pint (1½ dl.) thick cream	⅔ cup whipping cream

Cooking time 10 minutes
Makes 12 tartlets
Advance Preparations Cook tartlet cases.

Ideally the bread should be very fresh, so it can be moulded easily, but if inclined to be firm in texture roll each slice with a rolling pin until thin and pliable. Cut off the crusts if desired. Brush patty tins (tartlet pans) with a little melted butter, press the slices of bread into these – they can be cut in rounds to give a neat tartlet case (shell), but squares of bread give almost a 'tulip' shape. Brush the bread with melted butter and sprinkle with a very little sugar. Bake for approximately 10 minutes above centre of a hot oven, 425°F. (220°C.), Gas Mark 7, until crisp and golden brown. Cool. Fill with fresh fruit and top with whipped cream. Glaze the fruit by brushing with a little melted apple or redcurrant jelly, if liked.

Tasmania Pudding

Imperial/Metric	American
4 sponge cakes	¼ lb. yellow sponge or layer cake
1 oz. (25 g.) glacé cherries	2 tablespoons candied cherries
3 egg yolks	3 egg yolks
1½ oz. (40 g.) sugar	3 tablespoons sugar
little vanilla essence	little vanilla extract
¾ pint (4½ dl.) milk	2 cups milk
little jam	little jam
for the meringue	**for the meringue**
3 egg whites	3 egg whites
3 oz. (75 g.) sugar	6 tablespoons sugar

Cooking time 1 hour 10 minutes
Serves 4–6
Advance Preparations Prepare ingredients.

Dice the sponge cakes, put into a greased dish with the chopped cherries. Beat egg yolks and sugar, add the vanilla essence and warm milk, pour or strain over sponge cakes. Bake for 50 minutes in the centre of a very moderate oven, 325°F. (170°C.), Gas Mark 3, until firm. Spread with the jam. Whisk the egg whites until very stiff, fold in the sugar, pile on top of pudding and return to oven for about 20 minutes until crisp and golden brown. Serve hot.

Cakes

The picture and recipe on page 159, opposite, show a very special cake, which is not difficult to make. On this page are some small cakes, which are even easier to make. Nowadays a special soft margarine means that you can mix all the ingredients together for a very short time only, see the recipe below. If you have not bought the soft margarine (often called luxury margarine) then you must cream the margarine and sugar together first until the mixture is soft and light, then add the eggs, then the sieved flour and baking powder.

Funny Face Cakes

Imperial/Metric	American
4 oz. (100 g.) plain flour	1 cup all-purpose flour
2 level teaspoons baking powder	2 teaspoons baking powder (double-acting)
4 oz. (100 g.) castor sugar	½ cup granulated sugar
4 oz. (100 g.) easy creaming (luxury) margarine	½ cup easy creaming (luxury) margarine
2 eggs	2 eggs
for the icing	for the icing
10 oz. (250 g.) sieved icing sugar	2½ cups sifted confectioners' sugar
3 tablespoons water or lemon juice or orange juice	4 tablespoons water or lemon juice or orange juice
to decorate	to decorate
chocolate sweets (see picture)	chocolate sweets (see picture)
angelica	angelica
currants	currants
chocolate vermicelli or grated chocolate	chocolate vermicelli or grated chocolate

Cooking time 10–12 minutes
Makes approximately 24
Advance Preparations Make the cakes, allow to cool ready for icing.

Sieve the flour and baking powder into a mixing bowl. Add the sugar, the margarine and the eggs. It is a good idea to break each egg into a cup first to make sure they are quite fresh. Stand the bowl on a folded glass-cloth (dish towel), so it does not slip on the table when you mix the ingredients. Beat all the ingredients together until well blended, this takes up to 2 minutes. Stand about 24 paper cases on flat baking trays or stand them inside patty tins (muffin pans); this makes them hold their shape better. Spoon the mixture into the paper cases. Bake for 10–12 minutes above the centre of a hot oven, 400–425°F. (200–220°C.), Gas Mark 6–7, until the little cakes feel firm to the touch. Let the cakes cool before topping with icing. Mix the icing (confectioners') sugar with the water, lemon or orange juice. Spoon a little on top of each cake and spread with a small flat bladed knife. Wait for about 20–30 minutes until the very soft icing begins to stiffen; do not let it become too stiff otherwise the decorations will not 'stick'. Decorate the top of each

Doll's House Cake

For the Cake Cream 14 oz. (350 g. – 1¾ cups) butter and 14 oz. (350 g. – 1¾ cups) castor (granulated) sugar. Mix 6 large eggs and 2 tablespoons (3 tablespoons) milk – make certain the tablespoons are absolutely full. Sieve together 12 oz. (300 g. – 3 cups) self-raising (self-rising) flour, 2 oz. (50 g. – ½ cup) cocoa powder and 1 *level* teaspoon of baking powder (double-acting). If you use plain (all-purpose) flour then add 4 *level* teaspoons baking powder. Gradually beat the egg and milk into the creamed ingredients, add a little flour and cocoa so the mixture does not curdle. Gently fold in remaining flour and cocoa. You should have a soft dropping consistency; if necessary add a few more *drops* of milk. Grease and flour an 8-inch (20-cm.) square and a 6-inch (15-cm.) square deep cake tin (pan). Divide mixture between the tins, put just over half into the larger one. Bake the smaller cake for approximately 40–45 minutes and the larger for at least an hour in the centre of a very moderate to moderate oven, 325–350°F. (170–180°C.), Gas Mark 3–4. If the cakes appear to be getting too brown after half an hour, lower the heat slightly. Turn out carefully; cool.

For the Decoration Cream 1 lb. (½ kilo – 2 cups) butter with 2 lb. (1 kilo – 7 cups) sieved icing (sifted confectioners') sugar. Cut the larger cake in half down the centre. Cut the smaller cake in half diagonally. Coat the pieces of cake with butter icing, put them together. The two rectangles become the house; the triangular pieces form the roof. Coat the whole of the outside of the house with a little butter icing. Put on to a cake board. Divide the remaining butter icing into three. Colour one-third green with a few drops of culinary colouring and use this for the grass with a marshmallow path. Blend the second third with 1 tablespoon cocoa powder, dissolved in a little boiling water, and use this to pipe the wood beams and side windows. Leave the remaining icing uncoloured. Take two small thin bars of chocolate: cut off one-third of one bar for a window, use the remainder for the door. Cut the second bar into two squares and four triangles. Press the door and windows etc., in position, see picture. Use a fine writing pipe and the uncoloured icing for the panes on the windows, door handle, etc. Make a chimney. Finally press chocolate buttons over the icing for the roof. *Serves up to 20 small portions.*

Thirty-Minute Dishes and Menus

This chapter gives some of the quick dishes in the book. Although there will be others you can make when short of time, I felt it would be useful to have several menus collected together so you can produce meals within approximately thirty minutes.

We are very fortunate today in having a wide range of canned, dehydrated and frozen foods; if you keep a reasonable selection of these in your home you should always be able to produce a meal for the family and friends within a very short time. Here are some suggested menus:

Crabmeat Appetiser (below)	Cold or Hot Grapefruit (page 125)
Grilled Lamb Cutlets (page 137) with Frozen Beans and	Tomato Piperade (page 161)
Potato Crisps	Sponge Croûtes (page 161)
Fresh Fruit	
Plantation Ham Rolls (page 162)	Prawn and Fruit Cocktail (page 163)
Mocha Sundae (page 162)	Savoury Omelette (pages 104–105)
Veal Lyonnaise (page 164)	Pâté with Speedy Cumberland Sauce (page 165)
Celery Mornay (page 164)	Plaice Jamaican (page 165) with Green Salad
Apple and Ginger Salad (page 164)	Mock Orange Babas (page 165)
Devilled Pork Chops (page 166) with Creamed Potatoes	Cold Meats and Salad
and Peas	Sweet Omelette (page 167)
Brown Bread Perdu (page 166)	

Crabmeat Appetiser

Imperial/Metric	American
1 medium dressed crab or 6–8 oz. (150–200 g.) frozen or canned crabmeat	1 medium dressed crab or ¾–1 cup frozen or canned crabmeat
2 oz. (50 g.) cream cheese	¼ cup cream cheese
¼ pint (1½ dl.) yoghourt	⅔ cup yogurt
1 tablespoon tomato purée or ketchup	1 tablespoon tomato paste or catsup
few drops Tabasco sauce	few drops Tabasco sauce
seasoning	seasoning
little shredded lettuce	little shredded lettuce
to garnish	**to garnish**
1 large firm tomato	1 large firm tomato
1 lemon	1 lemon

No cooking

Serves 4–6

Advance Preparations Prepare crab mixture, keep covered. Shred lettuce, keep in polythene or foil. Put together at last minute.

Flake the crabmeat (drain off any surplus liquid from canned crabmeat). Blend the cream cheese, yoghourt, purée or ketchup and sauce. Blend with the crabmeat. Season well. Put on a bed of shredded lettuce, top with slices of tomato and lemon.

For Economy Use flaked white (lean) fish instead of crabmeat.

Variations

Add finely chopped celery, green and/or red pepper (pimiento) to the mixture.
Use other shell fish instead of crab.

160

Tomato Piperade

Imperial/Metric	American
small can tomatoes	small can tomatoes
1 green pepper	1 green pepper
1 oz. (25 g.) margarine	2 tablespoons margarine
4–6 eggs	4–6 eggs
seasoning	seasoning
4–6 slices bread	4–6 slices bread
to garnish	**to garnish**
parsley	parsley

Cooking time 6–8 minutes
Serves 6–8
Advance Preparations Prepare vegetables.

Open can of tomatoes, drain off surplus liquid.
Chop green pepper (discard core and seeds). Heat
margarine, add tomatoes and pepper, cook for 2–3
minutes. Beat eggs, season, pour into tomato
mixture. Scramble lightly. Meanwhile, toast bread,
cut into triangles and fingers. Arrange round
piperade. Top with parsley.

Variations
Cook finely chopped onions or chopped mushrooms
with tomatoes, etc.

Sponge Croûtes

Imperial/Metric	American
1 egg	1 egg
2 tablespoons milk	3 tablespoons milk
1 oz. (25 g.) sugar	2 tablespoons sugar
few drops vanilla essence	few drops vanilla extract
4 portions plain sponge cake	4 portions yellow sponge cake
for frying	**for frying**
3 oz. (75 g.) butter	6 tablespoons butter
for the topping	**for the topping**
jam, etc.	jam, etc.

Cooking time few minutes
Serves 4
Advance Preparations Prepare just before cooking.

Beat the egg and milk with the sugar and essence,
put on to a flat plate. Stand the pieces of cake in this
and allow the mixture to soften the bottom then turn
over and leave for a further few minutes – do not
leave too long otherwise the cake will break. Heat
the butter in a large pan and fry the croûtes until
crisp and golden brown on both sides. Lift on to a
hot serving dish and top with hot jam, or as
variations below.

For Economy Use pieces of bread instead of sponge
cake but use double the amount of sugar.

Variations
Fresh Fruit Croûtes Top croûtes with fresh strawberries, raspberries, etc., dust with sugar and serve
with cream.
Canned Fruit Croûtes Prepare a glaze just before the
croûtes are cooked. Blend $\frac{1}{4}$ pint ($1\frac{1}{2}$ dl. – $\frac{2}{3}$ cup)
syrup from the can with 1 teaspoon cornflour
(cornstarch) or arrowroot and a squeeze lemon juice.
Cook until smooth and thickened. Pile the canned
fruit on to the croûtes, top with the hot glaze, serve
at once.
Frozen Fruit Croûtes Allow fruit to defrost, make
juice up to $\frac{1}{4}$ pint ($1\frac{1}{2}$ dl. – $\frac{2}{3}$ cup) – if necessary –
with water. Continue as above.

Plantation Ham Rolls

Imperial/Metric	American
for the filling	**for the filling**
1 package vegetable soup powder	1 package dehydrated vegetable soup
1 carton soured cream*	⅔ cup sour cream*
2 rings pineapple	2 rings pineapple
4 oz. (100 g.) cooked or canned sweetcorn	¾ cup cooked or canned sweetcorn
4 large slices ham	4 large slices cooked ham
to serve	**to serve**
salad	salad

* or use ¼ pint (1½ dl. – ⅔ cup) whipped cream and 1 tablespoon lemon juice.

No cooking
Serves 4
Advance Preparations Make filling a little time ahead
to allow dehydrated soup powder to attain full
flavour.

Dehydrated soup powder is not only useful for
making a soup, but it can be used for a stuffing as in
this particular recipe.
Mix the vegetable soup powder with the soured
cream. Add the finely chopped pineapple and the well
drained sweetcorn. Chill thoroughly. Divide the
filling equally between the slices of ham, roll up,
wrap in foil and chill until required. Serve with salad.

Variations

Mushroom soup is also extremely good in this recipe.
Blend the soup powder with 4–6 oz. (100–150 g. –
½–¾ cup) cottage or cream cheese. Omit soured
cream in recipe above.
Glazed Ham Rolls Use the above recipe, brush with
half-set aspic jelly. Allow to set, then garnish with
gherkin, tomato, etc.

Mocha Sundae

Imperial/Metric	American
4–6 oz. (100–150 g.) plain chocolate	¼–⅓ lb. semi-sweet chocolate
3 tablespoons strong coffee	4 tablespoons strong coffee
large block vanilla ice cream	1½–2 pints vanilla ice cream

Cooking time few minutes
Serves 6–8
Advance Preparations Put chocolate and coffee over
hot water, turn off heat so mixture does not
become dry.

Heat chocolate and coffee in basin (bowl) over hot
water. Pour over ice cream just before serving.

Prawn and Fruit Cocktail

Imperial/Metric	American
1 lettuce	1 lettuce
3–4 oz. (75–100 g.) shelled prawns	½–⅔ cup shelled shrimp or prawns
2–3 tablespoons mayonnaise	3–4 tablespoons mayonnaise
1 grapefruit	1 grapefruit
1 orange	1 orange

No cooking
Serves 4

Shred lettuce and put at the bottom of 4 glasses or small dishes. Mix the prawns with the mayonnaise and the pulp from the grapefruit and orange. Spoon over the lettuce.

Variation

A new flavour is given to a prawn or shrimp cocktail by adding pears and melon to the shell fish, see the picture above.

First make the dressing: mix the mayonnaise in the basic recipe with a little tomato ketchup (catsup), thick (whipping) cream, horseradish cream and lemon juice. Dice one or two ripe peeled pears and several slices of melon. Mix with the dressing, put into glasses with the prawns, add sliced tomatoes and sliced cucumber to garnish. Omit the lettuce.

163

Veal Lyonnaise

Imperial/Metric	American
4 or 6 fillets veal	4 or 6 veal slices
seasoning	seasoning
2 onions	2 onions
3 oz. (75 g.) butter or margarine	6 tablespoons butter or margarine
1 tablespoon oil	1 tablespoon oil
can potatoes	can potatoes
to garnish	**to garnish**
watercress	watercress

Cooking time 20—25 minutes
Serves 4—6
Advance Preparations Chop or grate onions.

Flatten veal fillets with rolling pin until very thin,
season well. Peel and chop or grate onions. Heat the
butter or margarine and oil, fry the veal until tender.

Celery Mornay Open a large can of celery, strain
off liquid, add enough milk to make 1 pint (6 dl. —
2½ cups). Pour half the liquid into a pan. Heat the
celery hearts in this liquid, drain celery and put
into a hot dish. Melt 2 oz. (50 g. — ¼ cup) butter in a
saucepan, stir in 2 oz. (50 g. — ½ cup) flour, add all
the liquid. Bring to the boil, stir until thickened,
season; add 4 oz. (100 g. — 1 cup) grated cheese,
pour over the celery. Serve with meat dishes such
as the veal above or by itself as a supper dish.
Serves 6—8.
For Economy Use diced cooked celery when cheap.

Add onions towards end of cooking time. Drain the
potatoes, slice thickly. Lift the veal on to a hot dish,
put the sliced potatoes into the pan, heat thoroughly.
Arrange the potato onion mixture round the veal
fillets. Garnish with watercress and serve with
celery mornay, see below.

Apple and Ginger Salad

Imperial/Metric	American
4—6 dessert apples	4—6 dessert apples
for the syrup	**for the syrup**
½ pint (3 dl.) water	1¼ cups water
2 oz. (50 g.) sugar	¼ cup sugar
1—2 oz. (25—50 g.) preserved or crystallised ginger	1—2 oz. preserved or candied ginger
to serve	**to serve**
ice cream	ice cream

Cooking time 15 minutes
Serves 4
Advance Preparations Cook and reheat if necessary.

Make the syrup with the water and sugar, add the
chopped ginger. Peel and slice the apples, put into

the boiling syrup. Simmer gently for 5—6 minutes,
then cover the pan with a lid, remove from heat and
allow the fruit to continue cooking in the steam in
the pan. Cool, or serve warm, or reheat for a few
minutes. Serve with ice cream.

Pâté and Cumberland Sauce Ready-made or canned pâté can be made more interesting if served with this quick version of one of the classic sauces. Put 4 tablespoons (5 tablespoons) redcurrant jelly, 1 tablespoon lemon juice, 1 tablespoon water and 1–2 teaspoons made mustard into a saucepan. Stir over a low heat until well blended; cool. Spoon the pâté on to lettuce, or cut firm pâté into slices and arrange on lettuce. Top each portion with a spoonful of the cool sauce. There is a recipe for home-made pâté en croûte and pâté on page 201.

Plaice Jamaican

Imperial/Metric	American
4 large plaice	4 flounder
4 small bananas	4 small bananas
squeeze lemon juice	squeeze lemon juice
seasoning	seasoning
1 tablespoon flour	1 tablespoon flour
$\frac{1}{2}$–1 teaspoon curry powder	$\frac{1}{2}$–1 teaspoon curry powder
for frying	**for frying**
2–3 tablespoons oil or 1$\frac{1}{2}$–2 oz. (40–50 g.) butter	3–4 tablespoons oil or butter
to garnish	**to garnish**
lemon	lemon

Cooking time 6–8 minutes
Serves 4

Skin bananas and halve lengthways so they heat through quickly, sprinkle with lemon juice, then seasoned flour blended with a good pinch curry powder. Heat the oil or butter and fry the plaice (flounder) and bananas together. Garnish with lemon.

Mock Orange Babas

Imperial/Metric	American
small fresh tin loaf	small fresh loaf
for the sauce	**for the sauce**
2 tablespoons golden syrup or sugar	3 tablespoons light corn syrup or sugar
$\frac{1}{4}$ pint (1$\frac{1}{2}$ dl.) fresh or canned orange juice	$\frac{2}{3}$ cup fresh or canned orange juice
2 tablespoons orange marmalade	3 tablespoons orange marmalade
2 tablespoons rum	3 tablespoons rum
to decorate	**to decorate**
8 glacé cherries	8 candied cherries

Cooking time few minutes
Makes 8
Advance Preparations Prepare earlier in day.

Cut off the crusts from the whole loaf, halve lengthways. Cut each thick slice in 4 pieces. Arrange the 8 'babas' on a dish. Heat all the ingredients for the sauce. Spoon carefully over the bread, top with cherries. If possible leave for a time before serving.

Devilled Pork Chops

Imperial/Metric	American
4 rosy dessert apples	4 rosy dessert apples
little oil	little oil
4 thick pork loin chops	4 thick pork loin chops
6 tablespoons crisp breadcrumbs (raspings)	½ cup crisp bread crumbs (raspings)
2 teaspoons dry mustard	2 teaspoons dry mustard
1 teaspoon curry powder	1 teaspoon curry powder
for the sauce	**for the sauce**
2 tablespoons oil	3 tablespoons oil
2 medium onions	2 medium onions
1 tablespoon cornflour	1 tablespoon cornstarch
½–1 tablespoon mustard, to taste	½–1 tablespoon mustard, to taste
1 teaspoon curry powder	1 teaspoon curry powder
½ pint (3 dl.) good brown stock or water and 1 beef stock cube	1¼ cups good brown stock or water and 1 beef bouillon cube
1 tablespoon Worcestershire sauce	1 tablespoon Worcestershire sauce
seasoning	seasoning

Cooking time 30–35 minutes
Serves 4

Core the apples, slit round the skins, brush with oil.
Put on to foil in grill pan, or over barbecue, and
cook for about 30–35 minutes. Put the pork chops
on the barbecue bars or over apples in grill pan.
Cook for 10 minutes only, remove chops, press both
sides into the crumbs, mixed with the mustard and
curry powder. Return to the heat, continue cooking
for a further 10 minutes. Meanwhile, heat the oil in
a saucepan, add the chopped onions, cook for
several minutes. Stir in the cornflour, mustard and
curry powder blended with stock, or water and stock
(bouillon) cube, sauce and seasoning. Cook until
thickened. Do not spoon this over the meat too soon
for it will spoil the crisp outside. Serve with jacket
potatoes (when time permits) or with creamed
potatoes.

Brown Bread Perdu Heat ½ pint (3 dl. – 1¼ cups)
milk with a little grated nutmeg, 1 oz. (25 g. –
2 tablespoons) butter and 2 oz. (50 g. – ¼ cup)
sugar. Add 2 oz. (50 g. – 1 cup) soft brown
breadcrumbs and stir together, leave until cold, then
fold in ¼ pint (1½ dl. – ⅔ cup) lightly whipped cream.
Serve in glasses topped with grated nutmeg and a
little thin (coffee) cream if wished. *Serves 4.*

Sweet Omelettes

These make delicious sweets, quickly prepared and cooked. They *must* be served as soon as possible after cooking.

Basic Sweet Omelette

Imperial/Metric	American
3 eggs	3 eggs
½–1 oz. (15–25 g.) sugar	1–2 tablespoons sugar
1–2 tablespoons cream	1–2 tablespoons cream
flavouring, etc., see below	flavoring, etc., see below
1 oz. (25 g.) butter	2 tablespoons butter
to decorate	**to decorate**
icing sugar	confectioners' sugar

Cooking time few minutes
Serves 2–3
Advance Preparations Prepare filling.

Separate the yolks from the whites of the eggs, beat the yolks until fluffy with the sugar and cream. Add flavouring, then fold in the stiffly whisked egg whites. Heat the butter in an omelette (omelet) pan. Pour in the mixture, cook steadily until brown on the underside – either lower the heat and continue to cook the omelette in the usual way – tipping the pan and moving the liquid egg so it runs to the sides, OR a better method is to put the pan under the grill (broiler), set to a moderate heat, and cook the upper side for a few minutes. Fold, tip on to a hot serving dish and decorate with the icing (confectioners') sugar.

Variations
Almond Omelette Add 1 oz. (25 g. – ¼ cup) chopped blanched almonds and a few drops almond essence (extract) to the egg yolks. Fold and top with icing (confectioners') sugar and blanched almonds. Brown for 1 minute under the grill (broiler).
Apricot Omelette Add 1 tablespoon crumbled macaroon biscuit crumbs to the egg yolks. Fill with apricot jam or apricot purée before folding.
Banana Omelette Mash 1 large banana with a little lemon juice. Beat into egg yolks and sugar then add cream. Cook as before.
Brandy Omelette Add 1 tablespoon brandy (or fruit-flavoured brandy, such as apricot or cherry) to egg yolks.
Coconut Omelette Add 1 large tablespoon desiccated (shredded) coconut or shredded fresh coconut to the egg yolks.
Jam Omelette Heat 3 tablespoons (4 tablespoons) jam or jelly and spoon on to omelette before folding.

Entertaining for all Occasions

This section of the Family Cookbook gives a selection of interesting dishes and covers the many and varied occasions when you may want to entertain. This ranges from informal cocktail or cheese and wine parties to the more formal dinner party. Christmas and Easter traditional dishes have also been included.

The first few pages cover 'dips', pâtés of various kinds and meal 'starters'. I find these invaluable for almost every kind of party, for they can be the first course of a dinner party or part of a 'help-yourself' buffet.

Hors d'Oeuvre and Dips

The 'dips' on this page are a modern, and very sensible, way of providing food for your guests. Serve 'dips' instead of cocktail savouries, they are quickly and easily made, and, as the picture on page 171 shows, a 'dip' tray looks most attractive.

Celery Tomato Dip This dip is shown in the picture on page 171. Make ½ pint (3 dl. – 1¼ cups) white sauce, as the recipe on page 61. Stir as the sauce cooks, then blend in 3 tablespoons (4 tablespoons) tomato purée (paste), 2 tablespoons (3 tablespoons) soured cream or fresh thick (whipping) cream, plus a squeeze lemon juice. Open a medium size can of tuna. Flake the fish very well, then add to the white sauce, etc. Taste and season the mixture. Spoon into the bowl, stand this on a tray. Top with chopped parsley. Cut a head of celery into 'bite' size pieces, arranged round the tray with potato crisps. *Serves 4–6.*

Cheesy Celery Sticks Another easy savoury is also shown in the picture on page 171. Wash a head of celery, dry well, then cut into short pieces. Blend 4 oz. (100 g. – ½ cup) cream cheese with 2 oz. (50 g. – ¼ cup) Roquefort or other blue cheese. Add a little grated onion or chopped chives to flavour, season well. Spoon or pipe the soft mixture into the celery pieces and top with paprika and black olives. *Serves 4–6.*

Danish Celery Dip

Imperial/Metric	American
4 oz. (100 g.) Danish Blue cheese	¼ lb. Danish Blue cheese
8 oz. (200 g.) cottage cheese	1 cup cottage cheese
¼ pint (1½ dl.) soured cream or thick cream and 1 tablespoon lemon juice	⅔ cup sour cream or whipping cream and 1 tablespoon lemon juice
heart only of a head of celery	heart only of a bunch of celery
seasoning	seasoning
little celery salt	little celery salt
to garnish	**to garnish**
chopped celery leaves	chopped celery leaves

No cooking
Serves 6–8
Advance Preparations Make dip, cover with foil to prevent drying.

Mash Danish Blue cheese and blend with the cottage cheese, soured cream or cream and lemon juice and the very finely chopped celery. Add seasoning and celery salt. Top with celery leaves and serve with biscuits or crisps or cold cooked sausages.

To Make a Fish Pâté

This is a very good choice if your main dish is to be meat, poultry or game. Fish pâtés have been neglected for too long a period, and as you will see from the recipes below, you can produce a wide variety of pâtés from different kinds of fish.

In addition to being served as the first course of a meal these make very good fillings for sandwiches, vol-au-vent cases, or to put in pieces of celery instead of the more familiar cheese mixture, shown in the picture, page 171 (recipe page 168).

Taramasalata (Cod's Roe Pâté)

Imperial/Metric	American
10 oz. (250 g.) smoked cod's roe*	10 oz. smoked cod roe*
1 lemon	1 lemon
2 oz. (50 g.) butter	¼ cup butter
1 clove garlic	1 clove garlic
shake black pepper	shake black pepper
to garnish	**to garnish**
1 lemon	1 lemon
to serve	**to serve**
toast	toast
butter	butter

* there will be wastage due to thick skin – check cod's roe is fresh, it should be soft on the outside and bright red in colour.

No cooking
Serves 4–6
Advance Preparations This can be prepared some days ahead and stored in the refrigerator or frozen, in which case, to prevent the pâté drying on top, cover with a layer of melted butter.

Slit the skin and scrape all the soft roe out; discard the skin. Grate the yellow rind (zest) of the lemon very finely (if you enjoy a fairly strong lemon taste – if not omit this), squeeze out the juice. Cream the butter and crush the garlic then blend all the ingredients together. Put into a dish and cover with foil or melted butter if storing this. Serve with lemon, hot toast and butter.

For Economy Blend 2–3 tablespoons (3–4 table-spoons) very fine soft breadcrumbs with the roe, etc.
Freezing This freezes excellently. Use within 6–8 weeks.

Variations
Smoked Salmon Pâté Use smoked salmon instead of cod's roe.
Fresh Cod's Roe Pâté Use cooked or well drained canned unsmoked cod's roe; add ½ teaspoon anchovy essence (extract) plus 1 tablespoon tomato ketchup (catsup).
Kipper or Bloater Pâté Use lightly cooked kippers or bloaters instead of cod's roe.
Salmon Pâté Use well drained canned or cooked salmon instead of cod's roe.
Smoked Fish Pâté Use lightly cooked smoked haddock (finnan haddie) or cod, add 2 tablespoons (3 table-spoons) thick (whipping) cream to mixture.

Mulligatawny Fondue

Imperial/Metric	American
2 large cans mulligatawny soup or home-made soup, see page 17	2 large cans mulligatawny soup or home-made soup, see page 17
½ pint (3 dl.) water	1¼ cups water
2 oz. (50 g.) long grain rice	just over ¼ cup long grain rice
4 tablespoons thick cream	5 tablespoons whipping cream
1 green pepper	1 green pepper
1 red pepper	1 red pepper
2 bananas	2 bananas
1 lemon	1 lemon
1 large onion	1 large onion
2 oz. (50 g.) salted peanuts or other nuts	just under ½ cup salted peanuts or other nuts
2 oz. (50 g.) raisins	⅓ cup raisins

Cooking time   20 minutes
Serves 6–8
Advance Preparations Cook the rice in the soup,
reheat when required.

Put the soup and water into a pan. Bring to the boil,
add the rice and cook steadily until the rice is tender.
Add the cream, taste the soup and blend in a little
curry powder if desired. Dice the green and red
peppers (discard cores and seeds). Slice the bananas,
sprinkle with a little lemon juice to preserve the
colour. Peel and chop the onion very finely. Serve
the fondue with small bowls of peppers, banana,
nuts, raisins and onion arranged on a tray.

Variations

Flavour a cream of chicken soup with curry, and use
instead of mulligatawny soup.
Chilled Mulligatawny Fondue Blend ¼ pint (1½ dl. –
⅔ cup) thin (coffee) cream or soured cream with the
cold canned soup. Omit the rice and water. Continue
as above. Serve well chilled or iced lightly with the
same garnishes.

Rillettes of Poultry This is an excellent way to use
the giblets from any poultry. Simmer the giblets in
the minimum of liquid. Season this lightly and add a
small whole onion to give flavour. Do not over-
cook the giblets. When tender remove from the
liquid. Take all the meat from the neck and dice
this with the liver, heart, etc., very finely. Blend with
a little creamed butter, cream, extra seasoning and a
small quantity of brandy or sherry, to taste. Put into
a container and top with melted butter. Serve with
hot toast and butter. It is, however, quicker to
produce this in the blender of your mixer. Melt a
little butter and put this in the goblet. Add a small
quantity of cream and brandy or sherry then put in
the meat from the giblets. Emulsify until fairly
smooth, season and proceed as above.

170

Celery tomato dip, cheesy celery sticks (see page 168) and celery vol-au-vent (see page 193)

Vegetable Hors d'Oeuvre

Vegetable dishes are a very pleasant start to a dinner party menu. The two recipes on this page would also be suitable for part of a buffet menu.

Aubergines Lyonnaise

Imperial/Metric	American
2 large aubergines	2 large eggplants
seasoning	seasoning
1 large onion	1 large onion
2–3 tablespoons oil	3–4 tablespoons oil
½ pint (3 dl.) chicken stock or water and ½ chicken stock cube	1¼ cups chicken stock or water and ½ chicken bouillon cube
to garnish	**to garnish**
chopped parsley	chopped parsley

Cooking time 40 minutes
Serves 4
Advance Preparations Cook; reheat or serve cold.

Wash, dry, but do not peel the aubergines. Slice thinly and sprinkle with seasoning. (If you do not like the rather bitter flavour of the skin, score the aubergines first, sprinkle with salt and leave for 20 minutes then slice and season only with pepper.) Peel and chop the onion fairly finely. Toss the sliced aubergines and onion in the hot oil until nearly tender, take care they do not become brown. Add stock, or water and stock cube, cover the pan and simmer for 15–20 minutes. Remove lid and continue cooking very gently until the liquid has been absorbed. Top with parsley and serve hot or cold as a vegetable with the main course, or hors d'oeuvre.

For Economy Use 1 aubergine and part of a small marrow or 2 courgettes when cheap.
Freezing Cook, but do not allow *all* the liquid to evaporate; reheat from frozen state. Can be stored for up to 12 months.

Variation

Aubergines Provençale Fry 1–2 crushed cloves of garlic and 3 medium skinned, chopped tomatoes with the onions and aubergines.

Caribbean Mushrooms

Imperial/Metric	American
1 lb. (½ kilo) mushrooms	1 lb. mushrooms
2 onions	2 onions
2 oz. (50 g.) butter	¼ cup butter
seasoning	seasoning
2 teaspoons Angostura Bitters	2 teaspoons Angostura Bitters
½ pint (3 dl.) thick cream	1¼ cups whipping cream
1½ oz. (40 g.) blanched almonds	just over ¼ cup blanched almonds

Cooking time 40 minutes
Serves 4–6
Advance Preparations Prepare ahead, reheat gently, add almonds.

Slice the mushrooms and onions. Heat the butter in a pan, add the onions and cook until nearly tender but not browned. Add the mushrooms and cook for a further 3 minutes. Season the ingredients. Have the pan really hot, pour in the Angostura Bitters and set it alight; allow the flames to burn out. Pour in the cream, heat gently then turn into a hot serving dish. Meanwhile, brown the almonds under the grill (broiler) then chop these and sprinkle over the top.

Ways to Serve Smoked Fish

If serving smoked salmon, trout, eel or mackerel as the first course of a meal, the fish should be garnished with lettuce and lemon and served with brown bread and butter. It is usual to offer horseradish cream with the trout, mackerel or eel, but the dressing below would blend with all smoked fish. Make small rolls of smoked bacon, or dice the other fish, when serving for a buffet.

Cucumber Horseradish Dressing

Imperial/Metric	American
½ small cucumber	½ small cucumber
½ pint (3 dl.) natural yoghourt	1¼ cups unflavored yogurt
shake pepper	shake pepper
1 tablespoon horseradish cream	1 tablespoon horseradish cream

No cooking
Serves 6–8

Peel the cucumber, then cut into wafer-thin slices or matchstick pieces. Mix with the other ingredients. Excellent with meat stews, including curry, or with a meat or cheese salad.

Freezing Do not freeze, you spoil texture of cucumber.

Variations
Omit the horseradish cream and add 1–2 teaspoons concentrated tomato purée (paste).
Add 1–2 crushed cloves of garlic plus 1 tablespoon chopped mint – this is excellent with lamb salad.

Avocado and Smoked Salmon

Imperial/Metric	American
2 oz. (50 g.) smoked salmon	2 oz. smoked salmon
½ oz. (15 g.) butter	1 tablespoon butter
2–3 tablespoons thick cream	3–4 tablespoons whipping cream
shake cayenne pepper	shake cayenne pepper
1–2 lemons	1–2 lemons
2 teaspoons chopped parsley or chives	2 teaspoons chopped parsley or chives
2 medium avocado pears	2 medium avocados
to garnish	**to garnish**
lettuce leaves	lettuce leaves
1 lemon	1 lemon
to serve	**to serve**
brown bread and butter	brown bread and butter

No cooking
Serves 4
Advance Preparations Prepare smoked salmon mixture. Keep covered in refrigerator or freeze. Thaw out at room temperature.

Chop the smoked salmon fairly finely, mix with the softened butter, *unwhipped* cream, pepper, lemon juice to taste and parsley or chives; the mixture should be soft and creamy. Halve the avocado pears, remove stones, sprinkle with lemon juice to prevent pears darkening. Fill with salmon mixture, put on to the lettuce and serve with wedges of lemon and brown bread and butter. This can be served with the cucumber sauce, page 198.

For Economy You may be able to buy smoked salmon pieces quite cheaply from the fishmonger, and you can use the cheaper quality salmon for this.

Pasta Party

As spaghetti, macaroni and other kinds of pasta are very popular today, why not have a Pasta Party?
Make several different pasta dishes and serve these with salad and red or white wine. There is a number of
pasta dishes in this book (see pages 27, 38, 109 and below). Information on the correct cooking of pasta
is on page 109. Prepare the dishes ahead, but use slightly more liquid than recommended in the recipe,
for pasta absorbs moisture with standing.

Macaroni and Eggs Lyonnaise Cook 6 oz. (150 g.)
short cut macaroni in boiling salted water. Hard boil
(hard cook) 4–6 eggs, shell and halve. Heat 2 oz.
(50 g. – ¼ cup) butter in a pan, and fry 2–3 thinly
sliced onions until just soft. Stir in 1½ oz. (40 g. –
⅓ cup) flour and ¾ pint (4½ dl. – 2 cups) milk. Bring
the sauce to the boil, stir until thickened, season well
and blend with the well drained macaroni. Put half
the macaroni mixture into an ovenproof dish, add
the halved eggs, cut side downwards, then the rest of
the macaroni mixture. Top with a good layer of
grated cheese and a little butter. Heat thoroughly for
about 30 minutes in a moderate oven. If preferred
put the very hot ingredients into a flameproof dish
and heat under the grill (broiler). Garnish with
paprika. *Serves 4–6. Illustrated opposite.*

Mussels and Pasta Shells in Wine Sauce First prepare
the mussels. Put 2 quarts (2¼ litres – 2½ quarts) well
scrubbed mussels into a large pan – discard any that
do not shut when tapped sharply. Add ½ pint (3 dl. –
1¼ cups) dry white wine, 2 tablespoons (3 tablespoons) chopped parsley, 1 tablespoon finely chopped
onion or shallot and seasoning. Heat gently for
10–15 minutes until the shells open. Meanwhile,
boil 8 oz. (200 g.) pasta shells in boiling salted
water, drain, mix with a generous amount of butter,
a little finely grated lemon rind and seasoning. Put
into a heated ovenproof dish, cover, to prevent the
pasta drying, and keep hot. Lift the mussels from the
wine liquid with a fish slice or a perforated spoon,
cool sufficiently to handle. Remove one shell; discard
any mussels that have not opened properly. Put the
fish in the remaining shells on top of the pasta.
Cover again. Tip a small can of tomatoes and a little
lemon juice into the wine liquid. Heat for a few
minutes, then cool slightly; whisk in 2–3 tablespoons
thick (whipping) cream. Heat gently, *without
boiling.* Spoon the creamy wine and tomato sauce
over the mussels and pasta. Serve as soon as
possible. If you want to prepare as much of this dish
beforehand as possible, cook the pasta *lightly*; drain,
rinse in boiling water, then keep in a pan of cold

water. When you require the pasta bring the water
to boiling point as quickly as possible, strain the
pasta and use in the recipe above. Open the mussels
and stand in the wine liquid; reheat for 1 minute
only. *Serves 4–6. Illustrated opposite.*
Note Where mussels have a hairy 'beard' this should
also be removed.

Spaghetti and Mushrooms Chop several rashers
(slices) bacon; skin and slice 4–5 tomatoes. Heat
1½ oz. (40 g. – nearly ¼ cup) butter with 1½ tablespoons (2 tablespoons) olive oil. Fry the bacon and
tomatoes for several minutes then add 1 teaspoon
chopped fresh basil, ½ teaspoon chopped oregano,
8–10 oz. (200–275 g.) small button mushrooms,
¼ pint (1½ dl. – ⅔ cup) brown stock, ¼ pint (1½ dl. –
⅔ cup) red wine and seasoning. Simmer steadily for
30 minutes; remove the lid of the pan towards the
end of the cooking time, so the liquid evaporates
slightly. Meanwhile, boil 8–12 oz. (200–300 g.)
spaghetti in boiling salted water until tender. Strain
the spaghetti, toss in a little melted butter and pile
on to a hot dish. Top with mushrooms as picture.

Cheese to Serve with Pasta Always have bowls of
grated cheese on the table to serve with pasta;
whatever the basic flavouring of the dish, grated
cheese seems to blend with this. The 'correct' cheese
is of course grated Parmesan, but any other cheese
can be used if preferred.

Top Macaroni and eggs lyonnaise (see page 174) Bottom Mussels and pasta shells in wine sauce (see 175
page 174)

Warm Weather Menus

Here are four menus that would be ideal for warmer days when fruit and vegetables are plentiful.

Poached Salmon with Hollandaise Sauce (page 180)	*Avocado Soufflé (see below)*
Chicken Terrine de Luxe (page 178) with Mixed Salad	*Roast Duckling (page 179) with New Potatoes and Peas*
Gâteau Bernhardt (page 181)	*Fresh Fruit Salad and Cream*
Iced Melon	*Asparagus with Hollandaise Sauce (page 180)*
Chicken Suprême (page 180) with Boiled Rice and Mixed Vegetables	*Cold Meats with Delhi Salad (page 177)*
Iced Camembert Cheese and Biscuits	*Rich Ice Cream (page 177) with Raspberries*
(Put the cheese in the freezer or freezing compartment for about 1 hour)	

A well chilled white wine or a rosé wine would complement these menus, except when serving duckling, when most people would prefer a red wine, which should be served at room temperature.

Avocado Soufflé

Imperial/Metric	American
1 medium ripe avocado pear	1 medium ripe avocado
juice ½–1 lemon	juice ½–1 lemon
1 oz. (25 g.) butter or margarine	2 tablespoons butter or margarine
3 tablespoons milk or thin cream	4 tablespoons milk or coffee cream
seasoning	seasoning
3 or 4 eggs	3 or 4 eggs

Cooking time 35 minutes
Serves 4
Advance Preparations Egg whites must be added just before being cooked – if preparing avocado mixture earlier use plenty of lemon juice to preserve colour.

Halve avocado, remove pulp and blend with lemon juice (it is advisable to use only the juice of ½ lemon and add extra juice later if additional 'bite' is needed). Warm the avocado pulp over a low heat, add butter or margarine, milk or cream, seasoning, egg yolks and any extra lemon juice if required. Whisk the egg whites until stiff, fold into the mixture and spoon into a 6–7-inch (15–18-cm.) soufflé dish. Bake for 30 minutes in centre of moderate to moderately hot oven, 375–400°F. (190–200°C.), Gas Mark 5–6. Serve as soon as cooked.

For Economy If you can buy slightly damaged avocado pears cheaply, use these.

Variations
Avocado pears are an unusual fruit in that they can be served as the basis for savoury or sweet dishes:
Savoury Soufflés Add 1–2 oz. (25–50 g. – ¼–½ cup) grated Parmesan cheese or diced smoked salmon to the avocado pear mixture.
Sweet Soufflés Add 1–2 oz. (25–50 g. – 2–4 tablespoons) sugar and 1 tablespoon brandy to the avocado pear mixture. Dust with sieved icing (sifted confectioners') sugar before serving.

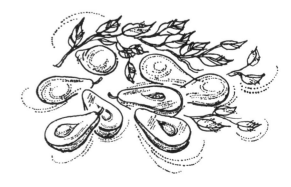

176

Delhi Salad

Imperial/Metric	American
8 oz. (200 g.) green beans (fresh or frozen)	½ lb. green beans (fresh or frozen)
seasoning	seasoning
8 oz. (200 g.) button mushrooms	2 cups button mushrooms
small bunch spring onions	small bunch scallions
2 teaspoons curry powder	2 teaspoons curry powder
5 fl. oz. (1½ dl.) soured cream or thick cream and 1 tablespoon extra lemon juice	⅔ cup sour cream or whipping cream and 1 tablespoon extra lemon juice
1 tablespoon lemon juice	1 tablespoon lemon juice
2 tablespoons mayonnaise	3 tablespoons mayonnaise
2–3 hard-boiled eggs	2–3 hard-cooked eggs
2–3 tomatoes	2–3 tomatoes
to garnish	**to garnish**
chopped chives	chopped chives

Cooking time 12–15 minutes
Serves 4–6
Advance Preparations Prepare mushroom mixture, boil eggs.

Cook the sliced beans in boiling salted water until tender but still fairly firm in texture. Drain well and set aside to cool. Slice the mushrooms and spring onions. Mix the curry powder, soured cream or thick cream, lemon juice, mayonnaise and seasoning. Turn the mushrooms, onions and beans in this sauce. Chill for 30 minutes. Serve in a dish edged with sliced hard-boiled eggs and tomatoes. Garnish with chopped chives.

Rich Ice Cream

Imperial/Metric	American
3 eggs	3 eggs
3–4 oz. (75–100 g.) sieved icing sugar	¾–1 cup sifted confectioners' sugar
½–1 teaspoon vanilla essence	½–1 teaspoon vanilla extract
½ pint (3 dl.) thick cream	1¼ cups heavy cream*
½ pint (3 dl.) thin cream	1¼ cups coffee cream*

* or use ⅔ whipping cream and ⅓ coffee cream.

Freezing time varies with individual freezing compartments or freezers, but allow several hours
Serves 6 or more if served with fruit, etc.
Advance Preparations See below.

Whisk the egg yolks and sieved icing sugar with the vanilla essence until thick. Whip the thick cream then whip in the thin cream, blend with egg yolks. Freeze for 1 hour, fold in the stiffly whisked egg whites. Freeze again until firm.

Variations

This is a basic ice cream which can be flavoured in very many ways, e.g., blend 2–3 tablespoons chocolate powder into the mixture or 1–2 teaspoons instant coffee, dissolved in 2 tablespoons (3 tablespoons) milk. For a fruit ice cream use ½ pint (3 dl. – 1¼ cups) thick fruit purée. Chopped nuts, dried fruit, etc., may be added to the ice cream (see page 199 for a very delicious ice cream using these). A little liqueur can also be added to the mixture, the best flavours being crème de menthe, curaçao and cherry brandy. As liqueurs are sweet use a little less sugar in the recipe, for too much sweetening prevents the ice cream from freezing properly.

Chicken Terrine de Luxe

Imperial/Metric	American
3½—4-lb. (1¾—2-kilo) roasting chicken with the giblets*	3½—4-lb. roasting chicken with the giblets*
seasoning	seasoning
bouquet garni	bouquet garni
8 oz. (200 g.) lean ham	½ lb. lean cooked ham
3 oz. (75 g.) blanched almonds	¾ cup blanched almonds
2 tablespoons brandy	3 tablespoons brandy
3 tablespoons thick cream	4 tablespoons whipping cream
2 oz. (50 g.) butter	¼ cup butter
to serve	**to serve**
toast	toast
salad	salad

* omit the giblets for a milder-flavoured stock. If using a frozen chicken in this recipe, thaw out thoroughly before cooking. This will take at least 12 hours at room temperature, and longer in the refrigerator.

Cooking time 1 hour for stock, 1½ hours for terrine
Serves 8—10 portions
Advance Preparations Make the stock; the terrine can be made 1—2 days beforehand, or frozen.

Cut the raw chicken flesh from the bones; keep the chicken skin. Simmer the bones and giblets with seasoning, *bouquet garni* and water to cover in a pan for 40 minutes. Remove lid, boil until only ¼ pint (1½ dl. − ⅔ cup) stock is left. Strain carefully. Cut the breast into neat slices, mince (grind) all the rest of the meat with the ham. Blend with half the stock, coarsely chopped nuts, brandy, cream and seasoning. Spread a generous layer of butter over the sides and bottom of a 2-lb. (1-kilo) loaf tin (pan). Arrange a third of the sliced chicken and stock on this then half the minced (ground) mixture. Add another third of the sliced breast and stock and the rest of the minced mixture. Top with the last of the sliced chicken, stock, chicken skin and butter. Cover with foil, stand in a tin of cold water and cook in the centre of a moderate oven, 300–325°F. (150–170°C.), Gas Mark 2–3, for 1½ hours. Remove from the oven, put a weight on top, leave to cool; if any stock rises to top of the tin pour this away. Remove chicken skin when cold. Serve sliced with toast and salad.

Freezing Cook and freeze. Use within 2—2½ months. Thaw out at room temperature.

Variations
Use a little less stock and add equivalent in sherry or brandy.
Game Terrine Use grouse, pheasant or hare instead of chicken.

Roast Duckling

If using frozen duckling, allow these to thaw out. One small duckling serves two people, but if you buy 2 large duckling you may be able to serve up to 6 people, especially if you have a fairly sustaining first course. The traditional accompaniments for duckling are sage and onion stuffing (page 60) and apple sauce (page 142), but duckling is equally good served with many other accompaniments, e.g. rings of fresh orange, as the picture on this page, and with an orange flavour given to the thick gravy, by adding a little finely grated orange rind and orange juice.

Put the stuffing into the body of the bird or birds. Weigh each duckling, generally they will need the same cooking time, but if one is slightly bigger put that into the oven first. Allow 15 minutes per lb. ($\frac{1}{2}$ kilo) and 15 minutes over. Put the ducks in the roasting tin (pan) or stand them on a rack if possible, so they are above any fat that runs out. Put into a moderately hot to hot oven, 400–425°F. (200–220°C.), Gas Mark 6–7. After 30 minutes cooking time, prick the skin gently, so the fat spurts out into the tin. Lower the heat slightly to complete the cooking. Serve garnished with orange rings, dipped in finely chopped parsley, watercress, potato crisps and with thickened gravy. New potatoes and green peas are the ideal vegetables to serve with duck.

Orange Sauce Cut the yellow part of the rind (the 'zest') from 2 sweet or bitter oranges. Simmer the rind in $\frac{1}{2}$ pint (3 dl. – 1$\frac{1}{4}$ cups) water for 15 minutes, then strain the liquid. Make a sauce with 1 tablespoon duck fat (from the roasting tin), add 1 oz. (25 g. – $\frac{1}{4}$ cup) cornflour (cornstarch), blended with the orange peel liquid, and $\frac{1}{2}$ pint (3 dl. – 1$\frac{1}{4}$ cups)

brown stock (from simmering the duck giblets), 2 tablespoons (3 tablespoons) port wine, and the orange juice. Simmer steadily for about 15 minutes until the sauce thickens, season well and add a little sugar to taste, or stir in 2–3 tablespoons redcurrant jelly to provide a glaze, a good colour, and additional flavour.

179

Some Special Sauces

A good sauce can turn a simple dish into a very much more sophisticated one, suitable for a special meal. Some of the most useful sauces are given below, together with the kinds of foods with which they blend.

Hollandaise Sauce Make ahead if you wish this sauce to be served cold; generally it is a hot sauce. If it is to be served cold, see suggestions in the recipe. Put the yolks of 2 eggs into a basin (bowl) – save the whites for meringues, see page 192. Add a good pinch of salt and pepper, a small pinch dry mustard or about ¼ teaspoon French mustard and 1 tablespoon lemon juice or white wine vinegar. Whisk hard over a pan of very hot, but not boiling, water, until the mixture thickens. Meanwhile, soften about 2 oz. (50 g. – ¼ cup) butter. Add small knobs of butter to the thick egg mixture, whisking all the time. Do not add this too quickly, otherwise the sauce becomes oily. Serve with poached fish, cooked vegetables – particularly good with asparagus and broccoli. If you want to serve the sauce cold, whisk as the mixture cools, and fold 2–3 tablespoons whipped cream into the cold egg mixture. This makes it a good sauce to serve with cold salmon or cold asparagus. *Serves 4–6.*

Poached Salmon This is given in the menus on page 176. You can poach this as the directions on page 27; but, when serving the fish as a cold dish, I prefer to put the salmon on a large piece of oiled greaseproof (wax) paper, season fish lightly, add a knob of butter and a squeeze of lemon juice, then fold the paper to make a neat parcel and tie this. Put into a pan of cold water, bring the water *slowly* to boiling point. Take the pan off the heat, cover this and let the salmon stand in the water until cold. Unwrap and serve. This method is ideal for a small piece of fresh salmon, but for cooking larger pieces and when serving the fish hot, it is better to follow the directions on page 27.

Suprême Sauce This is a very adaptable sauce in that it can be served with fish or with poultry (generally chicken or turkey). Naturally you will use the appropriate stock in the recipe, i.e. fish stock (made by simmering fish skins and bones) for a fish dish, or poultry (white) stock (made by cooking the poultry or by simmering the carcass). Put 2 oz. (50 g. – ¼ cup) butter into a pan, heat for 2–3 minutes, blend in 2 oz. (50 g. – ½ cup) flour, stir over a low heat for several minutes. Gradually stir in ¾ pint (4½ dl. – just under 2 cups) of very well

strained stock. Bring to the boil, cook until thickened, season lightly. Remove from the heat. Blend 2 egg yolks and ¼ pint (1½ dl. – ⅔ cup) thin (coffee) cream together with 2 tablespoons sherry. Whisk into the hot, *but not boiling*, sauce; cook gently until a coating consistency; season. If making in advance, make the sauce to the point where you add the egg yolks and cream, cover with damp paper. When ready to serve whisk sharply or emulsify, reheat gently, then continue as recipe. *Serves 6.*

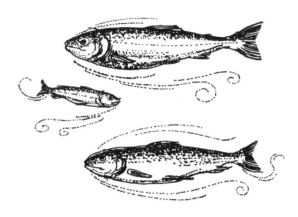

Chicken Suprême Chicken is given in the menus on page 176 to be served with the sauce above. Simmer the chicken gently in water to cover, or use water plus a little white wine. Add 1–2 onions, 1–2 carrots and a small bunch of fresh herbs. Season the liquid well. If the chicken is young, allow 20 minutes per 1 lb. (½ kilo) steady simmering, if older increase the time to 25–30 minutes per 1 lb. (½ kilo). If a really old boiling fowl then allow up to 40–45 minutes per 1 lb. (½ kilo). While you can use some of this chicken stock for the sauce, you will have a richer flavour if you joint or carve the chicken ready to serve, and keep this in a small amount of stock so it does not dry, then return any bones or carcass to the remaining stock, boil briskly until this is reduced to the amount needed for the sauce, then strain this.

To serve the dish: heat the chicken for a short time in the small amount of stock, strain, arrange on a hot dish, coat with the hot sauce. Top with paprika, triangles of toast, fried bread or puff pastry and sliced hard-boiled (hard-cooked) egg or asparagus tips.

Gâteau Bernhardt

Imperial/Metric	American
Victoria sandwich with 3 eggs, etc., see page 99*	Victoria sandwich with 3 eggs, etc., see page 99*
½ strawberry-flavoured jelly	½ package strawberry-flavored gelatin
½ pint (3 dl.) water	1¼ cups water
¾ pint (4½ dl.) thick cream	2 cups whipping cream
1¼–1½ lb. (⅝–¾ kilo) strawberries	1¼–1½ lb. strawberries
little sugar	little sugar
2 oz. (50 g.) flaked almonds	½ cup shaved almonds

* bake in 7–8-inch (18–20-cm.) tins (pans); allow a few minutes longer baking than on page 99.

Cooking time approximately 20 minutes
Serves 8
Advance Preparations Make gâteau, leave for some hours before serving.

Make the sponge cake and bake in two tins as page 99; split each half to give 4 layers. Make up the jelly with the hot water, allow to cool and begin to stiffen. Sandwich together the sponge layers with some of the whipped cream and half the strawberries, which should be sliced and sweetened. Meanwhile, brown the almonds and cool. Coat the cake sides with cream and press flaked browned almonds against these. Spread the top with the remaining cream and whole fruit. Top with the half-set jelly. Leave to set completely. Cut with a warm knife.

Freezing Freeze, then wrap. Thaw out slowly, use as soon as defrosted so strawberries do not lose their texture. Use within 6 weeks to 2 months.

Variations

Use raspberries and raspberry jelly (gelatin).
Use sliced chopped pineapple, fresh or canned, and pineapple or lemon jelly (gelatin).
Use apricots and lemon jelly.

Bavaroise or Bavarian Cream

Imperial/Metric	American
4 egg yolks	4 egg yolks
4 oz. (100 g.) icing sugar	1 cup confectioners' sugar
¾ pint (4½ dl.) milk	2 cups milk
scant ¼ oz. (7 g.) powdered gelatine	scant 1 envelope powdered gelatin
2–3 tablespoons cold water	3–4 tablespoons cold water
¼–½ teaspoon vanilla essence	¼–½ teaspoon vanilla extract
¼ pint (1½ dl.) thick cream	⅔ cup whipping cream

Cooking time approximately 10 minutes
Serves 4–6
Advance Preparations Prepare beforehand, chill thoroughly.

Beat the egg yolks with the sugar, add the hot but not boiling milk and cook in the top of a double saucepan until a smooth thick custard. Soften the gelatine in the water. Add to the custard together with the vanilla essence and stir over a low heat until thoroughly dissolved. Allow to cool but not set, then fold in the whipped cream. Spoon into glasses.

Variations

Chocolate Bavarian Cream Add 2 oz. (50 g.) grated plain (semi-sweet) chocolate or 1 oz. (25 g. – ¼ cup) cocoa to the egg yolks and milk.
Coffee Bavarian Cream Use just under ¾ pint (4½ dl. – 2 cups) milk, and 2 tablespoons (3 tablespoons) coffee essence (strong black coffee).
Raspberry Bavarian Cream Use raspberry essence (extract) instead of vanilla or cook egg yolks with ½ pint (3 dl. – 1¼ cups) milk, cool slightly and whisk in ¼ pint (1½ dl. – ⅔ cup) sieved raspberry purée. Other fruits suitable would be strawberries, blackcurrants, redcurrants.

Christmas Catering

For most of us catering at Christmas entails quite a lot of extra cooking and planning of meals. If you plan well ahead, and prepare most of the dishes, your work on Christmas Day should be appreciably easier. In the menu on this page I indicate just how much of the preparation can be done ahead.

Christmas Dinner Menu

Roast Turkey with various stuffings	*Simmer giblets a day or two beforehand for stock. Make the stuffings, either store for 1–2 days in the refrigerator or freeze*
Bacon Rolls and Sausages	*(see pages 56–60). Prepare Bacon Rolls on Christmas Eve. Make*
Bread and Cranberry Sauces (page 184)	*sauces and store or freeze.*
Brussels Sprouts and Chestnuts (page 184)	*Use canned chestnuts, or prepare and store or freeze. Prepare sprouts on Christmas Eve, store in covered container in the refrigerator.*
Ratatouille	*Store or freeze; see page 184.*
Duchesse Potatoes, Roast Potatoes	*Store or freeze Duchesse Potatoes (see page 108), peel potatoes on Christmas Eve, keep in cold water.*
Christmas Pudding with Brandy Butter (see opposite)	*Cook puddings some weeks ahead (opposite), make Brandy Butter several days ahead.*
Sherry Sauce (page 183)	*Make earlier, reheat over hot water, whisk sharply.*
Jellied Christmas Pudding (page 183)	*Make on Christmas Eve.*
Mincepies (see below)	*Make 1 or 2 days ahead, or freeze.*

Mincepies The picture on this page shows mincepies made with short crust pastry (page 72). Other kinds of pastry can be used if preferred. A recipe for home-made mincemeat is on page 116. Roll out the pastry cut rounds to fit into fairly deep patty tins (muffin pans). Put in a spoonful of mincemeat, top with a round of pastry (cut slightly smaller than the bottom round). Seal the edges of the pastry and make two slits on top with kitchen scissors. Bake mincepies in the centre of the oven for approximately 20 minutes. Use a hot oven, 425°F. (220°C.), Gas Mark 7, for short crust pastry, or a very hot oven, 450°F. (230°C.), Gas Mark 8, for the richer puff and flaky pastries. Reduce the heat after the first 10 minutes cooking time. Dust with sieved icing (sifted confectioners') sugar before serving.

Brandy Butter (Hard Sauce) This is the traditional accompaniment to Christmas pudding, but it is very good with mincepies too. Cream 4 oz. (100 g. – ½ cup) butter with 8 oz. (200 g. – nearly 2 cups) sieved icing (sifted confectioners') sugar, then gradually blend in several tablespoons brandy. Pile or pipe into an attractive container and decorate (as the picture opposite) with pieces of glacé (candied) cherry and angelica. *Serves 8–10.*

Christmas Pudding The quantities below make a pudding of the size shown in the picture above, i.e. sufficient for 8–10 generous or 12–14 smaller portions.

Mix together 4 oz. (100 g. – 2 cups) soft breadcrumbs, 4 oz. (100 g. – 1 cup) flour, 1 lb. 4 oz. ($\frac{1}{2}$ kilo plus 50 g. – $3\frac{1}{2}$ cups) mixed dried fruit, 5 oz. (125 g. – 1 cup) shredded (chopped) suet, 5 oz. (125 g. – generous $\frac{1}{2}$ cup) brown sugar, 2 oz. (50 g. – $\frac{1}{4}$ cup) chopped glacé (candied) cherries, 4 oz. (100 g. – 1 cup) chopped blanched almonds, 1 good size peeled grated cooking (baking) apple, 1 teaspoon mixed spice, $\frac{1}{2}$ teaspoon ground nutmeg, grated rind and juice 1 lemon, 2 eggs, 1 tablespoon black treacle (molasses), $\frac{1}{4}$ pint ($1\frac{1}{2}$ dl. – $\frac{2}{3}$ cup) liquid (milk or ale, or a mixture of ale and brandy). Put the mixture into a large well greased basin (mold), cover with greased greaseproof (wax) paper and foil. Steam for about 6 hours; remove wet paper and put on dry paper. Store in a cool dry place. Cook for another 2–3 hours on Christmas Day. Serve with brandy butter (page 182) and sherry-flavoured sweet white sauce.

Sherry Sauce Blend 1 oz. (25 g. – $\frac{1}{4}$ cup) cornflour (cornstarch) with $\frac{1}{4}$ pint ($1\frac{1}{2}$ dl. – $\frac{2}{3}$ cup) milk. Heat $\frac{3}{4}$ pint ($4\frac{1}{2}$ dl. – just under 2 cups) milk, pour over the blended cornflour. Return to the pan with 2 oz. (50 g. – $\frac{1}{4}$ cup) sugar, 1 oz. (25 g. – 2 tablespoons) butter. Stir until thickened, then whisk in 2 tablespoons (3 tablespoons) sweet sherry.

Jellied Christmas Pudding Make a fruit-flavoured jelly (gelatin) – preferably blackcurrant – in the usual way. Add dried fruit, few chopped glacé (candied) cherries and chopped nuts, then leave to set.

Roast Turkey

The accompaniments, etc., given for turkey are equally as good with chicken. Choose any of the stuffings from pages 56–60. The most usual for turkey are chestnut (page 57) and parsley and thyme (veal) on page 58. Put one stuffing in the neck end of the bird and the second stuffing inside the body. Weigh the stuffed bird, and allow 15 minutes per 1 lb. (½ kilo) and 15 minutes over for a bird up to 12 lb. (6 kilos) in weight. For every additional 1 lb. (½ kilo) above this weight allow only an extra 15 minutes up to the weight of 21 lb. (10 kilos). These times refer to fast roasting, i.e. in a moderately hot to hot oven, 400–425°F. (200–220°C.), Gas Mark 6–7. You can reduce the heat to moderately hot after 15 minutes for a chicken, or after 30 minutes for a larger turkey. Page 141 deals with covered roasting tins (pans) and foil. If you prefer to use slower roasting, as suggested on page 141 for meat, then increase the timing to 25 minutes per 1 lb. (½ kilo), reducing the time for larger turkeys to 20 minutes, then 15 minutes.
Serve with bread and/or cranberry sauces, as the recipes below, and with thickened gravy.

Sauces for Turkey and Chicken

The following sauces are served with roast turkey or chicken; portions are enough for 6.

Bread Sauce Peel an onion, press several cloves into this (optional). Put into ½ pint (3 dl. – 1¼ cups) milk. Heat for several minutes, stir in 3 oz. (75 g. – 1½ cups) soft breadcrumbs, a good knob of butter or margarine and seasoning. Leave in a warm place for as long as possible, then stir over a low heat; remove the onion before serving. A few tablespoons cream stirred into this sauce make a distinct improvement.
Freezing Make sauce when convenient; remove onion and freeze; defrost before heating. Use within 2 months.

Cranberry Sauce Simmer 1 lb. (½ kilo) cranberries in water to cover with sugar to taste. Sieve or emulsify if you require a smooth sauce. This sauce can be varied by adding a little port wine, orange juice or redcurrant jelly to the water, etc.
Freezing Either freeze the cranberries and make the sauce when convenient, or make the sauce, cool, then freeze; reheat when required. Keeps for up to 1 year.

Vegetables to Serve with the Turkey

Brussels Sprouts and Chestnuts These make an excellent combination. Split the skins of fresh chestnuts and boil for 10 minutes only. Remove the skins while hot, then simmer the chestnuts in fresh water for another 10–15 minutes until tender. Strain and mix with the cooked sprouts. Do not try and cook the nuts and sprouts together, for the vegetable turns a very odd colour.

Ratatouille Heat 3–4 tablespoons (4–5 tablespoons) olive oil or other good quality oil in the pan. Peel and slice 3–4 onions, 2–3 cloves garlic, 5–6 tomatoes, then toss in the oil for a few minutes, or until the juice flows from the tomatoes. Add 4–5 medium size sliced but unpeeled courgettes (zucchini) and 2 thinly sliced but unpeeled aubergines (eggplants). Season the mixture well, cover the pan and simmer for approximately 1¼ hours. Top with chopped parsley. Chopped red and green peppers and sliced mushrooms may be added if wished.
Serves up to 8.
Freezing This dish freezes admirably and will keep up to 1 year, although I find the texture better if used within 6 months. Thaw out slightly before reheating.

Braised Celery This is an excellent alternative to ratatouille. Simmer the giblets to give a good stock. Use some liquid for making gravy; save remainder. Wash large heads of celery, divide into neat pieces. Toss in margarine for a few minutes. Lift out of the pan; make a thick coating brown sauce (recipe on page 61) using the giblet stock. Season well, flavour with chopped onion, chopped parsley, etc. Replace celery in this, simmer gently until tender. Do this on Christmas Eve, reheat on Christmas Day. Not particularly good when frozen.

Rich Fruit Cake

This is suitable for a Christmas cake, for a not too rich wedding cake or for a celebration cake for older children and adults.

Imperial/Metric	American
10 oz. (280 g.) butter or margarine	1¼ cups butter or margarine
10 oz. (280 g.) moist dark brown sugar	1¼ cups moist dark brown sugar
1 level tablespoon black treacle	1 tablespoon dark treacle or molasses
finely grated rind 1 lemon	finely grated rind 1 lemon
4 large or 5 small eggs	4 large or 5 small eggs
3 tablespoons sherry, rum or brandy	4 tablespoons sherry, rum or brandy
1 tablespoon lemon juice	1 tablespoon lemon juice
12 oz. (340 g.) flour, preferably plain	3 cups flour, preferably all-purpose
1 oz. (25 g.) ground almonds	¼ cup ground almonds
½ teaspoon powdered cinnamon	½ teaspoon cinnamon
½ teaspoon allspice	½ teaspoon allspice
4 oz. (100 g.) chopped candied peel	½ cup chopped candied peel
4 oz. (100 g.) chopped glacé cherries	½ cup chopped candied cherries
1 lb. (½ kilo) currants	3 cups currants
8 oz. (200 g.) sultanas	1½ cups white seedless raisins
12 oz. (340 g.) seedless raisins	2¼ cups seedless raisins
2–4 oz. (50–100 g.) chopped blanched almonds	½–1 cup chopped blanched almonds

Note In view of the large amounts, metric quantities are sometimes given in excess of the normal 25 g. = 1 oz.

Cooking time 3½–3¾ hours, see method
Makes a 9-inch (23-cm.) round or 8-inch (20-cm.) square cake at least 3 inches (8 cm.) in depth, or a more shallow 10-inch (25-cm.) round or 9-inch (23-cm.) square cake

Advance Preparations Check fruit is clean; if washed allow 48 hours to dry at room temperature. Dry blanched almonds. Check you have paper to line tin (pan). Make cake at least a month ahead, so it has time to mature.

Line bottom of tin with a piece of brown paper. Make a double band of greaseproof (waxed) paper, snip along bottom edge at ½-inch (1-cm.) intervals; put this in position, the cut edges give a good fit. Cover base with a round or square of double greaseproof (waxed) paper; grease lightly. Tie a double band of brown paper round outside of tin.

Cream butter or margarine, sugar, treacle and lemon rind until soft and light, *do not over-beat*. Mix beaten eggs, alcohol and lemon juice. Sieve the flour, ground almonds and spices; add to the peel, cherries, fruit and almonds.

Stir the egg mixture, then the flour mixture, into the creamed butter or margarine, etc. Spoon into the tin, press down firmly (this makes the cake easier to slice). Press the top gently with damp knuckles, this helps to keep the top of the cake flat. Put into the centre of a very moderate oven, 325°F. (170°C.), Gas Mark 3; bake for 1 hour (check that your oven is the right temperature, for during this first hour the cake should not change colour very much; if beginning to brown too much, lower the heat at once). After 1 hour turn the heat to slow, between 275–300°F. (140–150°C.), Gas Mark 1–2, for a further 2½ to 2¾ hours (check again during baking – at the end of the second hour's cooking the cake should be pale golden, but still look soft). To test if cooked, press firmly on top, check the cake has shrunk away from the sides of the tin, bring out of the oven and listen – a *cooked* rich fruit cake is silent, an *uncooked* rich fruit cake gives a definite humming noise – this means the cake should be put back in the oven. Allow to cool in the tin, turn out and store in an airtight tin or wrapped in foil until ready to ice (frost).

Variations

For a very Moist Cake Prick the cake after baking and spoon a little sherry or brandy over the top. Repeat at intervals.
Golden Christmas Cake Use castor (granulated) sugar in place of brown sugar and golden (light corn) syrup in place of treacle (molasses).

Ways to Decorate a Rich Fruit Cake

Marzipan (Almond Paste) To make sufficient marzipan for the top and sides of the cake on page 185 use: 12 oz. (340 g. – 3 cups) ground almonds, few drops almond or ratafia essence (extract), 6 oz. (170 g. – $\frac{3}{4}$ cup) castor (granulated) sugar, 6 oz. (170 g. – $1\frac{1}{3}$ cups) sieved icing (sifted confectioners') sugar, 3 large egg yolks.

Blend all ingredients together, 3 egg yolks should be sufficient to bind mixture *without too much kneading*; if they are small you may need part of a fourth yolk Knead mixture lightly, roll out on a sugared board. There are two ways of putting the marzipan on the cake, see below. Depending on which method you choose, either roll the marzipan to a round sufficiently large to coat the whole cake, or roll out marzipan, cut a band the depth of the cake, plus $\frac{1}{4}$ inch ($\frac{1}{2}$ cm.) to 'fold over' at the top, then cut a 9–10-inch (23–25-cm.) round or 8–9-inch (20–23-cm.) square, the size of the top of the cake. (This second method is better for a square cake.)

To Coat Cake with Marzipan Prepare the cake by brushing away surplus crumbs. Coat with jam or egg white to prevent marzipan 'picking up' crumbs.
Method 1 Lift the round of marzipan over the cake and pull gently into position so cake is evenly covered.
Method 2 Roll the cake along the band of marzipan, so the sides are coated. Press the surplus $\frac{1}{4}$ inch ($\frac{1}{2}$ cm.) flat over top of cake, put the top round or square of marzipan in position.

Whichever method you choose, press the marzipan firmly against the cake, then neaten the bottom edge. Run a rolling pin lightly over top of the cake to make sure the marzipan is perfectly flat. Roll a jam jar round the sides of the cake (easier than a rolling pin) to neaten surface – remember the more perfect the marzipan coating the better the surface for the final icing.

If you are fairly expert at handling marzipan you can put the icing over this at once – this has the great advantage of keeping the marzipan softer.

If you feel you may have handled the marzipan rather a lot it is better to leave the cake for 48 hours for the oil to 'dry out'. Whichever method you choose, brush the marzipan with a little unbeaten egg white before coating with royal icing – this forms a seal for the icing, so it 'sticks' to the marzipan and also forms a protective layer against the oil in the ground almonds, which can discolour the icing.

Christmas Cake Cover the cake with icing, then 'pick up' for a snow effect, using the tip of a knife.

Wedding Cake Coat the cake as the instructions on this page and page 187. Allow the first coat to become quite dry before you give a second coating. When both coats are dry continue with the piping. Put the icing (frosting) into a piping bag or syringe (pastry bag), with the selected pipe (nozzle) in position. For a flowing border, as in the picture, hold the pipe at an angle to ensure a flow of icing. To pipe upright rosettes hold the pipe, etc., absolutely upright.

Royal Icing This is the icing (frosting) most suitable for both the Christmas cake and the wedding cake shown on the previous page. It becomes sufficiently hard to 'stand up' in peaks or to pipe well.

To make sufficient royal icing to coat the top and sides with one thick layer of icing plus the snow scene on the Christmas cake opposite or the piping on the wedding cake opposite you will need the following quantities. It must be pointed out, however, that you will have a better result if you use two layers of icing on the wedding cake before you do the piping. If you wish to make up all the icing for two layers, etc., at one time, you must keep the top of the bowl covered with a damp cloth or damp paper; check that this is kept damp all the time, otherwise the icing will harden and it will be unmanageable.

For one layer plus decoration or piping you need: 2 lb. (1 kilo — 7 cups) sieved icing (sifted confectioners') sugar, 4 egg whites, 2 tablespoons (3 tablespoons) lemon juice, up to 4 teaspoons glycerine (this prevents royal icing becoming too hard — it is not a wise thing to use on a wedding cake with several tiers, where you have to support the weight of each tier).

If you wish to make the icing for a second coat, I would use 3 lb. (1½ kilos — 10½ cups) sugar, etc. You must sieve the icing (confectioners') sugar; this is very important. Whisk the egg whites *lightly*; do not over-beat. Gradually blend in the sugar, add the lemon juice and glycerine. Beat until the icing is very smooth and white — *do not over-beat, particularly if making the icing with an electric mixer* — if you do over-beat you have large air bubbles in the icing that spoil a smooth coating.

Lift the marzipan-coated cake on to a 10–11-inch (25–28-cm.) cake board; stand this on an icing turn-table or an upturned basin or bowl which can be used as a substitute. Put just over half the icing in the centre of the cake; cover the remainder of the icing with a damp cloth or paper (keep this moist); this will prevent it becoming hard before you need it for piping, etc. Take a palette knife or icing spatula, hold at both ends then drag the icing over the top and down the sides of the cake — *cover the cake completely before you attempt to neaten the icing.* Clean the knife or spatula, and with long sweeping movements neaten the top of the cake (it helps to warm the knife or spatula in boiling water, then to shake it dry). Hold the knife or spatula upright and neaten the sides of the cake.

American Frosting This excellent icing is the type that never becomes really hard. The quantities will coat the cake on page 185 or a similar size of cake. Put 2 lb. (1 kilo) cube or granulated sugar and ½ pint (3 dl. — 1¼ cups) water into a really strong saucepan. Stir until the sugar has completely dissolved. Boil steadily until the mixture reaches 238–240°F. (114–115°C.), or until a little forms a soft ball when tested in cold water. Meanwhile, whisk 4 egg whites until stiff, gradually blend syrup on to these, whisking well; add a pinch cream of tartar. Continue whisking until icing is stiff enough to hold its shape, then spread over cake.

Butterscotch Layer Cake *(Illustrated)* Cream 6 oz. (150 g. — ¾ cup) butter or margarine, 3 oz. (75 g. — generous ⅓ cup) soft brown sugar, 3 oz. (75 g. — ¼ cup) golden (light corn) syrup and ½ teaspoon vanilla essence (extract). Sieve (sift) 6 oz. (150 g. — 1½ cups) self-raising (self-rising) flour or plain (all-purpose) flour with 1½ teaspoons baking powder (double-acting). Gradually add 3 beaten eggs to butter, etc., fold in a little flour if the mixture shows signs of curdling. Fold in remaining flour and 4 oz. (100 g. — 1 cup) chopped walnuts. Divide mixture between three 7-inch (18-cm.) sandwich tins (layer cake pans); bake above centre of a moderate oven, 350–375°F. (180–190°C.), Gas Mark 4–5, until firm to the touch. Turn out carefully and cool. Make the American frosting as above using half quantities. Sandwich the cakes together with some frosting (add a little melted chocolate to filling), spread remainder over the cake. Top with walnut halves, or decorate to suit the occasion. This is a good cake for a special occasion; it keeps well for 2–3 days.

Cold Weather Menus

Do not plan too substantial or 'stodgy' dishes for cold weather dinner parties; our homes are generally well heated and therefore the food can be almost as refreshing and light as in warmer weather. Use the foods that are at their best in cold weather, or traditional for that time of the year.

Caribbean Mushrooms (page 172)	*Dutch Menu – see the picture on page 191 and the*
Roast Goose (page 189) with Accompaniments	*recipes on page 196*
Brussels Sprouts and Creamed Potatoes	
Viennoise Pudding (see below)	
Fish Pâté (page 169)	*Aubergines Lyonnaise (page 172)*
Orchard Chicken (page 194)	*Moroccan Style Lamb (page 190) with Green Salad*
Creamed Spinach and Roast Potatoes	*Diced Mixed Vegetables*
Pumpkin Pie (page 204)	*Traditional Sherry Trifle (page 189)*
Tomato and Orange Soup (page 21)	*Iced Melon*
Pheasants in Calvados (page 205)	*Burgundy Oxtail (page 50)*
Celery, Sprouts and Game Chips	*Cauliflower and Duchesse Potatoes (page 108)*
Meringues Glacées (page 192)	*Citrus Fruit Alaska (page 205)*

Viennoise Pudding

This is an excellent alternative to a Christmas pudding, especially for older people or younger children who find the traditional pudding rather heavy.

Imperial/Metric	American
4 oz. (100 g.) bread (without crusts)	*¼ lb. bread (without crusts)*
4 oz. (100 g.) granulated sugar	*½ cup granulated sugar*
3 tablespoons water	*4 tablespoons water*
1 pint (6 dl.) milk	*2½ cups milk*
4 egg yolks	*4 egg yolks*
2 egg whites	*2 egg whites*
2 oz. (50 g.) sultanas	*⅓ cup seedless white raisins*
2 oz. (50 g.) chopped glacé cherries	*¼ cup chopped candied cherries*
2 oz. (50 g.) chopped nuts (optional)	*½ cup chopped nuts (optional)*
1 oz. (25 g.) chopped crystallised peel	*3 tablespoons chopped candied peel*
2 tablespoons sherry (optional)	*3 tablespoons sherry (optional)*

Cooking time   2 hours 40 minutes
Serves 6
Advance Preparations Make caramel mixture and pour over bread.

Dice the bread. Put 3 oz. (75 g. – generous ⅓ cup) sugar and the water into a strong pan, stir until the sugar has dissolved, then boil steadily until brown. Cool slightly, add the milk and heat, without boiling, until the milk has absorbed the caramel, then pour over the diced bread. Allow to soak for at least 30 minutes. Add all the other ingredients to the caramel mixture, beating the eggs well before they are put in. Pour into a greased basin (mold), cover with foil or

greased paper and steam gently, without boiling, for approximately 2½ hours. Turn out and serve hot with the sauces suggested for Christmas pudding, see page 183.

Freezing The Viennoise pudding, made as the recipe above, does not freeze well, since there is too much water in the milk. If, however, you like to make the pudding with half milk and half thick (whipping) cream it freezes well. Use within 2 months, and thaw out before reheating.

Roast Goose

The accompaniments and timing for cooking a goose are similar to those given for roast duckling on page 179, the only difference being that the goose should be pricked several times during cooking to allow the fat to run out. Take care to prick the skin gently; if you pierce the flesh too deeply the excess fat tends to run *into* the bird instead of spurting out into the tin. When buying a goose, remember that although it may seem very heavy it has large bones and relatively little meat on the breast; this is why it is a fairly extravagant purchase. To make a change from apple sauce to serve with goose, roast small cored, but not peeled, dessert apples round the goose. Add these to the tin about 45 minutes before the end of the cooking time. Prunes cooked until just tender are another excellent accompaniment to goose. Goose fat has an excellent flavour, so that it is worth keeping the fat, clarifying this (see below) and using it for cooking.

To Clarify Fat Pour the fat into a saucepan, cover with cold water. Heat slowly, then allow the fat to cool and become fairly solid (other fats are much harder than goose fat). Spoon or lift the fat away from the water, scrape away any sediments of meat and store in the refrigerator.

Traditional Sherry Trifle

Imperial/Metric	American
4–5 sponge cakes	¼ lb. yellow sponge or layer cake, or ladyfingers
jam	jam
4–8 tablespoons sherry	5–9 tablespoons sherry
2 oz. (50 g.) blanched chopped almonds	⅓ cup blanched chopped almonds
1 pint (6 dl.) thick sweetened custard, see page 131	2½ cups thick sweetened custard, see page 131
¼–½ pint (1½–3 dl.) thick cream	⅔–1¼ cups whipping cream
to decorate	**to decorate**
glacé cherries	candied cherries
angelica	angelica
blanched almonds	blanched almonds

Cooking time 10 minutes to make custard
Serves 5–6
Advance Preparations Improves by being made some hours beforehand.

Split the sponge cakes, spread with jam, sandwich together and put into a serving dish. Sprinkle the sponge with the sherry, add almonds. Cover with the *hot* custard. Leave until cold (covering with paper or a plate to prevent a skin forming). Whip cream and pipe or spread over the top of the sweet, and decorate with the cherries, angelica and almonds.

For Economy Simmer 4 tablespoons (5 tablespoons) water, 1 oz. (25 g. – 2 tablespoons) sugar together, then add 2 tablespoons (3 tablespoons) sherry and soak the sponge cakes with this.
Freezing Although a trifle does not freeze well for any long period, I find I can put it into my freezer for a week without spoiling the texture of the custard. Allow plenty of time to thaw out. If you make the custard with half thick or thin (whipping or coffee) cream and half milk, it freezes for 2–3 weeks.

Variation

Trifle Omit sherry, use canned fruit instead. Split the sponge cakes, spread with jam and put into the dish. Soak the cakes in the syrup from the can then add some of the chopped canned fruit – retain some whole pieces of fruit for decoration. Cover with the hot custard, put a piece of paper or a plate over the dish. When cold, decorate with whipped cream and fruit.

A New Look to Lamb

The casserole illustrated on this page, with the recipe below, gives an entirely new look to lamb. This dish is an adaptation of one of the well known Moroccan recipes, and I have made it in such a way that it should appeal to most people. It has the great advantage, when you are entertaining, that it can be left 'to look after itself'.

Moroccan Style Lamb

Imperial/Metric	American
6 oz. (150 g.) dried prunes	1 cup prunes
½ pint (3 dl.) water	1¼ cups water
8 best end of neck or loin chops or cutlets of lamb	8 lamb loin chops or rib roast cutlets
scant 1 oz. (25 g.) flour	just under ¼ cup flour
seasoning	seasoning
pinch curry powder	pinch curry powder
pinch cayenne pepper	pinch cayenne
1½ oz. (40 g.) margarine or butter	3 tablespoons margarine or butter
½ pint (3 dl.) white stock or water and 1 chicken stock cube	1¼ cups white stock or water and 1 chicken bouillon cube
½ tablespoon tomato purée	½ tablespoon tomato paste
2 oz. (50 g.) blanched* almonds	½ cup blanched* almonds
to serve	**to serve**
boiled rice or noodles	boiled rice or noodles

* to blanch almonds: put into boiling water for 1–2 minutes, remove, cool and pull away the skins.

Cooking time   1 hour 10 minutes
Serves 4
Advance Preparations Soak the prunes overnight in the water.

Strain the prunes, but retain the liquid. Trim any excess fat from the meat, mix the flour with seasoning, curry powder and pepper. Coat meat in this. Toss in the hot margarine or butter until pale golden. Transfer to a casserole, then blend the prune liquid and stock with the fat remaining in the pan and heat until a thin sauce. Add the tomato purée, taste and add extra seasoning. Pour the liquid over the lamb, add the prunes. Cover the casserole and cook in the centre of a moderate oven, 325–350°F. (170–180°C.), Gas Mark 3–4, for approximately 40 minutes. Add the almonds and continue cooking for 10 minutes. Serve with rice or noodles and a mixture of young vegetables.

Freezing This freezes well; do not over-cook before freezing. The liquid may seem a little thin after freezing and need a little extra thickening when reheated. Use within 3–4 months.

Variations

Moroccan Style Chicken Use jointed chicken in place of the lamb in the recipe above. Skin the chicken if you wish a softer coating on the outside of each joint. The curry powder can be omitted and a little ground ginger used instead.

A Dutch menu (see page 196)

Meringues

Meringues are a splendid standby and sweets topped with meringue look and taste delicious. A photograph of meringues is on page 6.

1 Make certain the egg whites are very stiff – you need a clean dry bowl, and egg whites at *room* temperature (so bring out of the refrigerator at least 1 hour before using) and *not less* than 24 hours old.

2 Whisk hard until the egg whites are very stiff; you should be able to turn the mixing bowl upside down without the egg whites falling out. *Do not*, however, over-beat until the egg whites are dry and 'crumbly'.

3 Either beat in half the sugar very gradually, then fold in the rest, or fold all the sugar gradually into the egg whites. If using an electric mixer add small amounts of the sugar gradually to the stiffly-whisked egg whites with the whisk still operating at *low* speed. All the sugar can be beaten in with an electric mixer.

4 When putting a meringue on a dessert you can set and brown this fairly quickly if the sweet is to be served hot; but it must be set very slowly if the sweet is to be served cold. This prevents the meringue shrivelling. It is also advisable to be more generous with the sugar to ensure a crisp meringue on a dessert.

Meringues

Imperial/Metric	American
2 egg whites	2 egg whites
4 oz. (100 g.) castor sugar (or you can use 2 oz. (50 g.) castor and 2 oz. (50 g.) sieved icing sugar)	½ cup granulated sugar (or you can use ¼ cup granulated and ¼ cup sifted confectioners' sugar)

Cooking time see method
Advance Preparations Meringues can be made and stored for weeks in an airtight tin.

Whisk the egg whites until very stiff, see point 2 above. Add the sugar, see point 3. Either pipe into neat shapes or spoon on to well oiled or buttered baking trays (sheets). Dry out in a very cool oven, i.e. 225–250°F. (110–130°C.), Gas Mark 0–½. This quantity makes:
8–10 large meringues: cook 2–3 hours
10–16 medium meringues: cook 2 hours
16–24 tiny meringues: cook 1½–2 hours.
To test if cooked, press firmly and they should be firm and hard. To remove from the trays, dip a palette knife in hot water, shake off surplus moisture, slide the knife under the cooked meringues and lift out. When quite cold, store in an airtight tin until ready to use.
Never fill the meringues with cream, etc., too soon before serving.

Variations

Chocolate Meringues Add 1 oz. (25 g. – ¼ cup) chocolate powder or ½ oz. (15 g. – 2 tablespoons) sieved cocoa to the sugar.
Coffee Meringues Add 1–1½ teaspoons instant coffee powder to the sugar.
Meringue Nests Form the meringue mixture into a nest shape and bake in the usual way. Fill with fresh or well drained canned or frozen fruit, and cream.
Meringues Chantilly Fill the meringues with sweetened whipped cream, flavoured with vanilla essence (extract).

Meringues Glacées

Imperial/Metric	American
meringues, see above	meringues, see above
ice cream, see page 177	ice cream, see page 177
little whipped cream (optional)	little whipped cream (optional)

Cooking time see above
Sandwich two meringue shells together with the ice cream. Pipe a little whipped cream round the edge if wished.

The Richer Pastries

The richer pastries, i.e. puff and flaky pastry (puff paste and rich flaky pie dough) are ideal for many purposes. One of the best pastry shapes for a party is to make the pastry into vol-au-vent cases, and instructions are below.

The richest pastry, i.e. puff pastry, is made by using equal amounts of flour and fat and giving the pastry 7 rollings and 7 foldings, so producing a very light texture. Details of puff pastry are on page 218. Flaky pastry, while light, will not rise quite as much as puff pastry; flaky pastry is made by using three-quarters the amount of fat to flour, see the recipe and sketches below. You can substitute this slightly more economical pastry for puff pastry.

Flaky Pastry (Rich Flaky Pie Dough) Sieve 8 oz. (200 g. – 2 cups) plain (all-purpose) flour with a pinch of salt. Rub 2 oz. (50 g. – $\frac{1}{4}$ cup) fat (this can be shortening, butter or margarine, or a mixture of fats) into the flour. Mix to an elastic dough with water, or water and lemon juice. Roll out to an oblong shape. Cover two-thirds of the dough with another 2 oz. (50 g. – $\frac{1}{4}$ cup) fat (type as above). *Sketch 1* shows how this is put on in small pieces. Fold the dough (*see Sketch 2*). Seal the ends of the pastry (*Sketch 3*) and turn at right angles. Depress the pastry at regular intervals as *Sketch 4*. Repeat the processes described by Sketches 1–4 with another 2 oz. (50 g. – $\frac{1}{4}$ cup) fat, then give the pastry a final fold and roll and it is ready for use. It is advisable to keep it in a cool place during the above stages, if it becomes sticky, and until ready for use. Bake as vol-au-vent below.

Vol-au-vent Roll out puff or flaky pastry until about $\frac{1}{2}$–$\frac{3}{4}$ inch (1–1$\frac{1}{2}$ cm.) in thickness. Cut into rounds – these can vary from tiny cocktail size rounds to the large size which would serve several people for a main meal. Take a smaller cutter (cookie cutter) and mark out a round in the centre of the pastry; this round should go about halfway through the pastry (*see Sketch 5*). Put on to a baking sheet and chill before cooking. Brush the top of the pastry rounds with a little beaten egg for a pleasant shine. Put into the centre of a very hot oven, 450–475°F. (230–240°C.), Gas Mark 8–9, for about 10 minutes until the pastry is well risen, then lower the heat to moderate, 350–375°F. (180–190°C.), Gas Mark 4–5, for a further 5–15 minutes (depending upon size of pastry cases) until firm. Remove from the oven. Gently lift out the centre round of pastry (*as Sketch 6*) then return the pastry cases to a cool oven for a short time to 'dry-out'. Fillings for vol-au-vent cases can be varied:

Sweet Fillings Fill with jam, fruit purée and whipped cream, etc.

Savoury Fillings Fill with vegetables, diced cooked chicken, ham, etc., in a thick sauce. The picture on page 171 shows a celery filling made by adding chopped raw celery and a chopped canned red pepper (pimiento) to a really thick cheese sauce, page 61, together with a topping of chopped parsley.

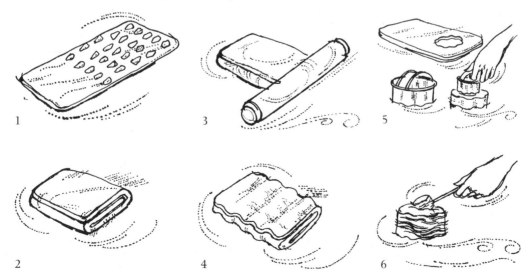

Fruit with Chicken

Do not imagine that one must serve vegetables with meat and poultry all the time. The picture opposite and the recipe below are clear indications that a fruit-flavoured chicken is not only unusual but delicious too.

Orchard Chicken

Imperial/Metric	American
6 chicken joints	6 chicken joints
1 bay leaf	1 bay leaf
sprig parsley	sprig parsley
seasoning	seasoning
2 tablespoons oil	3 tablespoons oil
1 oz. (50 g.) flour	¼ cup flour
2 onions	2 onions
¾ pint (4½ dl.) chicken stock	just under 2 cups chicken stock
1 teaspoon crushed coriander seed	1 teaspoon crushed coriander seed
¼ teaspoon ground cinnamon	¼ teaspoon ground cinnamon
¼ teaspoon powdered saffron	¼ teaspoon powdered saffron
1–2 tablespoons chopped preserved ginger	1–2 tablespoons chopped preserved (Canton) ginger
1 lb. (½ kilo) cooking pears	1 lb. baking pears
2–3 dessert apples	2–3 dessert apples
4–6 plums or apricots	4–6 plums or apricots
1 tablespoon syrup from preserved ginger	1 tablespoon syrup from preserved ginger
little lemon juice	little lemon juice
to garnish	**to garnish**
chopped parsley	chopped parsley

Cooking time 1¼ hours plus time for making stock
Serves 6
Advance Preparations Fry chicken, make the stock.

Skin the chicken joints and remove as many bones as possible, without spoiling the appearance of the chicken. Put the bones, bay leaf and parsley into a saucepan. Add about 1 pint (6 dl. – 2½ cups) water, season well. Cover the pan and simmer for at least 45 minutes. Strain off the liquid. Heat the oil in a pan and fry the floured joints of chicken for a few minutes. Lift out of the pan, add the chopped onions and cook for several minutes, then blend in the ¾ pint (4½ dl. – just under 2 cups) chicken stock. Replace the chicken joints in the liquid with the flavourings and simmer for 20 minutes. Add the peeled sliced pears and apples, halved plums or apricots, the ginger syrup and lemon juice to taste. Cover the pan and simmer for a further 40 minutes. Top with parsley. *Illustrated opposite.*

Pheasants in Calvados (see page 205)

Orchard chicken (see page 194)

Buffet Parties

A buffet party has the advantage that you can entertain a relatively large number of people within a small space, for all the food can be arranged on a table and the guests can help themselves. If there is no room for people to sit down it is important to provide the kind of food that can be eaten with a fork or served in some very simple manner; for example, if you want to include soup it is probably better to put the soup in cups from which people may drink, rather than trying to balance a soup bowl and use a soup spoon. Meat, etc., and salads, should be shredded finely so they can be eaten with a fork. The Dutch menu on this page, below, is for a quite different kind of buffet, in that it is fairly substantial and you would need to allow your guests to sit down at a table, or at least have a space on which to balance the food. As buffets vary so much I have not given set menus, but suggested some dishes that are always popular.

Dutch Menu

The Dutch Menu pictured on page 191 is very easy to make and economical too; it consists of:

Vermicelli Soup with Meat Balls
Egg Open Sandwiches with Red Cabbage
Spiced Apple Tart

Vermicelli Soup with Meat Balls (Vermicelli Soep met Balletjes) Put 2 pints (generous 1 litre – 5 cups) beef stock or water with 2–3 beef stock (bouillon) cubes into a pan. Add 2 blades of mace and seasoning and simmer for 10–15 minutes. Mix 4 oz. (100 g. – ½ cup, firmly packed) minced (ground) beef with seasoning and a little grated nutmeg. Form into tiny balls, roll in flour, add to the soup, together with a few tablespoons lightly crushed vermicelli. Cover the pan and simmer gently for 20 minutes. Remove mace and top with chopped parsley. *Serves 4–6.*

Egg Open Sandwiches (Uilsmijter) Butter one slice of bread for each person, top with a slice of cooked ham and a slice of Dutch Edam cheese. Fry 2 eggs for each person, drain and place on the cheese. Garnish with tomato, lettuce and gherkins or pickle, and with red cabbage. Serve at once.

Red Cabbage (Rode Kool) Although this is really served with hot meat dishes I find it excellent with the sandwiches above. Shred the heart of a red cabbage finely. Peel, core and quarter about 4 cooking (baking) apples. Put the cabbage, apple, ¼ pint (1½ dl. – ⅔ cup) water, good pinch salt, up to 1 tablespoon mixed spice (try a small amount to begin with) and 2–4 cloves into a large saucepan. Cover and simmer for approximately 45 minutes. Remove cloves and add 2–3 tablespoons vinegar and 2 oz. (50 g. – ¼ cup) butter. Season well.

Spiced Apple Tart (Appel Taart) Make pastry with 8 oz. (200 g. – 2 cups) flour as page 72. Line an 8-inch (20-cm.) sandwich tin (layer cake pan) or flan ring on an upturned baking tray (sheet) with half the pastry. Slice 1 lb. (½ kilo) peeled cooking (baking) apples, mix with 4 oz. (100 g. – ½ cup) sugar, 2 oz. (50 g. – ⅓ cup) sultanas (white raisins), 1 teaspoon ground cinnamon and the grated rind of ½ lemon. Put over the pastry. Roll out the remaining pastry to form a lid. Damp the edges and seal together. Make a few slits on top of the tart, see picture page 191. Bake for 15 minutes in the centre of a hot oven, 425°F. (220°C.), Gas Mark 7, then lower the heat to 350°F. (180°C.), Gas Mark 4, for a further 30 minutes, or even reduce the heat again slightly if the pastry seems to be getting too brown. Leave the tart in the tin for 5 minutes before turning out. Sprinkle with sieved icing (sifted confectioners') sugar. Serve hot or cold with cream. *Serves 6.*

Cheese and Wine Parties

Cheese and wine parties have, during the last few years, gained a great deal of popularity, for they are simple to prepare and yet can be extremely interesting. When planning such a party make certain you have a good variety of cheeses; you will need fairly familiar cheese for the conservative guest, i.e. Cheddar and/or similar hard cheeses. You then should choose a rather more sophisticated cheese, which can be a Camembert, a Brie or another of this type. Many people thoroughly enjoy the blue-veined cheeses and there is a big variety here, from the familiar Danish Blue to the classic Stilton and the very delicious Roquefort. Some people like very mild cheeses, so cream or processed cheese should be included. If you think any of your guests might be calorie-conscious, have bowls of cottage cheese as well. Look round the shops and try to include a very unusual cheese that will cause interest among your guests. If you have a lot of people and a restricted space it is a good idea to cut the cheese into convenient pieces and arrange these on trays with grapes, radishes, segments of orange, celery, etc. Serve biscuits, French bread, crispbread and butter. You may like to offer one hot dish and it could be something containing cheese, e.g. the tomato gouda pie (page 156), or savouries such as the recipe below.

Your choice of wine is unlimited, for practically every wine blends with cheese. Some people will insist that it should be a red wine, but in my opinion that is not essential. If you have too big a choice of wines it does make serving a little difficult; it is probably better to have one white wine and one red wine, or to compromise by having just a well chilled rosé wine.

Stuffed Mushrooms

Imperial/Metric	American
6 large slices bread	6 large slices bread
4 oz. (100 g.) fat or dripping	¼ cup shortening or drippings
24 medium cap mushrooms	24 medium cap mushrooms
1 medium onion	1 medium onion
8 oz. (200 g.) cooked chicken	½ lb. cooked chicken
8 oz. (200 g.) cooked ham	½ lb. cooked ham
3 oz. (75 g.) soft breadcrumbs	1½ cups soft bread crumbs
2 eggs	2 eggs
2 tablespoons thick cream	3 tablespoons whipping cream
seasoning	seasoning
1 tablespoon chopped parsley	1 tablespoon chopped parsley
to garnish	**to garnish**
watercress	watercress

Cooking time 30–35 minutes
Makes 24
Advance Preparations Fry bread. Prepare mushrooms, put on bread, heat 15 minutes before required.

Remove crusts from bread and divide each slice into four pieces, fry in just over half the fat or dripping until pale golden and crisp, drain on absorbent paper. Wash and dry mushrooms, remove stalks. Fry the finely chopped onion and chopped mushroom stalks in any fat or dripping remaining in pan, lift out and put into basin; then heat rest of fat or dripping and fry the whole mushrooms. Drain well on absorbent paper. Mince or chop chicken and ham finely, mix with onion, mushroom stalks, half the crumbs, eggs, cream, seasoning and parsley. Place mushrooms on fried bread, spoon stuffing into mushroom caps, top with rest of crumbs. Heat for 15–20 minutes in centre of very moderate oven, 325–350°F. (170–180°C.), Gas Mark 3–4. Garnish with watercress.

Freezing Either prepare to stage of filling mushrooms, then freeze; thaw out and cook as above; or cook, freeze then reheat. Use within 2 months.

With the Minimum of Cooking

Although in no sense a formal buffet menu the recipes on these two pages could form a very good meal. The Christmas dessert, opposite, is equally good at any other time of the year.

Celery Dressing

Imperial/Metric	American
½ heart of medium head celery	½ heart of medium bunch celery
few celery leaves	few celery leaves
¼ pint (1½ dl.) soured cream* or use yoghourt	⅔ cup sour cream* or use yogurt

* or thick (whipping) cream plus 1 tablespoon lemon juice.

No cooking
Serves 4—6
Advance Preparations This is better if made several hours before required, and chilled thoroughly.

Chop the celery and the leaves, mix with the soured cream or yoghourt. It is delicious with any poultry or meat dishes that are fairly dry in texture, as well as the beef and egg cutlets, page 209. Carry in a carton for a picnic.

Freezing Spoiled by freezing, the celery loses its crisp texture.

Variation
Cucumber Sauce Use finely shredded cucumber in place of celery, add a few drops Tabasco sauce plus 1 tablespoon tomato purée (paste).

Prawns with Celery Dressing Serve large cooked shelled prawns (jumbo shrimp) around a bowl of celery dressing, which is also an excellent dressing for a picnic meal to serve with ham, etc.

Sausage Boatees Allow 2 sausages, a little chutney, 2 slices of cheese (this should be processed, or Dutch cheese that rolls easily), plus 2 pineapple chunks for each person. Prick the sausages lightly and cook under a hot grill (broiler) until brown, turn several times during cooking so they cook evenly. Allow to cool thoroughly before continuing. Split down the centre and insert a little chutney. Place each one corner-to-corner across a slice of cheese. Lift up two loose corners and skewer with a cocktail stick. Cut the pineapple chunks into halves and put a piece on either end of each stick to keep cheese upright, see photograph.

Australian Ice Christmas Dessert

Imperial/Metric	American
1 oz. (25 g.) sugar	2 tablespoons sugar
¼ pint (1½ dl.) water	⅔ cup water
4 oz. (100 g.) raisins	⅔ cup raisins
4 oz. (100 g.) sultanas	⅔ cup seedless white raisins
4 oz. (100 g.) currants	⅔ cup currants
1 pint (6 dl.) vanilla ice cream*	2½ cups vanilla ice cream*
1–2 oz. (25–50 g.) glacé cherries	2–4 tablespoons candied cherries
2 tablespoons brandy or sherry ⅝	3 tablespoons brandy or sherry
10–15 sponge finger biscuits	10–15 ladyfingers

* bought or home-made, see recipe page 177.

Cooking time few minutes
Serves 6–8
Advance Preparations Can be frozen.

Dissolve the sugar in the water to make a syrup, and add the dried fruit. Bring to the boil, pour immediately into a basin and leave to cool completely. Drain the dried fruit of all the syrup and mix with the ice cream, together with the halved cherries and the brandy or sherry. Pack into a suitable dish (mold) and put into the refrigerator freezing compartment or home freezer for about 10 hours. Turn out and place the sponge fingers around the edge. Tie them in place with a piece of brightly coloured ribbon, see photograph. Store in the freezer until ready to use.

Variations
Add chopped nuts; add 2–3 oz. (50–75 g. – 1–1½ cups) soft stale cake or sweet biscuit (cookie) crumbs.

Chocolate Truffles First melt 2 oz. (50 g. – 2 squares) plain (semi-sweet) chocolate, then mix with 3 oz. (75 g. – generous ⅓ cup) creamed butter or margarine (do not use the 'soft luxury' type), 1¼ tablespoons cocoa powder, 2 tablespoons (3 tablespoons) drinking chocolate powder, 2 oz. (50 g. – ½ cup) sieved icing (sifted confectioners') sugar. Blend well, then add 1½ tablespoons (2 tablespoons) very strong coffee and 1 tablespoon brandy or rum. Allow the mixture to stand for several hours, or overnight in the refrigerator. Roll into tiny balls and coat with cocoa powder or chocolate vermicelli. Serve with after-dinner coffee. *This makes about 18 sweetmeats.*

Economical Truffles Add 2 oz. (50 g. – 1 cup) soft fine cake crumbs to the mixture, plus 1 extra tablespoon coffee and a few more drops brandy or rum. This will roll in balls almost at once. Chopped nuts, chopped glacé (candied) cherries, etc., may also be added to the mixture, and the balls may be rolled sufficiently large to serve as small petits fours.

199

Choux Pastry

This makes an ideal pastry for a buffet, for the buns or cases can be served as a savoury or a sweet.

Imperial/Metric	American
1 oz. (25 g.) margarine or butter	2 tablespoons margarine or butter
¼ pint (1½ dl.) water	⅔ cup water
1 teaspoon sugar for sweet cases or good pinch salt for savoury cases	1 teaspoon sugar for sweet cases or good pinch salt for savory cases
3 oz. (75 g.) flour (plain or self-raising)	¾ cup flour (all-purpose or self-rising)
approximately 2 whole eggs and 1 egg yolk	approximately 2 whole eggs and 1 egg yolk

Cooking time see recipes below
Makes approximately 8 large buns; 12–14 medium size buns; 20 tiny profiteroles; 8–10 good size eclairs, or approximately 20 very tiny cocktail size eclairs
Advance Preparations Weigh out ingredients or bake earlier in the day, or the day before required. Choux pastry does not keep well unless it is frozen after cooking.

Heat margarine or butter in water in a saucepan until melted, add sugar or salt. Remove from heat, stir in flour and continue stirring over low heat until a really *dry* mixture. Take off heat, add first egg – beat in very thoroughly until smooth mixture, add second egg – beat in again, then add as much egg yolk as is needed to give a sticky consistency.
The pastry is then ready to use and can be made into a variety of shapes, see below. All the shapes may be made earlier in the day.

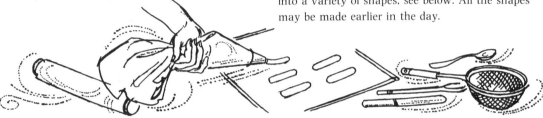

Bun Shapes Either put spoonfuls of the mixture on to well greased and floured baking trays (sheets), or pipe rounds of the mixture on to the trays using a ½–1-inch (1–2-cm.) plain pipe (nozzle). If you can cover the baking trays with a light, deep tin, you encourage the pastry to rise and swell into a more attractive shape. If you are covering the pastry, you must allow an extra 5–10 minutes cooking time. Bake in the centre of a hot oven, 425°F. (220°C.), Gas Mark 7, for about 12–15 minutes for small buns, or 18–20 minutes for larger ones, then reduce heat to moderate, 350°F. (180°C.), Gas Mark 4, for a further 10–20 minutes. Allow buns to cool away from a draught, then slit at the side and remove any uncooked pastry. Return for a few minutes to a cool oven to 'dry out', then fill, etc., as directions.
Freezing Fill buns, freeze, then wrap. Use within 2 months. Thaw out at room temperature.

Profiteroles These are exactly the same as bun shapes, but use only a very small teaspoon of the mixture and bake for approximately 10 minutes in a hot oven, and a further 5 minutes in a moderate

heat. There is no need to cover profiteroles with a tin.

Eclairs Either put 2-inch (5-cm.) lengths of the mixture on to the greased and floured baking tray (sheet), or pipe the mixture on with a ½-inch (1-cm.) plain pipe (nozzle), or put the mixture into straight, well greased and floured finger-shape tins. Bake as bun shapes, allowing 10 minutes in a hot oven, and 10 minutes in the moderate heat. Do not cover.
For a cocktail-size éclair, bake as for profiteroles. Cool away from a draught. Split open and remove any small amount of uncooked mixture in the centre, return to oven for a few minutes to dry out, cool again and fill.
If baking the day before required, re-crisp for a short time before filling.

Fillings for Savoury Buns or Eclairs

Choose any of the fillings suggested for vol-au-vent on page 193, but keep the mixture a little stiffer. Mashed sardines, cottage or cream cheese, or a very thick cheese sauce (page 61) are excellent for choux pastry.

Fillings for Sweet Buns or Eclairs
Cream Filling Whip cream lightly, sweeten if wished, and flavour with a few drops of vanilla essence (extract). Put into the bun shapes and top with sieved icing (confectioners') sugar.

Chocolate Eclairs Fill with cream as above and coat the tops either with melted chocolate or a chocolate icing.
To make sufficient icing for 12 éclairs: blend 4 oz. (100 g. – nearly 1 cup) sieved icing (confectioners') sugar, 1 oz. (25 g. – ¼ cup) chocolate powder or ½ oz. (15 g. – 2 tablespoons) cocoa with ½ tablespoon warm water and 2 or 3 drops of oil.

Profiteroles Fill with cream, pile into a dish and serve with hot chocolate sauce, see below.

Chocolate Sauce Melt 4 oz. (100 g.) plain (semi-sweet) chocolate, ½ oz. (15 g. – 1 tablespoon) butter, 1–2 tablespoons water in a basin (bowl) over hot water.

Ice Cream Buns Fill bun shapes with coffee or vanilla ice cream, serve with chocolate sauce.

Fruit Buns Blend equal quantities of thick fruit purée and whipped cream. Put into the buns and serve with extra pouring cream.

Bacon Liver Pâté en Croûte

Imperial/Metric	American
8 oz. (200 g.) frozen puff pastry or pastry made with 4 oz. (100 g.) flour, etc., see page 218	½ lb. frozen puff paste or pastry made with 1 cup flour, etc., see page 218
8 oz. (200 g.) streaky bacon (cut in one piece)	½ lb. slab bacon
4 oz. (100 g.) calves' liver or chicken livers	¼ lb. calf liver or chicken liver
1 onion	1 onion
1 tablespoon flour	1 tablespoon flour
2 tablespoons milk	3 tablespoons milk
2 eggs	2 eggs
2 tablespoons sherry	3 tablespoons sherry
¼ teaspoon grated nutmeg	¼ teaspoon grated nutmeg
seasoning	seasoning
6 thin rashers streaky bacon	6 thin bacon slices
to serve	**to serve**
salad	salad

Cooking time 1 hour
Serves 5–6
Advance Preparations Make or buy pastry, keep in cool place until needed for cooking. The pâté may be made and cooked 1–2 days before being required, or it can be frozen.

If using frozen pastry, defrost this. Mince the piece of bacon three times until it is very fine; add the liver and onion when mincing the bacon for the third time. Stir the flour, milk, 1 egg and sherry into the liver mixture, mix well; add the nutmeg and seasoning. Line a 1-lb. (½-kilo) loaf pan with the rashers of bacon, put in the liver mixture and cover with greased paper or foil. Bake for 30 minutes in the centre of a moderate oven, 325–350°F. (170–180°C.), Gas Mark 3–4; allow to cool in the pan for

10 minutes, turn out very carefully. Roll out the pastry very thinly so it will cover the pâté. Wrap round the pâté, so it is completely enclosed, brush with the beaten second egg. Bake for 30 minutes in the centre of a very hot oven, 450–475°F. (230–240°C.), Gas Mark 8–9, reducing the heat to moderate after about 15 minutes. Serve cold with salad.

Freezing Freezes well. Use within 6 weeks.

Variation
Liver Pâté Omit the pastry and bake the pâté as the recipe above. Keep in the pan until cold. Cover with a layer of melted butter if storing for any time. You can omit the minced bacon and use 12 oz. (300 g.) liver instead.

Easter Celebrations

Easter, like Christmas, has its own traditional fare. On Good Friday hot cross buns are generally served at breakfast time, but I would make rather a lot of these for I find most people enjoy them for tea on Good Friday, and they freeze extremely well, so you can bring them out on other occasions.

As this holiday coincides with spring, I always try to choose rather spring-like food — new season's lamb with young vegetables is a favourite luncheon menu. I use the early spring fruits in salads and light desserts.

It may well be that the weather will be sufficiently fine to eat out-of-doors, and you will find some typical picnic fare in the chapter starting on page 206.

Hot Cross Buns

Imperial/Metric	American
½ oz. (15 g.) fresh yeast	½ cake compressed yeast
1 teaspoon sugar	1 teaspoon sugar
¼ pint (1½ dl.) milk	⅔ cup milk
4 tablespoons water	5 tablespoons water
12 oz. (340 g.) plain flour	3 cups all-purpose flour
pinch salt	pinch salt
1–2 oz. (25–50 g.) margarine*	2 tablespoons–¼ cup margarine*
1 oz. (25 g.) sugar	2 tablespoons sugar
4–6 oz. (100–150 g.) dried fruit*	¾–1 cup dried fruit*
3–4 oz. (75–100 g.) candied peel*	½–¾ cup candied peel*
1 teaspoon mixed spice	1 teaspoon mixed spices
to decorate	**to decorate**
short crust pastry made with 2 oz. (50 g.) flour, etc., see page 72	basic pie dough made with ½ cup flour, etc., see page 72
2 tablespoons sugar	3 tablespoons sugar
2 tablespoons water	3 tablespoons water

*use the larger quantities for a richer bun.

Cooking time 10 minutes
Makes 12
Advance Preparations Make the buns and reheat on Good Friday, or freeze, see page 93.

Cream the yeast and sugar, then add the warm milk and water. Sprinkle a little flour over the top and leave in a warm place for 10–15 minutes until the surface is covered with bubbles. Sieve (sift) the flour and salt into a warm bowl, rub in the margarine, add the sugar, fruit, peel and spice. When the yeast liquid is ready, work in and knead thoroughly. Put in a warm place for approximately 1 hour to prove (rise), i.e., until the dough doubles in size. Form into round buns and prove for 15 minutes on a warm baking tray (sheet). Make the pastry as page 72 and cut into thin strips; arrange in the form of a cross on top of the buns. If preferred omit the pastry and mark a cross on the buns *before* proving. Bake for

10 minutes towards the top of a hot to very hot oven, 450–475°F. (230–240°C.), Gas Mark 8–9. Mix the sugar with the water. Immediately the buns come from the oven, brush with this glaze.

Simnel Cake

The tradition attached to this cake started many years ago when a fruit cake was made by maids to take home to their mothers when they were given time off duty for Mothering Sunday. However, over the years the occasion for eating this very delicious cake has changed. and now it is generally made for Easter Sunday. Decorated eggs will cause great pleasure to the younger members of your family for breakfast on Easter Day.

Imperial/Metric	American
6 oz. (150 g.) butter or margarine	¾ cup butter or margarine
6 oz. (150 g.) sugar	¾ cup sugar
3 eggs	3 eggs
8 oz. (200 g.) plain flour	2 cups all-purpose flour
1 teaspoon baking powder	1 teaspoon baking powder (double-acting)
1 teaspoon mixed spice	1 teaspoon mixed spices
1 lb. (½ kilo) mixed dried fruit	3 cups mixed dried fruit
3 oz. (75 g.) chopped glacé cherries	generous ½ cup chopped candied cherries
3 oz. (75 g.) chopped candied peel	½ cup chopped candied peel
2 oz. (50 g.) chopped blanched almonds (optional)	½ cup chopped blanched almonds (optional)
2 tablespoons milk	3 tablespoons milk
for the marzipan	**for the marzipan**
8 oz. (200 g.) ground almonds	2 cups ground almonds
4 oz. (100 g.) castor sugar	½ cup granulated sugar
4 oz. (100 g.) sieved icing sugar	1 cup sifted confectioners' sugar
2 egg yolks or 1 egg to bind	2 egg yolks or 1 egg to bind
to decorate	**to decorate**
egg white for glaze	egg white for glaze
chickens, ribbon, etc.	chickens, ribbon, etc.

Cooking time 2¼ hours
Serves 10–12
Advance Preparations Make some days before required.

Cream the butter or margarine and sugar until soft and light. Gradually beat in eggs. add little sieved (sifted) flour if mixture shows signs of curdling. Sieve flour, baking powder and spice. fold into egg mixture, add fruit, almonds and milk.

Make the marzipan by mixing ingredients together, roll out just under half to an 8-inch (20-cm.) round. Put half cake mixture into greased and floured 8-inch (20-cm.) cake tin (pan), cover with marzipan and then rest of the cake. Bake in the centre of a very moderate oven, 325°F. (170°C.), Gas Mark 3 for 2¼ hours, reduce the heat slightly after about 1–1¼ hours. Test to see if cooked by pressing firmly and listening. If cooked there is no 'humming' noise. Allow cake to cool on wire tray (rack). Roll out rest of marzipan, cover the top, make small Easter eggs (colouring these if wished) with marzipan. Brush top with egg white and brown for a little time under a low grill (broiler). Decorate with chickens, etc.

Birthdays and Anniversaries

The way in which you celebrate a birthday will obviously depend upon the age of the person, but it does not matter whether it is a small child, or an elderly adult, I am quite sure they will enjoy a birthday cake. Choose a plain sponge mixture as the recipes on pages 99 and 100 for small children or someone who is rather old, but you can use the rich fruit cake recipe on page 185 for other birthday cakes, and ice it as suggested on those pages. The way in which you decorate the cake will, of course, depend upon the interest of the person celebrating their birthday. Children's cakes can be topped with toy figures to fit in with their particular hobbies.

If making a cake to celebrate a silver or golden wedding, then it should look very much like a wedding cake with the decorations in the appropriate colour. To celebrate a coming-of-age birthday the cake could reflect the interests of the particular person.

The rest of the food will, of course, depend upon the time of day, etc. On the following page I have two recipes which, with a delicious hors d'oeuvre – and you will find a very big selection in this book – would make a special celebration meal. You may find it better to have a buffet or a tea party.

If you are celebrating the birthday of someone from another country, try and find a typical dish that reflects their own cuisine. You will find recipes from various countries in this book which could form part of the menu. As an example of this, I give below the famous pumpkin pie, which would be a very good choice for an American celebrating a special occasion.

Pumpkin Pie Line an 8–9-inch (20–23-cm.) flan dish or flan tin (layer cake pan) on an upturned baking tray (sheet) with short crust pastry (basic pie dough) made with 6–8 oz. (150–200 g.– $1\frac{1}{2}$–2 cups) flour, etc., (depending upon the depth of the dish or tin). Meanwhile, peel, dice and steam approximately 1 lb. ($\frac{1}{2}$ kilo) pumpkin until soft. Mash this and blend with 2 eggs, $\frac{1}{2}$ pint (3 dl. – $1\frac{1}{4}$ cups) thin (coffee) cream and 4–6 oz. (100–150 g. – $\frac{1}{2}$–$\frac{3}{4}$ cup) sugar. Flavour with a little ground cinnamon, ground ginger or other spices, or even with grated lemon rind instead. Spoon into the pastry case. Bake for 20 minutes in the centre of a hot oven, 425°F. (220°C.), Gas Mark 7, then reduce the heat to moderate, 350–375°F. (180–190°C.), Gas Mark 4–5, for a further 15–20 minutes, until the filling and pastry are firm. Serve hot or cold with cream or ice cream. *Serves 6.*

Danish Apple Cake

Imperial/Metric	American
4–6 oz. (100–150 g.) soft breadcrumbs	2–3 cups soft bread crumbs
$1\frac{1}{2}$ lb. ($\frac{3}{4}$ kilo) apples	$1\frac{1}{2}$ lb. apples
5 oz. (125 g.) butter	$\frac{5}{8}$ cup butter
2–3 oz. (50–75 g.) sugar, plus sugar to sweeten apples	$\frac{1}{4}$–$\frac{3}{8}$ cup sugar, plus sugar to sweeten apples
to decorate (optional)	**to decorate** (optional)
whipped cream	whipped cream

Cooking time 15–20 minutes
Serves 4–6
Advance Preparations This improves with standing, so make some hours before required.

Put the breadcrumbs on a tray in a moderate oven, and leave until a pale golden brown. A better texture is given to this dessert if the breadcrumbs are not completely even and are fairly coarse. Peel the apples and slice thinly. Cook gently in half the butter until soft, adding sugar to taste. Mix sugar and breadcrumbs and crisp in the remaining butter. Use a frying pan (skillet) so the crumbs brown evenly. Allow to cool in the frying pan. Use individual serving dishes for this, or one shallow glass dish. Put a thin layer of the crumb mixture at the bottom of the dishes or dish, then a topping of apples, then a sprinkling of crumbs, more apples and a final topping of crumbs. Decorate with whipped cream if desired.

Pheasants in Calvados

Imperial/Metric	American
2 pheasants	2 pheasants
3 oz. (75 g.) cream cheese	generous ⅓ cup cream cheese
about 20 grapes	about 20 grapes
2 oz. (50 g.) butter	¼ cup butter
¼ pint (1½ dl.) Calvados	⅔ cup Calvados
1 oz. (25 g.) flour	¼ cup flour
½ pint (3 dl.) stock (good beef or pheasant)	1¼ cups stock (good beef or pheasant)
¼ pint (1½ dl.) thick cream	⅔ cup whipping cream
seasoning	seasoning
to garnish	**to garnish**
grapes and watercress	grapes and watercress

Cooking time   1 hour 20 minutes
Serves 4–6
Advance Preparations De-seed grapes, stuff pheasants.

Wash and dry the pheasants, then stuff with the cream cheese and de-seeded and skinned grapes. Heat the butter in the roasting tin or casserole, turn the pheasants in this. Cook for 20 minutes just above the centre of a moderately hot oven, 400°F. (200°C.), Gas Mark 6. Add the Calvados, cover tin loosely with foil (do not wrap the birds) or put lid on the casserole, lower heat to moderate, 350–375°F. (180–190°C.), Gas Mark 4–5, and continue cooking for an hour. Lift the pheasants from the cooking container on to a hot dish, keep hot. Strain the liquid into a saucepan, blend the flour with the stock, add to liquid, and cook gently, stirring well, until the sauce thickens slightly. Remove from the heat, whisk in the cream and heat *without boiling*, season well. Coat the pheasants with a little sauce, garnish with de-seeded grapes and watercress. Pour remaining sauce into a sauce boat. *Illustrated on page 194.*

Citrus Fruit Alaska

Imperial/Metric	American
2 large grapefruit	2 large grapefruit
4 large oranges	4 large oranges
sugar to taste	sugar to taste
1 tablespoon brandy	1 tablespoon brandy
1 round sponge cake, see page 99	1 round sponge cake, see page 99
large block vanilla ice cream, or see page 177	1 pint vanilla ice cream, or see page 177
for the meringue	**for the meringue**
4 egg whites	4 egg whites
4–6 oz. (100–150 g.) castor sugar	½–¾ cup granulated sugar

Cooking time   3–4 minutes
Serves 6–8
Advance Preparations Make or buy sponge. Prepare fruit.

Cut away the peel and pith from the grapefruit and oranges. Cut the segments of fruit neatly, discarding skin and pips. Put into a bowl, sprinkle with a little sugar and the brandy. Leave until ready to make the dessert. Put the sponge cake on to an ovenproof plate. Spoon the citrus fruit over the top of the sponge. Use all the liquid, so this soaks into the sponge and makes it pleasantly moist. Top with the ice cream, then the meringue, made by whisking the egg whites until stiff, then gradually beating in the sugar (I prefer the smaller quantity). Brown for 3–4 minutes only in a very hot oven, 450–475°F. (230–240°C.), Gas Mark 8–9.

Eating out-of-Doors

The following pages give a number of recipes for food to be eaten out-of-doors, whether for a picnic, a barbecue or when camping.

Picnics and Barbecues

Curried Egg Pie

Imperial/Metric	American
shortcrust pastry made with 8 oz. (200 g.) flour, etc., see page 72	basic pie dough made with 2 cups flour, etc., see page 72
for the filling	**for the filling**
6 eggs	6 eggs
1 onion	1 onion
1 medium apple	1 medium apple
1 oz. (25 g.) fat	2 tablespoons shortening
2 tablespoons flour	3 tablespoons flour
1 tablespoon curry powder	1 tablespoon curry powder
¼ pint (1½ dl.) plus 3 tablespoons water	⅔ cup plus 4 tablespoons water
juice 1 lemon	juice 1 lemon
1 tablespoon tomato purée or 2 ripe tomatoes	1 tablespoon tomato paste or 2 ripe tomatoes
seasoning	seasoning
to glaze	**to glaze**
egg or milk	egg or milk

Cooking time 1 hour 20 minutes
Serves 4–6
Advance Preparations Make pie, keep in cool place or bake and allow to cool.

Hard boil (hard cook), then shell the eggs; peel and chop onion and apple. Melt fat, fry onion and apple for a few minutes. Stir in flour and curry powder then blend in the water, stir until a smooth sauce. Add the remaining ingredients, except the eggs. Cover the pan and simmer the curry sauce for 30 minutes, then allow this to cool. Make the pastry, roll out thinly and line a 9–10-inch (23–25-cm.) pie plate with half the pastry. Halve the eggs and place cut-side down on the pastry. Spread the cold curry sauce over and between eggs. Cover the filling with the remainder of the pastry, damp the edges and press together to seal. Flute neatly, as picture. Brush top with beaten egg or milk, decorate with leaves of pastry. Bake in the centre of a hot oven, 425°F. (220°C.), Gas Mark 7, for 25–30 minutes, lower heat after 15 minutes if necessary.

Freezing Do not freeze this pie as the hard-boiled eggs become tough and 'rubbery'.

Barbecues

Although modern barbecues can be heated by electricity or gas the most popular are heated with charcoal. Allow time for the charcoal to heat through (this varies a great deal, but a minimum of 35 minutes is usual). The barbecue is ready to use when the charcoal glows red. If using electricity or gas make sure the barbecue is well heated before adding the food. Brush the bars of the grid well with melted fat (shortening) or oil so the food does not stick, and keep the meat, etc., well basted during cooking so it does not become dry. Use either butter, oil, fat (shortening) or one of the sauce recipes, below, or on page 209. Barbecue sauces traditionally are hot and well flavoured. Turn the food several times during cooking.
The simplest foods to barbecue are steaks, chops and jointed chickens. Whole onions and jacket potatoes can be wrapped in foil and cooked over the barbecue.

Scallops St. Hubert This is a delicious way of cooking venison, or other meat, over a barbecue fire. The meat must, of course, be tender and, in the case of venison, it must be well hung. Use small, rather thin slices of meat. Season the meat very well, melt a large knob of butter in a pan and fry the meat until golden brown. Remove the meat from the pan and keep warm (use a piece of foil and stand the meat on the foil at the edge of the barbecue fire). Add a little extra butter to the pan and fry strips of any vegetables available, plus a little crushed garlic if you enjoy this fairly strong flavour. Cook the vegetables until tender, then pour over enough red wine to moisten. Just before serving, return the meat to the pan with strips of mature Dutch Gouda cheese and freshly chopped parsley. *Illustrated above.*

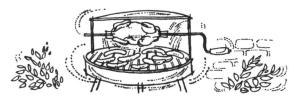

Speedy Barbecue Sauce Blend 1–2 tablespoons made mustard with a small can of condensed tomato soup. Heat, then add 2–3 tablespoons olive oil, seasoning and brown sugar to taste. Use for basting meat, etc.

Meat Loaves

These are extremely adaptable meat dishes for you can carry the loaf in the tin in which it was baked and slice it when you reach your picnic spot. On the other hand, should the weather prove disappointing the loaf can easily be reheated and served with hot vegetables.

Beef Loaf

Imperial/Metric	American
1½ lb. (¾ kilo) minced beef	1½ lb. ground beef
2 chopped onions	2 chopped onions
3 oz. (75 g.) soft breadcrumbs	1½ cups soft bread crumbs
seasoning	seasoning
1 teaspoon chopped fresh herbs or ¼ teaspoon dried herbs	1 teaspoon chopped fresh herbs or ¼ teaspoon dried herbs
2 eggs	2 eggs
4 tablespoons brown stock	5 tablespoons brown stock
little fat for greasing the tin	little shortening for greasing the pan

Cooking time 1½ hours
Serves 5–6
Advance Preparations Cook and store for a day in the refrigerator, or freeze.

Mix all the ingredients together and put into a well greased 2-lb. (1-kilo) loaf pan. Cover the top of the loaf with greased greaseproof (wax) paper or foil and stand in a tin containing cold water; this ensures that the outside of the loaf does not become too firm. Bake in the centre of a very moderate oven, 325°F. (170°C.), Gas Mark 3, for 1½ hours. If serving hot, wait about 5 minutes before turning out the loaf; if serving cold put a light weight on top of the loaf and do not remove this until the meat mixture is cold, this makes certain the loaf is a close texture and easy to slice. Turn out of the pan very carefully.
For a picnic you will find it easier to carry if you leave the loaf in the pan.

Freezing This freezes well. Use within 2 months. Defrost at room temperature.

Variations

Beef and Sausagemeat Loaf Use only 1 lb. (½ kilo) minced (ground) beef and 1 lb. (½ kilo) pork sausagemeat. Omit the breadcrumbs and flavour the loaf with a little chopped fresh or dried sage.
Creamy Loaf Use thick (whipping) cream instead of stock in the recipe.
Crisp Coated Loaf Grease the pan well and coat with crushed potato crisps (chips), or crushed cornflakes, or crisp breadcrumbs (raspings). Brush the top of the loaf with melted margarine and sprinkle with potato crisps, cornflakes or crumbs.
Egg and Veal Loaf Use minced (ground) veal in the loaf. Put half the mixture into the pan; top with several shelled hard-boiled (hard-cooked) eggs, then the rest of the meat mixture. Bake as before.
Sweet-Sour Loaf Add 1 tablespoon brown sugar, 4 tablespoons (5 tablespoons) apple juice or canned pineapple juice and the grated rind and juice of 1 lemon. Flavour with a few drops soy sauce also.
Upside-down Loaf Melt 1 oz. (25 g. – 2 tablespoons) butter in the loaf pan and arrange rings of raw cored and peeled dessert apple on top of this; sprinkle with a very little brown sugar, mixed with ½ teaspoon mixed spice. Top with the meat mixture. Although any meat can be used for this purpose, choose minced (ground) pork for preference.

Beef and Egg Cutlets

Imperial/Metric	American
2 medium onions	2 medium onions
$\frac{1}{4}$ pint (1$\frac{1}{2}$ dl.) water	$\frac{2}{3}$ cup water
seasoning	seasoning
8 oz. (200 g.) cooked beef or corned beef	$\frac{1}{2}$ lb. cooked beef or corned beef
2 hard-boiled eggs	2 hard-cooked eggs
2 oz. (50 g.) soft breadcrumbs	1 cup soft bread crumbs
to coat	**to coat**
1 tablespoon flour	1 tablespoon flour
1 egg	1 egg
2 oz. (50 g.) crisp breadcrumbs (raspings)	$\frac{1}{2}$ cup crisp bread crumbs (raspings)
for frying	**for frying**
2–3 oz. (50–75 g.) fat	$\frac{1}{4}$–$\frac{1}{3}$ cup shortening

Cooking time 20 minutes
Serves 4
Advance Preparations Prepare cutlets, cook as required.

Peel and chop the onions. Put into the water, add seasoning and cover the pan. Simmer for 10 minutes or until onions are just tender. Mince the beef or chop finely, then chop the eggs. Mix with the onions and any liquid left in the pan. Add the crumbs and season again. Cool mixture then form into 4 or 8 small cutlet shapes. Coat in a little seasoned flour, beaten egg and crumbs. Fry in the hot fat until crisp and brown. Drain on absorbent paper. These are delicious served with celery dressing, see page 198.

For Economy Coat in a thicker layer of seasoned flour only; omit egg and crumbs.
Freezing These do not freeze well with the hard-boiled eggs (they become 'leathery'), but you can omit the eggs and use more meat, then prepare and freeze, or fry, drain and freeze. Cook or reheat from frozen state. Use within 3–4 months.

Variations
Use cooked poultry (mince skin with flesh) or other meat instead of beef. When meat is not available use more eggs, or add a little grated cheese.
Use cooked rice in place of breadcrumbs.

Steaks with Barbecue Mustard Sauce

Imperial/Metric	American
2 tablespoons French mustard	3 tablespoons French mustard
1 tablespoon made English mustard	1 tablespoon made English mustard
4 tablespoons frying oil	5 tablespoons frying oil
good shake pepper	good shake pepper
pinch salt	pinch salt
$\frac{1}{4}$ pint (1$\frac{1}{2}$ dl.) brown stock or water and $\frac{1}{4}$–$\frac{1}{2}$ beef stock cube	$\frac{2}{3}$ cup brown stock or water and $\frac{1}{4}$–$\frac{1}{2}$ beef bouillon cube
6–8 steaks	6–8 steaks

Cooking time depends on the thickness of the steaks, but approximately 10 minutes
Advance Preparations Mix all the ingredients together.

This sauce gives a fairly liquid mixture so you can be generous with the amount put on to the steaks (or chops). It is sufficient for 6–8 portions of meat. Blend everything together, brush over the food before cooking and continue basting the meat with this sauce as it cooks.
Brush the bars with oil, put the steaks on the grid and brush with the sauce. Cook for 2–3 minutes, turn with tongs or a long-handled fork if the fire is fierce. Brush again with sauce. Continue cooking to personal taste. Serve with rolls heated over the barbecue, and with salad. *Illustrated on page 211.*

Rissoles

The recipe below, and the cutlets on page 209, are good examples of rissoles. If you wish to make vegetable cutlets use either of these recipes and omit the meat or poultry. Use finely diced cooked vegetables instead.

Creamed Chicken and Ham Cutlets

Imperial/Metric	American
1 lb. (½ kilo) cooked chicken (weight without bones)	1 lb. cooked chicken (weight without bones)
8 oz. (200 g.) lean ham	½ lb. cooked lean ham
1 oz. (25 g.) butter	2 tablespoons butter
1 oz. (25 g.) flour	¼ cup flour
⅓ pint (2 dl.) chicken stock	generous ¾ cup chicken stock
¼ pint (1½ dl.) thick cream	⅔ cup whipping cream
seasoning	seasoning
2 oz. (50 g.) soft breadcrumbs	1 cup soft bread crumbs
to coat	**to coat**
1–2 eggs	1–2 eggs
3 oz. (75 g.) crisp breadcrumbs	¾ cup crisp bread crumbs
to fry	**to fry**
little fat or chicken fat	little shortening or chicken fat
to serve	**to serve**
salad	salad

Cooking time   15 minutes
Makes 12–15 cutlets
Advance Preparations Make cutlet mixture. Chill before forming into cutlet shapes and again after coating.

Put all the chicken and just over half the ham through the mincer (grinder): choose the coarse or fine cutter. Dice the rest of the ham neatly and mix with the minced chicken, etc. Melt the butter in a pan, stir in the flour, cook for 2–3 minutes, gradually add the stock. Bring to the boil, cook until thickened, add the cream and seasoning. Stir in the chicken, ham and the breadcrumbs. Divide into 12–15 portions on a flat dish, chill so the mixture is no longer too soft to handle. With damp fingers, form into cutlet shapes. Coat with beaten egg and crumbs, then chill again if possible. Fry until crisp and brown on either side; drain on absorbent paper. Serve with salad.

Note These can be cooked over the barbecue.

For Economy Use less chicken and more crumbs.
Freezing Cook and freeze, or freeze the prepared cutlets. These can be reheated or cooked from the frozen state. Use within 3 months.

Variation
Make small cutlets for cocktail savouries.

Sausage kebabs with sweet and sour sauce (see page 213)

Steaks with barbecue mustard sauce (see page 209)   *Liver and bacon kebabs (see page 213)*   211

Meat Patties

The most famous meat patty in the world is a hamburger, see below; while this should be made with really good quality beef you can use the more inexpensive minced (ground) beef, although naturally you must then cook the hamburgers more slowly for a longer period.

Hamburgers

Imperial/Metric	American
1 lb. ($\frac{1}{2}$ kilo) finely minced beef	1 lb. finely ground beef
seasoning	seasoning
$\frac{1}{2}$–1 tablespoon oil or 1 oz. (25 g.) melted butter if the meat is very lean	$\frac{1}{2}$–1 tablespoon oil or 2 tablespoons melted butter if meat is very lean
good pinch mixed herbs (optional)	good pinch mixed herbs (optional)
for frying	**for frying**
little fat or oil	little shortening or oil

Cooking time   5–6 minutes
Serves 4–5
Advance Preparations Prepare and store in refrigerator, or freeze.

Mix the ingredients together with a wooden spoon, or your hands, so you bind it well. Form into 4–5 patties and cook in a little hot fat or oil, turning after 2–3 minutes. Cook the patties for the same length of time as you would pieces of steak, for many people prefer hamburgers 'rare' as they do steak. Serve on toasted buns, toast, or with salad or vegetables.

For Economy Blend equal quantities of smooth mashed potato and minced (ground) beef together. Fry 2 finely chopped onions in 1 oz. (25 g. – 2 tablespoons) fat or 1 tablespoon oil, add to the mixture, together with 1 tablespoon chopped parsley, seasoning and a good pinch mixed herbs. This version can be given extra flavour by adding curry powder; soy sauce; Worcestershire sauce.
Freezing These freeze well; separate each hamburger with a piece of greaseproof or waxed paper so the burgers may be 'peeled off' as required. Cook from the frozen state. Use within 3–4 months.

Variations

The mixture may be bound with an egg or egg yolk (this makes it slightly stickier to handle but gives a firmer texture when cooked).
Add 1 large grated potato and 1 large grated onion. This is particularly good when using cheaper quality meat which takes longer to cook.
Add chopped fresh parsley to the mixture.

Hamburgers Roma Flavour the meat mixture with garlic salt, or 1–2 crushed cloves garlic, and add 2 oz. (50 g. – $\frac{1}{4}$ cup) grated Parmesan cheese to the meat, etc. Choose good quality meat for this variation since the cheese mixture must not be cooked for too long a period.
Slimmers' Burgers Follow the basic recipe, omitting oil, etc., in the ingredients. Wrap each burger in a little oiled foil and bake in a hot oven for 10–15 minutes.
Devilled Burgers Blend 2 teaspoons made mustard and 1 teaspoon Worcestershire sauce and $\frac{1}{2}$–1 teaspoon curry powder with the mixture.
Crisp Coated Burgers Make the hamburgers; dip in seasoned flour, then in beaten egg and finally into crushed potato crisps (chips), fry as before.
Nutty Burgers Coat the hamburgers with finely chopped nuts.
Fruity Burgers Add 2 oz. (50 g.– $\frac{1}{3}$ cup) dried fruit, the grated rind of 1 orange and 1 lemon and 1 oz. (25 g.– $\frac{1}{4}$ cup) chopped walnuts to the meat mixture.
Sweet and Sour Burgers Add 2 tablespoons (3 tablespoons) chopped mustard pickles and 2 tablespoons (3 tablespoons) sweet chutney to the meat mixture. Since this makes it rather moist add about 1$\frac{1}{2}$ oz. (40 g.– $\frac{3}{4}$ cup) soft breadcrumbs to the meat.
Lamburgers Choose minced (ground) lamb and flavour with a little finely chopped mint and parsley, and add 1 oz. (25 g. – 3 tablespoons) sultanas (seedless white raisins) to the mixture.

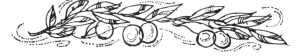

Liver and Bacon Kebabs

Imperial/Metric	American
4–6 medium onions	4–6 medium onions
oil	oil
seasoning	seasoning
1 lb. (½ kilo) lamb's liver	1 lb. lamb liver
8–10 rashers streaky bacon	8–10 bacon slices
2–3 small oranges	2–3 small oranges
for the sauce	**for the sauce**
1 can mandarin oranges	1 can mandarin oranges
1–2 tablespoons French mustard	1–2 tablespoons French mustard
to serve	**to serve**
boiled rice, see page 146	boiled rice, see page 146

Cooking time 1 hour
Serves 4–6
Advance Preparations Prepare onions and kebabs.

Peel the onions, brush with oil and season. Put the onions on to foil, wrap loosely and cook the onions over the barbecue for about an hour. Cut the liver into neat dice; remove the bacon rinds, halve each rasher and roll firmly. Cut the oranges into rings, remove any pips. Put the liver, bacon and orange rings on 4–6 skewers. Season lightly, brush with oil and cook over the barbecue for about 10 minutes, turning once or twice. Heat the mandarin oranges, plus the syrup from the can, in a pan with the mustard. Serve the kebabs with boiled rice, see page 146, orange sauce and the cooked onions. *Illustrated on page 211.*

Variation

Sausage Kebabs The picture on page 211 shows sausages being cooked over the barbecue. Baste these with the sauce below to give a good flavour. The corn must be pre-cooked then heated only and basted with a little oil or butter to keep it moist.

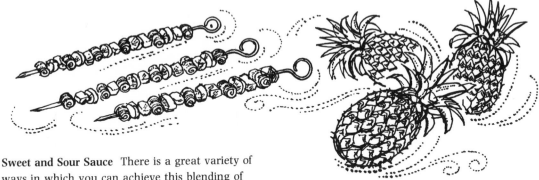

Sweet and Sour Sauce There is a great variety of ways in which you can achieve this blending of flavours. The ideas below may be varied by adding more sweetening or more vinegar to give the balance of flavour you prefer.
Blend 2 teaspoons cornflour (cornstarch) with ¼ pint (1½ dl. – ⅔ cup) brown stock. Put into a saucepan and stir until thick. Add 2 tablespoons (3 tablespoons) honey or sugar, 2 tablespoons (3 tablespoons) vinegar, 2 tablespoons (3 tablespoons) tomato purée (paste) and a little seasoning. Stir in 2–3 tablespoons (3–4 tablespoons) sherry or extra stock to give a coating consistency. This sauce is shown in the picture on page 211. *Serves 4–6.*

Pineapple Sauce Blend the cornflour with ¼ pint (1½ dl. – ⅔ cup) brown stock and 6 tablespoons (½ cup) pineapple syrup from canned pineapple. Omit the tomato purée (paste) and sherry, etc., from the sauce recipe, but use all the other ingredients listed. Chopped pineapple and chopped pickled onions are a good addition to this particular sauce.
Quick Sweet and Sour Sauce To make a very quick sauce blend equal quantities of vinegar and honey together. Add a little seasoning. If serving hot, this sauce is rather thin.

Making Sandwiches

Never imagine that sandwiches need be dull; they can be as simple or elaborate as you like, small and dainty or substantial as the occasion demands. A very quickly made sandwich for a hungry family is shown in the picture on this page. Make hamburgers as page 212, and sandwich them between soft rolls, or really thick slices of fresh bread and butter, and serve at once, while the meat patties are hot.

If carrying sandwiches on a picnic, wrap well or put into polythene boxes, so they do not dry. Open sandwiches can be carried quite easily; top each sandwich with a square of greaseproof (wax) paper and pack in boxes.

Cutting Sandwiches the Easy Way

1   It is easier to cut sandwiches if the bread is fresh, but not over-fresh. However, if you have very fresh bread, dip the bread knife in hot water, shake dry, but use while warm.

2   It is probably easier, however, to choose sliced bread for sandwiches and, remember, you can buy either thin or thick slices.

3   If you are buying unsliced bread and have to cut a lot of sandwiches in a hurry, then slice the bread lengthways, so giving you a large area to butter and cover at one time.

4   Make certain the butter is not too hard. If it is hard, beat with a very little warm milk to soften and make it go further. You may, however, prefer to use one of the modern excellent margarines, most of which are now sufficiently soft to spread even if they come from the refrigerator.

5   If you are cutting a large amount of sandwiches, line up the butter or margarine and the filling neatly, so that you work quickly and efficiently.

Open Sandwiches for Hungry People

Any visitor to Scandinavia, particularly Denmark, knows the wonderful selection of open sandwiches you will be offered. These may be small enough for a cocktail party or large enough for a complete meal. Choose a variety of breads for open sandwiches — brown, white, rye or split rolls. Butter the bread generously and then top with the colourful mixtures.

Fish Top bread with crisp lettuce, rollmop herrings, a little red cabbage and rings of uncooked onion.
Arrange fillets of cooked fish on bread and butter with lettuce, top with tartare sauce and Russian salad, garnish with lemon.
Meat Serve sliced cooked pork on buttered bread, with rings of dessert apple or a little apple sauce and cooked prunes.
Top sliced cooked beef on buttered bread with a little horseradish cream, potato salad and gherkins.
Top sliced cooked ham on buttered bread with scrambled egg and a little diced beetroot (beet).
Cheese Cover crisp lettuce on buttered bread with chutney and slices of cheese, twists of orange, sliced tomato and cucumber.
Cover luncheon meat or liver pâté with crisp bacon rashers (slices) and crumbled Danish Blue cheese.
Egg Cover buttered bread with sliced tomatoes then one or two fried eggs, garnish with crisp bacon.
Cover crisp lettuce on buttered bread with fillets of cooked herring, scrambled egg. Garnish with tomato.

Hamburger sandwiches

214

Party Open Sandwiches

Make these small, and ensure that the filling will not drop off when served. Keep covered lightly with polythene, aluminium foil, greaseproof (wax) or slightly damp kitchen paper after preparation. Unless stated to the contrary, the bread may be cut into rounds, squares or fancy shapes.

Fish Top brown bread and butter with caviare blended with chopped egg yolk. Garnish with finely chopped egg white.
Top smoked salmon with tiny shapes of gherkin and/or asparagus tips.
Put small pieces of smoked eel over crisp lettuce, top with scrambled egg and/or horseradish cream — small pieces of smoked trout could be used.
Make a pâté of salmon by pounding with butter.
Use as the base and top with twists of cucumber.
Meat Arrange thin strips of pâté and asparagus tips and sliced olives in neat lines on buttered bread.
Chop ham finely, blend with little butter and mustard.
Pile on crisp lettuce on buttered bread — garnish with Maraschino cherries.

Cover rings of salami with cream cheese and pieces of gherkin.
Cheese Crumble Danish Blue cheese with a little butter. Pile or pipe over bread and butter. Garnish with grapes, or pineapple, or pieces of preserved ginger.
Blend cream cheese, strips of smoked salmon and chopped shrimps. Garnish with minute pieces of skinned lemon.
Egg Blend chopped hard-boiled (hard-cooked) egg with cream and lemon juice and top with whole prawns or shrimps.
Blend chopped hard-boiled egg with cream, little curry powder and few drops chilli sauce. Garnish with salted peanuts.

Two-decker Sandwiches

Choose two sandwich fillings and three slices of bread and butter. You will then have brown bread and butter, **filling 1**), white bread and butter, **filling 2**), and a final layer of white bread and butter.
Here are some ideas:

1) smoked salmon and lettuce
2) cream cheese and chopped shrimps
1) caviar and hard-boiled (hard-cooked) egg-white
2) chopped hard-boiled egg yolk and mayonnaise
1) cottage cheese mixed with chopped glacé cherries

2) cottage cheese blended with finely chopped nuts
1) finely chopped ham or corned beef and chopped gherkins or cucumber, blended with mayonnaise
2) finely chopped hard-boiled egg, blended with chopped parsley and mayonnaise

Sweet Sandwiches

Sweet sandwiches are generally popular with children; remember that they also need savoury sandwiches to provide protein. Try some of the following and serve with fruit, as the picture.
Blend peeled grated dessert apple with chopped dates, and whipped cream or cream cheese.
Mash bananas, add a little sugar and lemon juice then mix with chopped nuts and/or chopped dates.
Dice or grate peeled dessert apples and blend with grated raw carrot, sultanas (white raisins), mayonnaise or cream cheese.
Whip cream firmly, add seasoning, plus a pinch sugar, then add a little grated cheese, diced well drained pineapple and chopped nuts.
Halve grapes, remove the seeds, then blend with a little honey and a pinch mixed spice.

Caravan Cookery

Caravan Living

Here are a few recipes that would be particularly suitable when you decide to holiday in a caravan. They are very delicious, but depend upon originality, rather than complicated cooking processes or a great number of ingredients. They also make wise use of canned foods which can be stored in the caravan.

The rolls on page 218 could be made with frozen, instead of home-made, puff pastry; or you could buy a packet of flaky pastry mix and use that instead. Remember though that your own home-made pastry and pastry dishes can be frozen, so you could prepare these rolls, and many other dishes too, then freeze them at home, so you can enjoy a leisurely holiday in your caravan (providing you have a refrigerator with a good frozen food compartment).

Pot Roasting

If you do not possess an oven it is possible to roast a joint of meat in a really strong saucepan or flameproof (not ovenproof) casserole. This is the type of casserole that can be put on top of a cooker as well as in the oven. Tie the joint so that it will fit neatly into the cooking container. Heat a very little fat in the bottom of the container and brown the joint on both sides, and then lift it out of the pan, pouring away all the fat except about 1 tablespoon. Put a good layer of rather large vegetables (for you do not want them to cook too quickly and become over-soft) into the bottom of the pan. Add just enough liquid (water, stock or a mixture of stock and wine) to cover the vegetables, season these then place the joint back again into the pan. Put on the lid, make sure it fits very tightly, lower the heat and cook steadily. Allow approximately 40 minutes per lb. ($\frac{1}{2}$ kilo) for most meats, except rare beef and chicken, which should have only about 30 minutes per lb. ($\frac{1}{2}$ kilo).

Nutty Apricot Pie

Imperial/Metric	American
1 lb. ($\frac{1}{2}$ kilo) cooked apricots or large can apricots	1 lb. cooked apricots or large can apricots
small can condensed milk	small can condensed milk
4 oz. (100 g.) butter or margarine	$\frac{1}{2}$ cup butter or margarine
8 oz. (200 g.) flour	2 cups flour
2 oz. (50 g.) rolled oats	just over $\frac{1}{4}$ cup rolled oats
2 oz. (50 g.) brown sugar	$\frac{1}{4}$ cup brown sugar

Cooking time 30–35 minutes plus time to cook apricots
Serves 6
Advance Preparations Make pie, keep in the refrigerator until ready to cook.

Strain most of the cooked or canned apricots. Keep a few halves for decoration and the syrup for a sauce. Sieve the fruit or put into the liquidiser (blender) and switch on until a smooth pulp. Mix the pulp with the condensed milk. Rub the butter or margarine into the flour until the mixture resembles breadcrumbs, add the rolled oats and sugar. Grease a round or square 7-inch (18-cm.) loose-bottomed sandwich tin (layer cake pan) and press two-thirds of the crumb mixture over the bottom and sides of the tin. Put apricot filling into lined tin and cover with the rest of the crumbs (do not press these too hard on to the filling). Bake in the centre of a moderate to moderately hot oven, 375–400°F. (190–200°C.), Gas Mark 5–6, for 30–35 minutes until golden. Decorate with apricot halves and serve hot or cold with the fruit syrup. You can also serve cream or ice cream with this dessert.

Freezing This freezes well. Use within 3–4 months.

Variations
Nutty Pineapple Pie Use canned pineapple, chopped.
Nutty Raspberry Pie Use fresh mashed uncooked but sweetened raspberries.

Fish Cobbler

Imperial/Metric	American
8–12 oz. (200–300 g.) tomatoes	½–¾ lb. tomatoes
1 medium onion	1 medium onion
3–4 courgettes (tiny marrows)	3–4 small zucchini
1 aubergine	1 eggplant
1¼ lb. (⅝ kilo) fresh cod or haddock	1¼ lb. fresh cod or haddock
2 tablespoons oil or 2 oz. (50 g.) margarine	3 tablespoons oil or ¼ cup margarine
seasoning	seasoning
for the topping	**for the topping**
4–5 rounds of bread	4–5 rounds of bread
little oil or butter	little oil or butter

Cooking time 45 minutes
Serves 4–5
Advance Preparations Make vegetable mixture, put into dish, do not top with bread until reheated.

Skin and slice the tomatoes and onion. Wash and slice the courgettes, slice the aubergine fairly thinly and dice the fish. Fry the tomatoes and onion for a few minutes in the oil or margarine then add the courgettes and aubergine, season lightly. Simmer for 20 minutes, stirring once or twice. If the mixture has become rather dry add a little white wine or water. Add the fish and extra seasoning if wished and continue simmering for 10 minutes. Turn into an ovenproof serving dish, top with rounds of bread, brush with a little oil or melted butter and cook for about 10 minutes in a hot oven.

Freezing This dish can be cooked and frozen. Add bread when reheated. Use within 4–6 weeks.

Variation
This can be turned into a thick type of fish soup if you use at least ¾ pint (4½ dl. – 2 cups) liquid with the vegetable mixture.

Pork and Orange

Imperial/Metric	American
4 pork chops	4 pork chops
seasoning	seasoning
2 oz. (50 g.) flour	½ cup flour
1 tablespoon oil	1 tablespoon oil
½ pint (3 dl.) canned orange juice	1¼ cups canned orange juice
2 oz. (50 g.) raisins	⅓ cup raisins
to garnish	**to garnish**
1 orange	1 orange
watercress	watercress

Cooking time 25 minutes
Serves 4

Coat the pork chops in seasoned flour, then fry steadily in the hot oil until nearly tender. Pour over the orange juice, add the raisins and simmer for 10 minutes. Garnish with orange rings and watercress. Serve with rice or noodles or spaghetti and a green salad.

For Economy Use half orange juice and half stock.

Variation
1 teaspoon Worcestershire sauce or Angostura bitters gives a piquancy to the sauce.

Ham and Pork Rolls

Imperial/Metric	American
for the puff pastry	**for the puff paste**
8 oz. (200 g.) plain flour	2 cups all-purpose flour
pinch salt	pinch salt
squeeze lemon juice	squeeze lemon juice
water to mix	water to mix
8 oz. (200 g.) butter, preferably unsalted	1 cup butter, preferably sweet
for the filling	**for the filling**
12 oz. (300 g.) can chopped ham and pork	12 oz. can chopped ham and pork
to glaze	**to glaze**
1 egg	1 egg
to serve	**to serve**
salad	salad

Cooking time 20 minutes
Makes 18 rolls
Advance Preparations Make the pastry, or prepare
the rolls and keep in the refrigerator for 24 hours
before cooking; or cook, store carefully and reheat
gently when required. See also information on
freezing.

To make the puff pastry: sieve flour and salt into a
bowl. Mix with lemon juice and water to an elastic
dough, roll out to an oblong. Put butter in centre of
dough, then fold the bottom third over this, then
bring down top third. Turn pastry, seal ends, roll out
to an oblong again, repeat until pastry has had
7 rollings and 7 foldings, put in cold place for 10–15
minutes in between each rolling to keep it firm. Cut
the ham and pork into neat fingers – about ¾ inch
(1½ cm.) wide. Roll out pastry to a strip about 2 inches
(5 cm.) wide. Put filling along the pastry, then brush
edges of pastry with beaten egg, and fold over to
enclose meat. Seal edges firmly, flute, then cut into
individual portions and make 2 slits on top of each.
Brush each roll with egg. Bake for 20 minutes above
centre in a very hot oven, 475°F. (240°C.), Gas
Mark 8–9, until crisp and golden brown, reduce heat
if necessary. Do not pack these for a picnic until
pastry is quite cold, otherwise it becomes soft. Serve
cold with salad.

Freezing These freeze extremely well and can be
warmed through from the frozen state. Use within
3 months.

Variations
Use freshly minced boiled bacon or ham, or other
cooked meat.
Sausage Rolls Use uncooked sausagemeat instead of
the canned ham and pork. Cook as the method above
but be very certain you do not under-cook since the
sausagemeat is raw. It would be advisable to lower
the heat after about 15 minutes and continue
cooking at a lower temperature.
Use a different type of pastry, e.g., short crust, page
72; or flaky, page 193.

Index